CONTENTS

Acknowledgements

The visit of Professor Castells would not have been possible without the generous financial contributions received by the Centre for Higher Education Transformation from the following organisations and institutions:
Anglo-Gold
Ford Foundation
Human Sciences Research Council
National Economic Development and Labour Council
National Research Foundation
University of Cape Town
University of Natal
University of the Witwatersrand
United States Agency for International Development

Our thanks go to the following individuals

- Professors Brenda Gourley, Ahmed Bawa and Ari Sitas for hosting the Durban leg of the visit and Sharon Dell for keeping things together in Durban.
- Professor Brian Figaji and his staff at Peninsula Technikon for hosting the public meeting in Cape Town.
- Professor Njabulo Ndebele for chairing and participating in the Cape Town seminar during his first week of assuming office as the new Vice-Chancellor of the University of Cape Town.
- Professors Wiseman Nkhulu and Saleem Badat of the Council on Higher Education for hosting the lunch seminar in Pretoria.
- Bobby Godsell of Anglo-Gold for hosting a dinner at which Professor Castells was able to interact with representatives of labour and business.
- Murphy Morobe of the Finance and Fiscal Commission for chairing the two-day seminar in Gauteng.
- Robert Mopp for ensuring that two meetings occurred between President Thabo Mbeki and Professor Castells.
- Linda Benwell from Sure Millennium Travel for her logistic support.
- Julie-Anne Justus and Fathima Dada for editing the manuscript.
- The Board and staff of CHET for their constant support.

Manuel Castells: A brief biography

Spanish-born Manuel Castells is Professor of Sociology and City and Regional Planning at the University of California, Berkeley, where he was appointed in 1979 after a twelve-year teaching stint at the University of Paris.

Born in Barcelona and exiled under Franco, Castells studied sociology with Alain Touraine in Paris, and in 1966 at the age of 24, became the youngest professor at the University of Paris. He has also taught and researched at the Universities of Madrid, Chile, Montreal, Campinas, Caracas, Mexico, Geneva, Copenhagen, Wisconsin, Boston, Southern California, Hong Kong, Singapore, Taiwan, Amsterdam, Moscow, Novosibirsk, Hitotsubashi and Barcelona. He has published over 20 books, including the 1 400-page trilogy *The Information Age: Economy, Society and Culture* (which is being translated into ten languages) and *The Informational City* (1989).

He has been the recipient of many awards and distinguished appointments, including a Guggenheim Fellowship, the C Wright Mills Award, the American Society for the Study of Social Problems Award and the Robert and Helen Lynd Award for life-long outstanding contribution in urban sociology. He is a member of the European Academy and the European Commission's High Level Group of Experts on the Information Society. In 2000 he was invited to become part of Kofi Annan's United Nations Advisory Council on Information Technology. He has also accepted President Thabo Mbeki's invitation to serve on the Presidential International Task Force on Information Society and Development which will assist the South African government in bridging the digital divide.

Castells has lectured around the world on issues related to sociology of information technology, urban sociology, economic development strategies and social theory. He has also addressed the World Economic Forum in Davos, Switzerland, the State of the World Forum in San Francisco and the United Nations Economic and Social Committee in New York. He has also been an advisor to Unesco, the United Nations Development Programme, the International Labour Office (UN), the European Commission, Organisation for Economic Development and Co-operation, US AID, the World Bank and the governments of Portugal, Spain, Andalusia, Asturias and the Russian Federation.

Introduction: Plugging in

Manuel Castells is a Spanish-born political economist, sociologist and urban analyst at the University of California, Berkeley. Author of numerous publications, he is best known for his magisterial trilogy *The Information Age*, a publication that is widely seen to have helped establish globalisation as the pre-eminent social phenomenon of our time. In June and July 2000, Castells, together with his long-time friend and intellectual collaborator, Stanford University political economist and educationist Martin Carnoy, visited South Africa to present a series of seminars and to engage in serious debate with South African scholars, politicians and policy-makers. This book is an intellectual record of that engagement.

The visit was at the invitation of Nico Cloete, the Director of the Centre for Higher Education Transformation (CHET). A Steering Committee was formed to organise the programme, with representatives from the National Economic Development and Labour Council, the Council on Higher Education, the Development Bank of Southern Africa, the Human Sciences Research Council, the Universities of Cape Town and Natal, and Technikon South Africa. The visit was co-ordinated and managed by CHET. Six seminars were held, in Pretoria, Cape Town, and Durban, and participants included senior government officials, policy-makers, academics, business people and trade unionists. In addition to the seminars, a public meeting was held in Cape Town which attracted a broad popular audience. Taken together, more than six hundred South Africans were afforded the opportunity to engage with the views of Castells and Carnoy on globalisation, the knowledge economy and the role of the state. This book comprises a selection of the papers that were delivered at the seminars. Some were academic papers, while others were less formal addresses. Some of them have been included to give a flavour of the debate and discussion that took place.

Castells is often taken to be an analyst of globalisation, in fact *the* analyst of globalisation. He is even taken by some to be an apologist for it, but this is surely wrong and says more about the inability to distinguish analysis from advocacy than it does about Castells. Certainly there is an ideology of globalisation, sometimes called neo-liberalism, which depicts the driving force of global capital flows as a natural one to which states must adapt or die. But Castells is critical of this position, as this book makes evident.

Therborn (2000: 149) has commented that '"globalisation" is the most immediate legacy to the new century of the social sciences of the outgoing 20th century'. This is an ambiguous phrasing, and can be read to insinuate that social scientists have, through persistent performative endeavours, literally talked this abstraction into existence. While this probably is the case in some wilder realms of social science, there does seem to be too much smoke here for there to be no fire at all. But what kind of fire? The range of sub-discourses on globalisation is extensive, and they do not necessarily refer to one another. There is competition economics that compares international competitive performance in relatively stark economic terms; international political theory that examines its impact on the state form and new forms of global regulation (Held 1995; Rosenau 1969); cultural studies that stress the concurrent production of diversity, or glocalisation, that comes with globalisation (Robertson 1992; Appadurai 1996; Lash and Urry 1994); as well as a host of other positions identified with their authors – world system analysis (Wallerstein 1974); risk society (Beck 2000) and others. Castells does not fit neatly into any of these. In fact a case could be made that Castells is not in these senses primarily an analyst of globalisation.

The central problem with 'globalisation' as an explanatory category is its analytical limitations. As Tony Judt (2000: 69) says: '"Modernisation", "Americanisation", or "globalisation" are at best descriptions ... they don't explain anything.' Rather, they mark the problem requiring explanation. What is this problem? It is to understand the changing conditions for productive life in the wake of an informational technological revolution, one that leaves no state untouched. Castells' endeavour is to explain the motor of this new mode. To do so required an effort of conceptual and empirical synthesis, to find, as he quotes Confucius in the prologue to his trilogy, 'one thread which links up all the rest'. Visvanathan (see Section One Chapter 3 in this volume), after Isaiah Berlin, depicts Castells as a fox (who knows many things) rather than as a hedgehog (who has only one great idea). He may be right, but it would be a grave error to miss Castells' hedgehoggish aspiration, and to refrain from evaluating the credence of his enterprise accordingly.

This is not unambitious, but then, the magisterial syntheses of Marx and Weber, with which this work bears comparison, were also ambitious. It helps to consider that Castells writes as a classical political economist, in a very particular tradition. This tradition is that of the analysis of post-industrialism, whose key iconic figures are Daniel Bell (1976) and Alain Touraine (1998), and now Manuel Castells. This tradition is primarily interested in delineating changes in the mode of development, which is broader than the mode of production. The fundamental thesis is well-known: states worldwide are moving from an industrial to a post-industrial mode of development based on science and technology. Castells' great innovation is to be much more precise about post-industrialism, which he revealingly calls informationalism, that is, the new dependence of productivity on the ability to deal with (generate, process and apply) knowledge-based information.

If the first distinctive aspect of this approach is its focus on the informational mode of development, then the second is the consistent balance it maintains, in common with the best traditions of European critical theory, between the system and the actor. The sub-title of the trilogy – 'Economy, society and culture' – indicates a triple focus, on production (action on nature), power (action over others) and experience (action on self). As Castells says:

> A new society emerges when and if a structural transformation can be observed in the relationships of production, in the relationships of power, and in the relationships of experience. These transformations lead to an equally substantial modification of social forms of space and time, and to the emergence of a new culture. (Castells 1998: 360)

We are seeing just such a change at the moment, says Castells, and it leads to a new social structure, called the network society, which is made up of networks of production, power and experience. The structural opposition that underlies this analysis is that between function, representing an abstract, universal instrumentalism; and meaning, representing historically rooted particularistic identities. Castells' names for these are the net and the self respectively, and the arc of this structural opposition is the lynchpin of his analysis: the language of the Information Age is, as he says, the power of flows (the logic of the net) versus the power of identity (the heavens and havens of cultural meaning).

Castells' work, then, is not really about globalisation as such. It is rather about the vicissitudes of this grand opposition playing itself out in different ways in different places under an emergent new development regime. Since the cultural or actional element in his work is strong, the analysis, even when grim, imparts a certain long-term optimism. This should not be taken to indicate either approval for globalisation or undiluted faith in the possibilities of human opposition against it. Unlike Touraine, Castells is not engaged here in activist theorising, in seeking conditions to optimise opposition to the system. His project is not to strengthen the arm of civil society or cultural movement: the anti-globalisation social movements and cultural projects in any case display an alternative logic to that of civil society (Castells 1998: 371). His aim is analytic, and it is to understand the conditions for enhanced productivity and hence enhanced life conditions for as many people as possible. He is as interested in the systemic conditions of possibility as he is in the actional opportunities for self-definition. The closest he comes to policy prescription – in his proposals for European citizenship (see Section Two Chapter 1 of this volume) and for a new Technological Marshall Plan (see Section Three Chapter 1) – attend to both sides of the equation.

'Globalisation' is usually associated with the thesis that the (role of the) nation-state will diminish, or has diminished. For many, this is a scandalous notion to be repulsed, and a number of the arguments at the first seminar target this issue as the reader will see in Section One in this volume. On the one hand, most observers will agree that finance markets are truly global, and that since states cannot control capital flows, economic policy now operates under new constraints. This is the view put forward very clearly by Castells and Carnoy. This though doesn't eliminate the state, although some commentators take this to be the claim. But it does impose a new role, which is to create the conditions for capital to flow in. States become not superfluous, but on the contrary, by facilitating capital flows, the premier agents of globalisation. This in turn inclines states to look outward rather than inwards which, depending on the legitimacy quotient the state enjoys, creates a greater or lesser problem for its popular base. Touraine puts it pithily: 'the elected look only at the world market and the electors look only at their private life' (quoted by Jeffrey Alexander 1999: 102). Castells lays bare the problem in one of his most poignant paragraphs, analysed further by Neville Alexander in Section Two Chapter 2 of this volume:

> Thus, the more states emphasise communalism, the less effective they become as co-agents of a global system of shared power. The more they triumph in the planetary scene, in close partnership with the agents of globalisation, the less they represent their national constituencies. End of millennium politics, almost everywhere in the world, is dominated by this fundamental contradiction. (Castells 1997: 308)

Successful and unpopular (USA) or unsuccessful and popular (Zimbabwe), the state now has some difficult choices. Gelb makes an incisive contribution toward our understanding of the dilemmas (or 'trilemma') involved at the macroeconomic level in Section One Chapter 5 of this volume.

No matter how carefully Carnoy and Castells put the case that the state role is changed, not eliminated (see particularly Castells 1996; Carnoy in Section One Chapter 2 of this volume), there are many writers who habitually overstate the case. For example, taken almost at random, Ulrich Beck has said recently: 'A return to nation-state democracy is purely illusory. There can no longer be any democracy in Europe unless it is transnationally expanded' (Beck 2000: 176).

From the perspective of a country such as South Africa, or indeed Africa as a whole, such a view sounds alarming indeed. Having only recently achieved indigenous statehood, views like this sound like a trick or a joke, or both. We can expect ordinary people to continue looking to the state for material succour and cultural cushioning. But the truth is, this is no longer its preferred option. From the point of view of Castells and Carnoy, without the state paying serious attention to the developmental fundamentals, and not just to macroeconomic policy or to the symbolism of sovereignty, we can expect the 'fundamental contradiction' above to deepen. This is a serious warning for all countries, but for the excluded and semi-excluded countries of the South – South Africa too – it is critical.

What then are the new developmental fundamentals? They come down to two sets of capacity: communications capacity and human resource capacity. The former refers to telecommunications infrastructure and information technology; the latter refers to the proportion of knowledgeable labour available. Knowledgeable labour, or as Castells calls it in Volume 3 of his trilogy, self-programmable labour, comprises the 'informational producers' of the informational economy, the labour that can make the new informational technology productive (see Carnoy in Section One Chapter 2 and Hall in Section Four Chapter 2 of this volume). Non-self-programmable or generic labour cannot generate productivity in the same way. Without a significant cohort of self-programmable labour, no national economy can plug profitably into the network society. The critical factor distinguishing self-programmable from generic labour, and that thus connects the two developmental fundamentals, is high quality education. It is impossible to stress this point too strongly. One might even say that communications technology and quality education are the two factors that should top the list of priorities of any state trying to move up the productivity pole. Indeed, Castells and Carnoy stress that a determined move in the direction of these two fundamentals will enable states to 'leap-frog'. The only two alternatives to leap-frogging are in any case hardly an attractive option. Firstly, business as usual will lead to 'trickle-down' growth, which will simply move too slowly and take too long, while the second option of de-linking from the net into a survival economy merely delays the inevitable.

The book has four sections. The first section, 'The network society', presents the Castells/Carnoy case for the key economic changes of globalisation, and some unavoidable implications for the way the state can consequently govern. The papers that follow comment on, or take issue with, various features of this argument, with the principal focus being where the new limits to state power are to be drawn.

The second section, 'The net and the self', confronts Castells' second central point, that the new global networks cannot be understood outside of differential human engagements with them – that is, without considering matters of meaning, culture and identity. Castells discusses successful (French) and unsuccessful (Soviet Union) attempts to impose a national identity, and argues against the viabilty of such attempts under globalisation. The discussions in Section Two try to situate South Africa in this debate.

The third section, 'Technology and development', makes the case for the one indispensable component of successful contemporary development – technology – and discusses the key site for its deployment, the region. The chapters in Section Three discuss aspects of South African technological capacity.

The final section, 'Higher education and the network society', makes the case for the other indispensable component of successful development in the network society – education, in this case, higher education. The discussion in Section Four considers whether and how information technology can expand access to higher education, and looks also at the new possibilities and limits of expanded access presented by the reconfiguration of higher education institutions under globalisation.

This book represents the first sustained, interdisciplinary engagement by South Africans with some of the consequences for the network society of the Information Age, which, after Castells, we know we all, enthusiastically or reluctantly, perforce now inhabit.

References

Alexander, JC (1999) 'Why we might all be able to live together: an immanent critique of Alain Touraine's *Pourrons-Nous Vivre Ensemble?*', *Thesis Eleven*, 58: 99–105.

Appadurai, A (1996) *Modernity at Large: Culture Dimensions of Globalisation.* Minneapolis: University of Minnesota Press.

Beck, U (2000) *The Brave New World of Work.* Cambridge: Polity Press.

Bell, D (1976) *The Coming of Post-Industrial Society: A Venture in Social Forecasting.* New York: Basic Books.

Castells, M (1996) *The Information Age: Economy, Society and Culture. Volume 1: The Rise of the Network Society.* Oxford: Blackwell.

Castells, M (1997) *The Information Age: Economy, Society and Culture. Volume 2: The Power of Identity.* Oxford: Blackwell.

Castells, M (1998) *The Infomation Age: Economy, Society and Culture. Volume 3: End of Millennium.* Oxford: Blackwell.

Held, D (1995) *Democracy and the Global Order.* Cambridge: Polity Press.

Judt, T (2000) 'The story of everything', *The New York Review of Books*, XLVII, 14: 66–69.

Lash, S and J Urry (1994) *Economies of Signs and Space.* London: Sage.

Robertson, R (1992) *Globalisation: Social Theory and Global Culture.* London: Sage.

Rosenau, JN (ed.) (1969) *Linkage Politics: Essays on the Convergence of National and International Systems.* New York: Free Press.

Therborn, G (2000) 'Introduction: from the universal to the global', *International Sociology*, 15, 2: 149–150.

Touraine, A (1998) *Return of the Actor: Social Theory in Post-Industrial Society.* University of Minnesota.

Wallerstein, I (1974) *The Modern World System.* New York: Academic Press.

section one

the network society

1

.... the new economy ... is the economy of all kinds of businesses and all kinds of activities whose organisational form and source of value and competition are increasingly based on information technologies, of which the Internet is the epitome and the organising form.

manuel castells

The new global economy

What is the new economy?

We are indeed in a new economy. This new economy is not only the California economy but it has extended worldwide with different manifestations. It is of course a capitalist economy. Never before in history has capitalism been the only economy on the planet, as it is now. To say that it is capitalism is important, but it is not enough to understand it. However, I'm not going to enter into the ideological discussion of whether it is capitalism or not capitalism. What I would like to develop are notions about what exactly this new economy is, on the basis of empirical observation and how it manifests itself throughout the planet in different forms, depending on where you are. I will then focus on some of the key dimensions of this new economy and economies of other kinds, which depend very much on the kind of labour and labour process on which economic activity is based.

Labour is still the basis of any economy – and this is particularly so of the new economy. It is the source of value creation. I wouldn't say that I believe in the labour theory of value but I believe in the value theory of labour in the sense that labour is the source of productivity and competitiveness in this new economy, as it was in other economies.

I want to emphasise that the new economy is not the Internet economy. It is not the economy of the Internet companies. It is the economy of all kinds of businesses and all kinds of activities whose organisational form and source of value and competition are increasingly based on information technologies, of which the Internet is the epitome and the organising form.

The new economy can be defined as the combination of three inter-related characteristics that cannot function without each other. Firstly, it is an economy in which productivity and competitiveness are based on knowledge and information. Knowledge and information have always been very important but they are now more important than ever in the sense that new information and communication technologies allow information and knowledge to be processed and distributed throughout the entire realm of productive activity. So, productivity is generated through knowledge and information, powered by information technology.

Secondly, this new economy is a global economy. A global economy does not mean that the entire world is one single economic system. In fact, in terms of jobs, most jobs are not global, they operate in local, regional and national labour markets at the level of planning. But I would say that most jobs, if not all jobs, are influenced by what happens in this global core of the economy. In more precise terms, the global economy is that particular economy which has the capacity to work as a unit in real time, on a planetary scale. This capacity refers fundamentally to its core activities, not to everything.

... the global economy is that particular economy which has the capacity to work as a unit in real time, on a planetary scale.

This capacity is, thirdly, technological, organisational and institutional. Technological capacity refers to its ability to structure the entire planet through telecommunications and informational systems. It has organisational capacity because the firms and networks working in this economy organise themselves to be active globally, both in terms of the supplies they receive and the markets they look for. It is also based on institutional capacity which basically means deregulation and liberalisation, which opens up the possibility for this economy to operate globally. In that sense governments are the main globalisers by creating the institutions of the new economy throughout the world. After that they lose control.

Dimensions of globalisation

Globalisation is at this point both a code word for the new system emerging in the world (actually already fully consolidated) and at the same time, the banner to rally both the determined march of global corporate capitalism and the worldwide sources of resistance to it. But besides acknowledging these connotations of globalisation, we can try to understand the term in a more analytical way.

Globalisation is not only economic. It also refers to media, to information systems, to international institutions and to the networking of states. But for the sake of simplicity and to focus the analysis, I will concentrate mainly on the economic dimension of globalisation.

Financial globalisation

The heart of the global economy is the global financial market. To say that capital is global in a capitalist economy is not a small thing. Global financial interdependence has been enhanced even further recently by the combined process of financial deregulation and electronic trading. By building electronic networks at the heart of the global financial markets, we are in a process in which savings are mobilised and invested constantly from anywhere to anywhere.

We thought that we were in the mature phase of financial globalisation, but in fact we are just starting. The attempted merger of the London and Frankfurt Stock Exchanges was a major step in that direction – but only a first step, because the critical moment is the integration of the American Nasdaq, the London-Frankfurt Nasdaq and the Tokyo Nasdaq as one electronic market. Also the fact that Eurex has overtaken the Chicago Board of Trade as the main futures and liberties market, which is absolutely essential in the global financial economy, signals the way that the electronic marketplace largely removes control.

Here is one empirical indicator so you have some idea. I don't know how they do it, but serious people put the value of the derivatives of the financial market at about twelve times global gross domestic product (GDP). Also, the current trading in the currency markets in 1999 reached about US$2 trillion, which was about 20 per cent more than the GDP of the United Kingdom per day. In other words, there is the circulation of capital, unrestrained in the entire world, and this is part of the economy.

I said that globalisation refers to the core activities. What are these core activities? Fundamentally they are the following. Firstly, at the heart of the process of globalisation is the emergence of global financial markets, the integration of capital markets and money markets, in a system which works as a unit in real time.

> ... at the heart of the process of globalisation is the emergence of global financial markets, the integration of capital markets and money markets, in a system which works as a unit in real time.

These global financial markets have increased phenomenally in the last twenty years and in fact, this is what allows us most firmly to talk about the acceptance of the global economy. Our planet is at this point entirely capitalist, save some small exceptions such as North Korea, but not Cuba, which is quite fully integrated into the capitalist system. So, if we consider that the capitalist economy is based on capital and capital is globally integrated, this allows us to talk about globalisation.

By way of illustration, if we measure the cross-border transactions of bonds and equities as proportional to GDP, between 1970 and 1996, these cross-border transactions increased by a factor of about 54 in the United States. Not 54 per cent, 54 times; 55 times in Japan; almost six times in Germany. The total financial flows from industrialised countries to developing countries increased by a factor of seven between 1960 and 1996. Another measure: in the global economy, by 1996, mutual funds, pension funds and institutional investors in general controlled about US$20 trillion, that is ten times more than in 1980, an amount equivalent to about two thirds of global GDP. Currency markets are exchanging about US$2 trillion per day. If we take another key financial development, financial derivatives alone these days suppose an annual value of transactions equivalent to 12 times global GDP.

Last year I calculated the relationship between some of the dotcom companies and economies of countries. One calculation that may be interesting: Amazon.com, which has never made a profit, is valued in market capitalisation at twice as much as the entire Russian economy traded in the stock exchange market. Of course, now Amazon.com is down and the Russian economy is up, but the simple scale of the comparison between one relatively small company and the whole economy of a country as important as Russia seems to be meaningful.

This global interdependence of financial markets is the result of a number of developments. First and most important is the deregulation of financial markets and the liberalisation of cross-border transactions in most countries. Let's place the rise of financial markets on one date (historians like to fix dates): 27 October 1987. It was the moment of the Big Bang in the City of London when financial flows were fully liberalised.

A second development is the existence of a technological infrastructure, including advanced telecommunications, Internet, interactive information systems and powerful computers capable of high-speed processing of models required to handle the complexity of transactions. So speed, size and complexity are the three key characteristics of this market.

Third, the connectedness results also from the nature of financial products such as derivatives which include futures, options, swaps and other products. Derivatives are synthetic securities that combine everything that can be combined, from any market to any market. This means that anything that happens in any market goes through the derivative system into other markets.

> ... the integration of financial markets is also linked to a speculative movement of financial flows ...

Fourth, the integration of financial markets is also linked to a speculative movement of financial flows, moving swiftly in and out of a given market security or currency to take advantage of the small differences in valuation which become amplified by the swift movements.

Fifth, market valuation firms such as Standard and Poor or Moody's are very powerful elements for the integration of financial markets by establishing certain rules and certain criteria, and enforcing them. It seems to me that this process is not very scientific. This is not as a result of a lack of professionalism or corruptive influences. It is simply not hard science. But once Moody says something in the market, it happens, not because that is the reality, but because Moody has said it – as in Korea in 1997. These criteria are criteria which are communicated throughout the world markets. In other words, markets have to fit into these criteria because the system is unified.

Sixth, international financial institutions such as the International Monetary Fund make sure that these criteria actually work, particularly for most developing countries, as rules of the game. In other words, if you want to be in the global 'club', you have to accept these rules or else not only will you not receive a loan, you will be judged and considered an unreliable market. So, instead of being an emerging market, you will be a submerging market, and that will stop capital flows coming in. Again, all this depends not so much on hard science. In the book that was published recently in London, by people like Hutton, Giddens, Soros, Volcker and myself, there is a wonderful paper by Paul Volcker, the former chairman of the Federal Reserve Board in the United States, who writes: 'Flows of funds and their valuation in free financial markets are influenced as much by perceptions as by objective reality – or perhaps more precisely, the perception is the reality' (Volcker 2000: 78).

Which means, in my view, that it's not that profits don't matter, but valuation mechanisms include profits as well as many other elements, which contribute to the ups and downs of the market so that we are in a systemic volatility situation. Not simply in a bubble, a bubble is not a real notion. Some companies are in a bubble, some segments of industry in some countries at one point are in a bubble, as it was in the case of Japanese real estate a few years ago. But fundamentally, the notion of a bubble refers implicitly to a market equilibrium in which the bubble bursts and then we go back to the equilibrium of the market. Well, this is not what's happening. We have bubbles that burst and go down and go up – the Nasdaq index in April 1999 went up and down eleven times across five per cent of its value. But that's not a bubble, that is sparkling water. So in that sense, what we have is a new kind of system in which global financial markets are integrated, interdependent and at the same time, highly unstable in their processes.

If capital markets and currencies are interdependent, so are monetary policies and interest rates, and therefore, so are economies everywhere. Capital flows become global and increasingly autonomous, at the same time, *vis-á-vis* the actual performance of the economies. What is the relationship between the performance of an economy and what happens with its financial system? It is a very undetermined equation.

The transformation of international trade

A second major dimension of globalisation is the transformation of international trade. I will be quite brief on the matter, even if it is an important one, because this is the best known dimension. International trade has continued to grow but it is affected fundamentally by two elements or trends that one has to consider.

The first trend is the transformation of the composition of international trade. Commodities and raw materials are increasingly displaced as sources of value by manufactured goods and manufactured goods are being displaced by advanced services. And within manufactured goods you have a growing discrepancy between low value added, low-tech manufactured goods and high value added, high-tech manufactured goods, which is the heart of international trade today.

Commodities and raw materials are increasingly displaced as sources of value by manufactured goods and manufactured goods are being displaced by advanced services.

The second trend is that the developing countries' share of international trade has increased quite substantially. Obviously the intertrade of the Organisation for Economic Co-operation and Development (OECD) countries still accounts for the bulk of international trade. Actually at this point, OECD countries which have 19 per cent of the world's population account for about 74 per cent of the world's total export of goods and services. So the notion that we have a development of trade in the developing countries is true *vis-á-vis* the importance of this trade in developing countries – but it's not true that developing countries now represent a substantial share of OECD countries.

By the way, the most internationalised region in the world, measured in terms of the external sector over GDP is – surprise, surprise – Africa. Sub-Saharan Africa has a proportion of export and imports over GDP of close to 30 per cent, in comparison to 21 or 22 per cent for OECD countries. This completely belies the notion that the only thing you have to do is to trade and to open up your economies, because it depends what you trade, for whom, at which price. If you trade cocoa and coffee and cotton against microchips and advanced business services, I don't think you are in a great business, even though you go all over the place to achieve your 40 per cent or 50 per cent of the economy.

Just one additional remark on this. There has been a major debate on whether international trade is creating regions in the world, such as the European Union or South America, the United States, the

Asian Pacific, or whether on the contrary, it is creating a global economy. Well, it is neither. It is neither integrated regions nor one simple global economy. Instead, there are networks of trade. In other words, the European Union is not a trading bloc – it is one economy. Remember, that's what has changed. You have one central bank and one currency (except for the pound, for political purposes for a couple of years more), you have one economy. The European Union is one economy, not one trading bloc.

Nafta is also one economy, not one trading bloc, and there is no Asian Pacific economy, regardless of which indicator is used to test this. But what there is, is an extraordinary integration of the productive sectors and their trade. This is what led me to the third and most important dimension of globalisation after the financial markets, which is the internationalisation of production.

The internationalisation of production

What really has happened in the world in the last twenty years is that the core of production of goods and services in every sector has been internationalised through transnational networks of production, distribution and management. This is the core of the matter.

Multinational corporations and their ancillary networks only employ a fraction of the global labour force but they account for 30 per cent of global GDP and two thirds of international trade, of which, in fact, about half is trade within the same corporation and its ancillary networks. In other words, what we consider to be internationalisation of the economy through trade is in fact the consequence of the internationalisation of the production process through networking.

This is also linked to production as well as to foreign direct investment. Foreign direct investment usually takes the form of mergers and acquisitions. In other words, rather than multinational corporations investing, what they do is buy assets and integrate these assets into their production system.

I also want to remind you of one key item of empirical information. When people talk about multinational corporations, they usually refer to a small number of usual suspects, ten, twelve corporations. Well, let me remind you, there are 53 000 multinational corporations with 415 000 subsidiaries, so it's a much wider network than is commonly believed. A network which, in addition, is completely networked within itself. So there are multinational corporations, highly decentralised in terms of their departments and markets, but these units of multinational corporations are connected with each other.

Then you have small and medium business networks that work together, co-operate together, export and also link to multinational corporations. And in addition, this system is often linked to the informal sector in developing countries. So you have a layer and network structure that goes from the heart of the corporate centres to the shanty towns of the scavengers processing paper, processing debris for the paper mills, for example in Kali, Colombia.

Globalisation of science and technology

The fourth dimension of globalisation is the selective globalisation of science and technology. Science and technology are absolutely critical components of the production process and, not only that, of the capacity for development of societies as well. Science and technology are globally integrated in the sense that all major research centres have connections to developing countries. At the same time it's highly asymmetrical. And here, I want to insist only on two notions. First, we have an extraordinary concentration of science and technology and particularly information technology, research and development, in the leading economies. In other words, instead of diffusing, information technology has concentrated research and development capacity. That's one part of this dimension.

Second, while they are concentrated in terms of research centres, their networks are interactive and therefore you have the ability to diffuse technological capacity to a number of developing countries, while at the same time being connected to the centres of information processing. Let me give you just one example. The main process of circulation of science and technology is the human mind. Science and technology are not embedded in machines, they are embedded in people, in minds, and minds are usually connected to bodies. Let's take, for instance, what has happened in Silicon Valley in the last ten years. My colleague, Anna Saxenian, conducted a survey in 1999 and found that 30 per cent of the new companies created in Silicon Valley in the 1990s were headed either by an Indian or a Chinese chief executive officer (CEO). Many of the Indian CEOs are from Bangalore, Bombay. So they come to Silicon Valley, but this is not a brain drain. They get their freedom first, they get their Green Card, that's the key thing. Once they are free people with their Green Card, they establish their own company and then once they are successful, well, if they are not successful they do it again and again and again, seven times on average. And when they finally are successful, they go

The main process of circulation of science and technology is the human mind.

back to India, establish a company there and go back and forth. A similar pattern exists with Taiwan, with Singapore, and a similar pattern is emerging now with China, and so on. So, in other words, there are networks of diffusion of science and technology, but, at the same time, a high concentration of research capabilities in the core economies.

Technological basis of the new economy – the Internet

A key characteristic of the new economy is that it is organised in networks. By networks I simply mean a set of interconnected nodes. These networks are networks that are within the large corporations, they are decentralised as networks. Small and medium businesses connect to each other, forming networks, and these small networks connect to these decentralised networks of the corporation, forming a network of networks. And, in addition, increasingly many of these networking operations are on-line, in terms of management, in terms of selling, in terms of production. People are fascinated by e-commerce over the Internet. Well, 80 per cent of economic transactions over the Internet are business to business, not business to consumers.

Business-to-consumer transactions are also increasing but that's a minor part. The real heart of what's happening is that the actual production system is being produced on-line. The new technological basis of this new economy is the Internet. The Internet is not simply one more technology. The Internet is the equivalent of electricity and of the electrical engine of industrialisation. It induces the networking form, just as the fusion of the electrical engine allowed the formation of the industrial factory, at the heart of the development of the large capitalist corporation.

Global reach of the new economy

This new economy has global reach. Certainly, it has a different weight in different countries. In California, it's a very important segment of the economy but this new economy is expanding its logic so that in a few years, there will be only two kinds of economies in the world. What is called the new economy will transform the old economy. The new economy is not one segment of the economy. It is a new economy growing within the old economy and the most important thing is not electronics or Internet companies and so on, it's what's happening in the automated production sector, in the consumer goods production sector, in agriculture, in services. That's where the new economy is transforming everything. So, new economy and survival activities are the two key sectors of the new world.

This new economy is organised in networks throughout the world. These networks which have a technological and organisational basis have one particular quality. They search for everything that is valued or can be valued according to the criteria of the networks, ultimately money-making, to integrate into these networks, and discard from these networks everything that has no value from the point of view of these networks. So it's a very lean, efficient system of including and excluding at the same time and it works for firms, it works for labour, for management, for regions, for cities, for everything.

The double logic of inclusion and exclusion cuts across countries, so the notion of a North and South divide no longer prevails.

The double logic of inclusion and exclusion cuts across countries, so the notion of a North and South divide no longer prevails. We now have global networks which integrate and disintegrate. Certainly it is not the same thing if 80 per cent of the countries are disintegrated, than if only 20 per cent of the countries are disintegrated. It makes a great deal of difference, particularly for the people who are part of the disintegrated 80 per cent. But if you are part of the disintegrated 20 per cent of East Palo Alto in California, you feel that you are also excluded. And therefore, the notion of this new economy as a North economy, I think, is misleading. For example, Bangalore is highly integrated in this new economy. But if you look to most of rural India or to the shanty towns of Calcutta, certainly they are not part of the new economy and they are part of a different, basic survival economy.

In that sense, it's a very different system which replaces the old notions of North and South, developed and developing or underdeveloped, with the notion of networks – global networks. These global networks articulate and disarticulate so that at the same time we have a world made of global networks and local societies which certainly are relatively independent of these networks, but at the same time they all suffer or enjoy the consequences of these global networks. In other words, globalisation does not integrate everybody. In fact, it currently excludes most people on the planet but at the same time, affects everybody.

Leap-frogging through technology

In his report to the Millennium Summit of the United Nations, Kofi Annan (2000) emphasises the notion that developing countries need to 'leap-frog' development. And not just leap into the high technology of the leading societies and continue along the traditional path of industrial development, manufacturing services, and so on. On the contrary, what is critical is Internet-based agriculture, Internet-based services, Internet-based health, Internet-based education, particularly for developing countries that need a faster process of development. This poses all kinds of policy problems about how we jump from the current state of dereliction and under-development to an Internet-led economy. But once we know the principle, we can discuss policy matters.

In advanced societies there were all kinds of metaphysical discussions about how new technologies would destroy jobs, would destroy labour markets, and so on. In fact, the empirical evidence is that there is no relationship between information technology or technology *per se* and the destruction of jobs. Unlike what some of the proponents of technology say, there is no evidence on either side. Under some conditions, certainly the introduction of new technology destroys some jobs. So if you don't create a dynamism in other sectors at the same time, then the net effect is destruction of jobs.

Nevertheless, societies that most probably introduced this information technology such as the United States, Japan and Scandinavia are the ones with the lowest unemployment rate. Societies in the advanced countries with lower technological development, such as Greece and Spain, are the ones with higher unemployment rates.

Transformation of labour markets

On the other hand, though, technology does have a tremendous effect on the kind of work and on the kind of labour market. I would say the two most important transformations are the following.

The first major development is that we have shifted to a process of flexible labour as a norm. What is fading away, not only in advanced economies but throughout the world, is the traditional form of stable employment in a standardised labour market, heavily institutionalised with a predictable career pattern and based on collective bargaining. This model of employment is being superseded. The natural tendency of this, of course, has all kinds of implications for people's protection and for industrial relations but it is possible, and many unions are working on the matter, to reconstruct the protection of workers' rights under the new conditions of flexible labour (see Patel in Section One Chapter 7 of this volume). It is possible to do it. But first you have to recognise the economic and technological movement together. It's not just technological, it's a fundamental and economic strategy of networking which allows for the flexibility of labour as a key condition for the development of the new economy. But because of information technology this flexibility can be brought into operation.

The second major development, together with the flexibility of the labour market and the individualisation of labour–capital relationships, is what I call self-programmable labour. Self-programmable labour is labour which has the built-in capacity to generate value through innovation and information, and that has the ability to reconstruct itself throughout the occupational career on the basis of this education and this information. Therefore it is always at the source of the creation of value.

Self-programmable labour is labour which has the built-in capacity to generate value through innovation and information, and that has the ability to reconstruct itself throughout the occupational career on the basis of this education and this information.

Together with this labour there is a very large mass of workers, including in the advanced societies, which I call generic labour. Generic labour has no specific skills apart from some basic level of education. This labour co-exists with unskilled labour, semi-skilled labour and machines in developing countries in the same sequence depending on economic combination strategies between capital and labour in every country.

Let's say that, these days as a rule, capital is global, labour is local, if you take things in quantitative terms. The highest estimates of people working outside their country of birth put them at about 200 million. I'm very careful about this. The United Nations Development Programme says 145 million, but it doesn't count a lot of undocumented workers. However, remember that about one third of those are in the region most unlikely to consider immigration, that's sub-Saharan Africa. So they are counted as people who are migrants but are not necessarily migrants for reasons of opportunity – although if you go to the Ivory Coast certainly migrants go there from the surrounding countries. So, 200 million over a three billion global labour force.

However, even in the European Union, where everybody is up in arms against immigrants, Britain and France have a lower proportion of immigrants now than ten years ago, of foreign-born populations. People call French citizens of Nigerian origin born in France immigrants, but that's a different matter.

What I want to emphasise is that there are two phenomena in terms of the globalisation of labour that have to be considered. One is a global search for talent and in that sense, highly skilled labour is increasingly situated in a global market. These are the financial analysts, computer software engineers, football players, professional killers. All this high-level skilled labour is globalised, but most of labour is certainly not.

The other thing is increasing pressure from countries with much lower standards of living, to access the developed world by any means. So we will see an increasing pressure from people from poor countries becoming migrants. If you take the European Union, the situation is that there are fewer than 100 million people in the northern rim and more than 400 million people in the southern rim of the Mediterranean. At the same time, a decreasing population growth in all European countries, even a stagnation in the case of Spain or Italy, will lead to more migration. But for the moment, labour is not the most globalised segment of the new economy.

Impact of the new economy in the developing world

In the developing world the impact of this new economy, for the moment, is the division between a highly dynamic information-based sector which is incorporated into these networks of production, including larger-scale manufacturing. Manufacturing is not a disappearing trend. It is diminishing proportionately in the core economies but there is more employment in manufacturing now than ever before in history. In China, in Brazil, in Thailand, still in Taiwan, by and large, still in Singapore, employment in manufacturing is exploding all over the world; certainly in India.

But it's a different type of manufacturing. It's not simply sweatshop manufacturing, it's manufacturing plus automation, it's manufacturing plus automation plus high technology plus a connection to information and global markets. Then, around this high-tech information-led sector which is global and built on networks of production, which are in India or Taiwan or Silicon Valley, around this, for a large part of the planet you have two phenomena. One, the devaluation of labour, that is, people simply being reduced to irrelevance as labourers, not irrelevant as people, naturally, but as labourers by the fast process of de-ruralisation and crisis of traditional agriculture, and the inability of the urban economy to incorporate them in this modern sector. And at the same time, therefore, the creation of extraordinary numbers of people in the informal sector, in the survival sector and in the criminal economy sector, which are three different but interrelated sectors.

In Brazil 50 per cent of urban employment is informal. The informal sector is connected to the modern sector – it's not disconnected – through a number of mechanisms, but it is a low productivity sector which works by providing cheap labour and cheap activities to these modern sectors. The survival unemployment sector, I would say, in this case is not employment – it's a survival of people, sometimes surviving through the family, sometimes surviving through self-production of food. This is happening on a very large scale.

... the criminal economy ... is booming all over and is probably the fastest growing segment in the world.

And thirdly, the criminal economy, I'm sorry to say, is booming all over and is probably the fastest growing segment in the world. To put things into perspective, a very conservative estimate by major institutional international organisations puts the value of money laundering in the formal economy at somewhere between US$1 trillion and US$1,5 trillion per year. This, by the way, is a little bit higher than the current value of the Internet economy in the United States.

So we have a world with extraordinary productivity, extraordinary creativity, which is increasingly concentrated in some sectors. Other sectors are linked to these sectors through informal mechanisms; another sector practises either survival or crime, which is in fact another form of survival. My last point is that sectors and countries that fall in-between are going to have very serious problems. Traditional manufacturing-based employment, traditional public sector employment, particularly in developing countries, do not have the political basis to resist change and do not have the ability under the current conditions to be integrated into the modern sector of competitive production based on information. So through this process of restructuring, what will result is not prescribed in the rules of the new economy. Instead, it depends on the interaction between societies, politics and the state, but within the context of the new technologies and global capitalism.

Globalisation, inequality and poverty

What I would like to emphasise is that this global economy is at the same time extraordinarily creative and productive, and extraordinarily exclusionary through this process of networking and segmentation. Which leads me to the obverse element of the analysis, which is that while this global economy has been extraordinarily productive and, on average, has increased standards of living measured by all kinds of indicators in the last twenty years, in the world at large, this process is extraordinarily uneven.

As you know, if one person dies young and another lives to 100 years, the average expected life is 50 years. So averaging is always misleading in terms of telling the story. That's why I think the number of observations that have related the expansion of the global economy to increasing inequality, poverty and social exclusion in the world at large has been important. The data is well known, so I'm not going to dwell too much on it but simply signal what the issues are.

But when signalling what the issues are, we have to remember that there are different dimensions, first of all, when we describe the process of inequality. Inequality is one thing. Inequality is bad but it's not the worst thing because if there's greater inequality but everybody is doing much better, the problems are not so serious.

Then there is poverty, which is in fact the institutional definition of how many people are below the poverty line in terms of whether they can survive, etc. Then there is polarisation. That is when the rich get richer and the poor get poorer, which is yet another process. And then there is social exclusion, which is the placing of part of the population in conditions of inability to develop an autonomous livelihood, which in capitalist, and therefore wage-based, societies, is usually linked to exclusion from a labour market in terms which are structurally reproduced.

If we keep these four axes in mind and use the United Nations Development Programme (UNDP) Human Development reports as a measurement, then overall, inequality has increased in almost every country, in both the developed and the developing world.

... inequality has increased in almost every country, in both the developed and the developing world.

Poverty is persistent in many countries but in some major countries such as China and India it has been reduced substantially in the last ten years. In Latin America, Chile has reduced inequality substantially, although, as I told them last year, Pinochet left the country with 45 per cent of people below the poverty line so it was easy to improve. But overall, Chile and a number of other countries have improved their conditions. Brazil continues to have a very high poverty level.

Polarisation has also increased. In almost every country that has been measured, the rich are getting richer and the poor are getting poorer. The most concerning point, however, is the massive increase in social exclusion throughout the world, from small starting proportions but high rates of growth in countries, even of the European Union. To give you one figure, child poverty in Germany in the 1990s has increased by 125 per cent. In the United States, depending on what you believe and how you count, either 20 per cent or 25 per cent of children live in poverty. Poverty has been reduced a little in the last few years by one single measure – the decision to increase the minimum wage. But overall you still have in this great new economy society of the United States, about one quarter of children living in poverty.

In the world at large, as you know, about 50 per cent of people in the world live (or actually die) on less than US$2 per day. It used to be 45 per cent in the mid-1990s; the UNDP says it's about 50 per cent now. And if we, in a very rough calculation, try to integrate every possible dimension of this global economy, about two thirds of people on the planet have either been stagnating or deteriorating in the last ten years under the development of this new global economy.

So, on the one hand, we have statistical, anecdotal and graphic evidence of the simultaneous development of an extraordinary, creative, innovative, productive economy at the heart of the planet, not just in the North but in networks between North and South. And on the other hand, discarded from these productive networks, the notion of the increase in the social exclusion of a large proportion of the population.

Well, as you know, correlation doesn't mean causality, so it's not necessarily clear who or what is responsible. Certainly it's not information technology *per se*. It is in fact the relationship between this new mode of development, which I call info development, and the overall process of integration. I have tried to identify some of the mechanisms that seem to be connecting the two processes. On the one hand we have the creation of this new economy on a global scale, and on the other hand the process of social exclusion and increase in polarisation.

... the networking and flexibility of the system make it possible to connect the valuable and discard the devalued for people, firms and territories ...

Let me elaborate. First, the networking and flexibility of the system make it possible to connect the valuable and discard the devalued for people, firms and territories; leading to a notion of a dynamic system which doesn't need and doesn't require all these other elements of our species.

Second, there is an extreme under-development of technological infrastructure in most of the world. The diffusion of the Internet has been very rapid: over 45 per cent of households in the United States and Scandinavia are connected, about 40 per cent in the United Kingdom, 25 per cent in the European Union. Within five years, connectedness will be almost universal, let's say over 75 per cent in all advanced countries. But in the world at large, only three per cent of the world population is connected and in areas that have been measured a little more accurately, such as South Asia, the figure is less than one per cent.

Some reliable estimates suggest that there will be two billion Internet users by 2007. But then the real problem arises, because educational ability and cultural capital are extremely unequally distributed. And this inequality of cultural and educational capital is amplified by the Internet.

Third, everybody agrees that in the new system education, technological literacy and research and development are key sources of production and of the ability to benefit from this production. Education, technological literacy and research and development are extremely unevenly distributed in the world. Now we know that there has been a major effort at schooling children throughout the world; for instance, Brazil has made an extraordinary effort. In primary education at this point, 96 per cent of the children are at school.

But about 40 per cent of the teachers have not completed primary education. In other words, what we are seeing throughout the world is what I call the warehousing of children rather than the education of children. It's a good idea, and it's better than having them on the streets. So it's a beginning but it doesn't mean that we are actually improving education *per se*.

Fourth, volatility of financial integration leads to recurring crises which have lasting, devastating affects in the more vulnerable areas. For instance, the crisis in East Asia in 1997–1998 is generally over in terms of the financial markets or in terms of investment flows. But entire regions in Indonesia, Thailand, the Philippines, even in Korea, are still devastated and according to some of the United Nations calculations, are regions which will take at least five years to recover to the previous level of employment.

Fifth, governments, which used to be the compensators, are often bypassed by flows of capital and technology, and are increasingly restrained by international financial institutions and private lenders.

Sixth, in this crisis, a criminal economy develops, further delegitimising governments and creating a parallel economy that benefits from globalisation. Estimates on the size of the criminal economy today value it at about US$1 trillion per year. I don't frankly believe too much in these estimates because I don't know how they are measured. Apparently this is done through accounting in terms of financial flows but let's say, to be precise, that it's a lot, and certainly it's at least as much as some of the key industries in the developed world.

As economies and societies come under stress, corruption, ethnic strife, crime and civil wars emerge in most of the world, disintegrating states and societies. Massive movements of population, migrations, vast urbanisation without conditions to integrate people in cities, follow. This leads to a permanent ecological crisis and ultimately to the development of epidemics of different kinds. And in this process, children are the most vulnerable and they are abused more than ever, not only in their families, as used to be the case, but in the economy at large.

So, in that sense, we have unleashed extraordinary creativity and technological innovation but the contradictions of development are sharper than ever.

... we have unleashed extraordinary creativity and technological innovation but the contradictions of development are sharper than ever.

Now, is this system sustainable? Is this process of globalisation creating value at unprecedented rates at one end of the networks and at the same time not integrating a substantial proportion of humankind? Is this sustainable? Well, believe it or not, many people think it is. Many people in the higher circles of decision-making believe that it will work, that there will be a 'trickle-down' effect. In the meantime, charity should smooth the transition to the new world. The underlying assumption is that the new economy is so powerful, it's so innovative, it's so creative, that all these will ultimately trickle down, so we just have to be patient for a while.

Now, I'm very hesitant to accept this position. Certainly for moral and ethical reasons, but morality doesn't get you a long way in this world. I think the system has built-in contradictions which make it highly unlikely that it will be sustainable. The first one is the volatility of financial markets being systemic. It's been, at this point, compensated for by the very rapid ups after the downs but this volatility is not what we used to know as the business cycle. The business cycle still exists and the key issue here is that on the one hand, you have a highly volatile financial system and on the other hand, you have a business cycle with which it sometimes coincides, sometimes doesn't. If, by simple statistical probability we have a downturn of the business cycle coinciding with a conjunctural downturn in volatility, then the extent of the plunge could be important enough to actually provoke not a catastrophic crisis of the 1929 kind but a crisis large enough to hamper elements of the key economies substantially.

And since at this point about 50 per cent of American households and about 35 per cent of German households have a susbtantial proportion of their assets in stock markets, together with their real estate (indeed, for the first time in history, more households in the United States have a larger proportion of their assets in stock markets than in their homes), well, the impact of volatility could be accumulative. The same thing with people being paid in stock options which are great when they become billionaires but have nothing when stocks go down.

So first of all, financial volatility is systemic, we do not have systems to regulate it. Electronic trading makes it very difficult and governments don't do it anyway. It's certainly not from South Africa that you are going to regulate the financial flows.

Second, the system may at this point be having some crisis of overcapacity. The notion that you can broaden markets at a speed and a size large enough to compensate for the extraordinary increase in productivity and economic growth in the core economies is also very questionable. Europe is only now reaching the stage of the new economy. The United States is increasing productivity, depending upon moments and years, between 2,6 per cent and four per cent per annum.

Therefore, it's real growth based on increasing productivity. Europe is jumping now from the 1,9 per cent productivity growth over the last two years, to an estimated 2,5 per cent this year and three per cent the following year. Well, if this is not economic growth but the growth of productivity (which is really the key growth), if this continues, then the notion that 19 per cent of the population of the planet is going to be able to absorb this extraordinary increase in innovation and productivity is actually, in my opinion, farfetched.

Third, it's not only the ratio of productivity over market expansion but the fact that this economy can only thrive on the basis of talent, of building up, bringing into the economy higher numbers of talented people able to be productive. The United States only works these days because of the 200 000 skilled engineers, scientists and technicians imported from the rest of the world. But even China, India and Russia can be exhausted very soon in these terms. So unless there is a process of development in which the entire world produces talent for the entire world and not only for Silicon Valley, precisely because of the extraordinary dynamism and creativity of the system, it's actually unsustainable.

Then, the notion that this system can proceed forever, while excluding two thirds of humankind, is simply naïve. Let's say that the 'trickle-down' theory works, which I don't believe. The whole matter here is the time frame. If it works in five years, all right, but if it works in twenty years, I see that the reactions that we are observing in terms of the global development process, in terms of the Seattle syndrome, fighting against the process of social exclusion, will make the system not only economically and technologically unsustainable but socially and politically unsustainable.

References

Annan, K (2000) *We the Peoples: The Role of the United Nations in the Twenty-First Century.* New York: United Nations.

Saxenian, AL (1999) *Silicon Valley's New Immigrant Entrepreneurs.* San Francisco: Public Policy Institute of Caliornia.

Volcker, P (2000) 'The sea of global finance', in W Hutton and A Giddens (eds) *On the Edge: Living in Global Capitalism.* London: Jonathan Cape.

martin carnoy

The role of the state in the new global economy

Introduction

I would like to address the very difficult issue of trying to understand the role of the state in the new global economy. Four important changes inform this analysis:

- the nature of labour markets is being transformed – workers are being separated from traditional collectivities and individualised into 'human capital portfolios'
- the world economy is increasingly a knowledge economy
- the national economy is increasingly less national, and so the national state has decreased influence over the definition of economic and social life
- the distance between those workers 'integrated' into the global economy and those who are not increases, creating a more limited space in which state social policies are relevant for most workers – such policies increasingly have to focus on reintegrating marginalised individuals into some notion of collectivity.

In the national industrial economy, the role of the capitalist state was crucial to reproducing capitalist society. That role was to convert class consciousness developed in the workplace and working-class communities into an individualised notion of identity and to an attachment to a national identity rooted in individual consciousness and action. This national identity was couched in individualistic terms and an individualistic notion of the workers' political role.

The organisation of work and the state

The state's role in individualising workers and separating them from their class was crucial in industrial capitalism precisely because of the organisation of industrial work. The factory system separated workers from their tools, but put them into a new organisation of work that gave them new social identity – despite employers' efforts to pit different groups of workers in the factory against each other. The factory system enabled workers to organise associations around particular workplaces and long-term employment. They created job-based, firm-based and industry-based unions that reproduced class identification. Job and occupational stability in the industrial system helped produce a new working-class consciousness. The development of this consciousness in the context of industrial work organisation is a crucial fact of late 19th century and much of 20th century political life. So is the democratic capitalist nation-state's role in combating and recasting this consciousness through creating individual citizen-nationalists, individual voters and individual subjects of the juridical process.

Today, a major change is taking place in the workplace. Globalisation and information technology are transforming work. The new organisation of work that characterises this transformation incorporates individualisation of workers directly into labour markets and the structure of production. This was made possible largely because of the success of democratic capitalist states in internalising individualisation of workers through the ideological apparatuses of the state. Globalised firms in those advanced capitalist countries where the ideology of individualisation was more developed and class consciousness more weakly developed are finding it easier to restructure their work organisations on the basis of individualised workers. Nonetheless, the transformation of work is occurring in all capitalist economies. What is the nature of this transformation and what does it imply for the ideological role of the nation-state?

More intense competition on a worldwide scale makes firms acutely aware of costs and productivity. The 'solution' they have settled on is to reorganise work around decentralised management, work differentiation and customised products, thereby individualising work tasks and differentiating individual workers in their relationship to supervisors and employers. This has made subcontracting, part-timing and hiring temporary labour much easier, since a lot of work can be narrowed down to specific tasks, even as other 'core' work is conducted in teams and is multitasked. Workers are gradually being defined socially less by a particular long-term job they hold than by the knowledge they have acquired by studying and working. This knowledge 'portfolio' allows them to move across firms and even across types of work, as jobs are redefined.

This transformation is occurring rapidly and with profound impact on labour markets. According to the estimates in my book (Carnoy 2000), 'non-standard' employment (part-time, temporary and self-employed) increased in almost all countries in the Organisation for Economic Co-operation and Development (OECD) between the mid-1980s and the mid-1990s, rising to 37 per cent in the United Kingdom, 30 per cent in France and Germany, almost 40 per cent in Italy, more than 40 per cent in Holland, almost 50 per cent in Japan and 50 per cent in Australia. In the United States, already characterised by a high degree of flexibility in industrial-era capitalist labour markets compared to European countries, the proportion of non-standard employment is relatively low, at about 27 per cent. But according to a recent survey, the proportion in California, a state in the vanguard of responding to globalisation, is much higher, at about 60 per cent.

In addition to the growth of non-standard employment, the new workplace is marked by less attachment to a particular job.

In addition to the growth of non-standard employment, the new workplace is marked by less attachment to a particular job. Turnover rates are increasing in a number of OECD countries, particularly among younger and middle-aged workers. Younger workers in the United States change jobs more frequently in order to increase their earnings; older workers are 'restructured' out of jobs, usually taking income losses. The result is flatter age-income profiles than in the past for all education groups after age forty. The 'traditional' relationship between earnings and seniority and the security that went with it is disappearing. Even though these figures pertain to a highly developed country, the United States, we can be certain that the behaviour of firms worldwide tend to emulate the United States model, and so labour markets worldwide will tend to move in the same direction. This will be just as true in the more developed parts of developing economies, including South Africa.

The conception underlying this relationship of a family–work structure that had men earning income and women taking care of children is also disappearing. In its place, a new work system is developing that includes women as part-time and full-time workers, a family that is generally much smaller, and jobs no longer embedded in a stable, working-class network dominated by male workers. Again, family structure varies greatly from society to society, but the trends in the developed countries are rapidly diffusing to developing countries.

The effect of individualisation and differentiation is to separate workers from the 'permanent', full-time jobs in stable businesses that characterised post-World War II development in Europe, Japan, the United States and other industrialised countries. Just as an earlier factory revolution drove a wedge between workers and products they made, the new transformation is dissolving the identity that workers developed with industrial organisations such as the corporation and the trade union. Workers are being individualised, separated from their 'traditional' identities built over more than a century, and from the social networks that enabled them to find economic security. The 'job' and everything organised around the job – the group of work friends in the company, the after-work hangouts, the trade union, even the car pool – lose their social function. They are as 'permanently temporary' as the work itself.

As Anna Saxenian (1994) has shown, some, mainly highly educated, professional and technical workers are building new networks. Instead of just talking to colleagues in the company where they work, they build electronic mail and informal information relations across companies and across countries. Network technology such as the Internet helps. Information exchanged in after-work, up-scale hangouts attracting professionals from a broad range of firms serves the same purpose. The main question is what happens to the vast majority of workers who do not have easy access to information about other companies or to workers in other companies, or those highly skilled workers who fall 'out of the loop'. They tend to be left in an individualised limbo, 'disaggregated' from traditional networks but not 'integrated' into new ones. New, private networks, such as temp agencies, are emerging to fill this void. These temp agencies have existed in various forms all over the world, in developing as well as developed countries. But, except for some striking exceptions, such as construction unions that traditionally allocate temp jobs among their members, these new networks are not organised for or by workers. They miss satisfying the need for social integration served by stable jobs, unions and professional associations.

If workers are now being successfully disaggregated from class identity at the workplace itself, the crucial role of the nation-state in individualising class-conscious workers becomes less central to capitalist hegemony. Rather, the ideological apparatuses of the nation-state – the juridical system, education and political parties – take on roles that have less to do with preserving capitalist class relations against an active potential of working-class consciousness, than in trying to keep isolated individuals in the global economic and political environment. The main project of the capitalist state changes from one of separating the worker from his or her class-based identity to one of bringing the isolated, individualised worker into a global, market identity. The legitimacy of the nation-state itself hinges on its capacity to reintegrate workers into a globalised notion of community and identity. Poulantzas' (1980) notion of the state as a locus of struggle remains, but the struggle inside the state shifts from one based solely on class to one based on group (including class) identity and its various and multifaceted conceptions of reintegration. At the same time, the centrality of political struggle in the ideological apparatuses of the nation-state is not as great as before.

The main project of the capitalist state changes from one of separating the worker from his or her class-based identity to one of bringing the isolated, individualised worker into a global, market identity.

Castells points out that one of the ironies of this is that the nation-state was and is the agent of globalisation, creating the contradiction of reducing its own power and also creating the need to reconstruct itself to manage and compensate for the exacerbation of inequality caused by globalisation. So the nation-state which pushes (particularly developed countries, but now even in developing countries) for globalisation by supporting free trade, trying to attract foreign investment and stimulate exports by adhering to International Monetary Fund and World Bank directives, essentially reduces its own definition of a nation-state. At the same time it creates conditions which make inequality even greater within the national border and therefore creates a greater task for itself even as it diminishes its power.

The knowledge economy

In the developed countries during the era of industrial capitalism, the production of knowledge could be characterised as largely national. The state was influential in defining a 'science' and 'values' that served the reproduction of power within national boundaries. Scientific knowledge became central to capitalist production in late capitalism. Much of this centrality emerged as part of the military–industrial complex that dominated post-World War II scientific development, not only in Western capitalist countries but also in the Soviet Union and China, the main state capitalist economies. Beyond the militarisation of scientific innovation, the post-World War II welfare state, with its vast public resources, was also able to define the social incorporation of marginalised groups through its knowledge apparatuses, namely the educational system, the health system and the welfare system.

In developing societies, knowledge has also been a 'monopoly' of the national state, with education systems defined by the state and almost all research and development, such as it exists, done by state-owned enterprises. The issue in developing countries concerning the 'nationality' of knowledge revolves much more around how much of the knowledge has its origins in the developed countries and is imported. In that sense, for the developing countries, knowledge never had its locus nationally.

In the globalised information technology environment, knowledge formation and power over knowledge moves out of the control of the nation-state. This is true for three reasons.

First, dominant bourgeois values and norms are in the process of being globalised. They are increasingly organised around knowledge and information that circulate globally and serve a globalised innovation and profit-making structure. The highest valued information and knowledge now have their locus in the global economy, not in any single national site, even though many kinds of knowledge with global value are produced in national locations or certain local aggregations of innovation, such as Silicon Valley. This transformation of knowledge formation from national into global space is still in its incipient stages, but the trend is clear. It results mainly from the globalisation of science-based, innovation industries, the rapid demilitarisation of high-tech companies beginning in the mid-1980s, and, finally, the rapid, global growth of telecommunications and information technology themselves. Thus, even though the most advanced forms of knowledge production still take place in the private and public sectors of a few countries, the public role is proportionately declining and knowledge production capacity to other countries is spreading, first to the newly industrialised countries, then further out. And because 'global values' are primarily those rooted in global finance and production, knowledge is increasingly defined in terms of economic value. Since the nation-state's monopoly of knowledge was at least partly determined by its ability to interpret and transmit bourgeois behavioural norms, including language and culture, this shift to greater valuation of profit-producing skills again means the reduction of the nation-state's control over knowledge.

... knowledge is increasingly defined in terms of economic value.

Second, many of the same forces are decentralising the control of knowledge production and transmission within countries away from the centrality of nation-states. Nation-state sponsored and controlled scientific innovation for military purposes, while still important, is declining rapidly compared to innovation that originates totally outside state control. For example, the Internet, which was originally state-sponsored as part of a university–military networking program (electronic mail), is spreading worldwide outside the state knowledge system. The near-ubiquity of personal computers and Internet access in the developed countries is gradually making it possible to access education, particularly at the university level, through privately financed and managed courses of study, many of them promising better training in globally valued knowledge than that provided by the state educational system.

Third, because of increased economic competition and aging populations, the industrial nation-states have been unable to sustain the level of welfare of the post-World War II period. This has decreased the influence of these states over those segments of the population already most marginalised in industrial capitalism. Global competition marginalises these segments – namely those with the least formal education, the least socialisation into the nation-state and the least capacity to increase the value of their human capital – even more than before. Because they have difficulty accessing knowledge deemed valuable by global markets, their members search for other forms of knowledge that reinforce their identity both outside global markets and outside the nation-state knowledge system.

Thus, the modern capitalist state developed into a successful market 'softener'. But the decline of that role in the face of powerful global marketisation of national economies pushes the 'dispossessed' to seek refuge in new and more exclusive collectives. These collectives generally do not have the power or the funds to help the dispossessed financially nor to develop the skills and knowledge valued by global markets. They can help develop self-knowledge and therefore self-confidence. They can provide community and therefore a sense of belonging. Cultural identity, or what I call 'self-knowledge', whether religious, ethnic, racial or gender, and whether local, regional or more global, is an antidote to the complexity and harshness of the global market as the judge of a person's worth. Although the production of such self-knowledge may be highly centralised in formal, sometimes global, religious organisations, it is generally disconnected from nation-states.

Thus, globalisation has eroded the nation-state's monopoly of scientific knowledge and its ability to use that knowledge to reproduce class power, even as the nature of class power relations itself moves away from nation-state control. Even as knowledge becomes increasingly important in shaping power relations, the state's role in this process is declining for the reasons discussed. Yet, that said, the state still has an important, albeit changing, role in defining knowledge, distributing it and using it to shape power relations. The state-financed and run educational system continues to dominate the educational process, hence the transmission of knowledge to the young as well as the production of new knowledge in universities. Those who want to acquire new knowledge therefore still have to pass through the apparatuses of the state.

... the state still has an important, albeit changing, role in defining knowledge, distributing it and using it to shape power relations.

The difference is that in the global environment, global markets, not national markets and moral values, determine the knowledge transmitted in the nation-state's educational system. This has long been the case in the developing countries most tied to capitalist metropoles. The nation-state increasingly uses its remaining control over knowledge production and transmission to develop a global ideology rooted in the singular value of productive skills. This ideology tends systematically to undermine the importance and legitimacy of the nation-state even as the nation-state attempts to use the educational system in this way to maintain political legitimacy.

Further, because knowledge is becoming more important in shaping power, those groups that were not well served by the state's education system in the past are now more willing to abandon the state in their drive to acquire globally valued skills. In the industrial era, mere graduation from secondary school or vocational school was sufficient to get a good, high-paying, permanent job in a manufacturing plant. In today's global, knowledge-based service economy, access to university education has become crucial to getting a high-paying job, and to establishing the networks needed for social mobility. Poor and many middle-class parents reason that if the state was not able or willing to deliver the knowledge needed for entry to university education in the past, why would it do so now. Although they continue to pressure the state to give their children better access to knowledge, they also push for alternative, privately run forms of education not under the direct control of the state.

In sum, knowledge formation and power over knowledge in the global economy is moving out of the control of the nation-state, because innovation is globalised, because the discourse on knowledge is outside the state's control, and because information is much more accessible than it was before, thanks to technology and communications. Self-knowledge, in the form of cultural identity, also pulls the discourse out of the 'scientific'. The nation-state is also losing control over the educational system, as education decentralises and privatises in response to pressures by parents to get the kind of education for their children that is needed by them to acquire globally valued skills.

The new relation between power and knowledge is negotiated increasingly in the global innovation system and global markets.

At the same time, knowledge and information continue to be distributed very unequally, probably more unequally than when they were a state 'monopoly'. The new relation between power and knowledge is negotiated increasingly in the global innovation system and global markets. Ironically, national and regional states, which before monopolised knowledge and shaped its distribution, are still a major site of organising knowledge transmission and production, but now for the global economy. And it is mainly through this knowledge production and transmission that the state both maintains its legitimacy and shapes the national economic/political space in terms of global investment and production. The better the state can 'reintegrate' its disaggregated workers into a smoothly functioning knowledge-based society, the higher the potential return to global capital in those national and regional sites, and the more rapid the economic development at those sites.

Globalisation and the network state

For the most part, national governments and even local and regional governments are still operating under the old model. They have not understood how to change and deal with these new conditions. So they are still busy isolating and disaggregating workers. Nation-states are still operating in ways that separate workers from social identities that are already disappearing. As a result, nation-states are becoming irrelevant politically to increasing fractions of their citizenry. We have evidence from many of the developed and developing countries that there is less and less attachment to national politics. This is not an issue of national identity, which is also declining. More importantly, people are involving themselves less and less in national politics. They find it less and less relevant to their world, in large part because the national politicians are still trying to do things in the old way. Rather than concerning themselves with collective identities that might undermine national capitalism, national politicians should now be concerned that over-individualisation and separation will undermine national, regional and local sites of global capitalism.

This changes the conception of an efficient state completely. Many have argued that globalisation means the end of the nation-state. Globalisation may indeed mean the end of the nation-state if the nation-state fails to redefine itself to meet the new conditions it faces in a globalised environment.

In other words, if the nation-state fails to become efficient in new ways that are appropriate to the new global economic conditions that Castells has described, it will certainly begin to disappear. The old discussion of a strong or centralised state versus a decentralised state is largely irrelevant here. The real issue in the global environment is how to define a new concept of an efficient state, whether or not that state is centralised.

What are the characteristics of this new efficiency? The first is that the state has to be able to create and sustain the underlying conditions for economic growth in a global economy. In a global economic environment, that means attracting global capital and generating capital at home. Many continue to argue that attracting global and creating local capital means suppressing labour and keeping wages low. I would argue that high labour productivity, good infrastructure including financial infrastructure and a high level of social capital – the trust and belief that you can write contracts and have them enforced – are far more important than low wages.

The second characteristic of this new state is that it is able to reincorporate separated, disaggregated workers into new forms of community. So much more than in the past, this means creating a competent, flexible bureaucracy that can deliver appropriate government services to a diverse constituency. This includes the very difficult task of separating informal labour markets from crime labour markets. An efficient state has to be able to control crime. That is abundantly clear in post-apartheid South Africa. A mass demand from the citizenry is the control of crime. Yet, it is difficult to differentiate crime from informal labour markets. The state has to be highly efficient to do that, particularly in a situation such as South Africa's where the state was used previously to exercise control under totally undemocratic conditions.

Castells and I call the new efficient state the 'network state'. It is a state made of shared institutions, and enacted by bargaining and interactive iteration all along the chain of decision-making: national governments, co-national governments, supra-national bodies, international institutions, governments of nationalities, regional governments, local governments and NGOs (in our conception, neo-governmental organisations). Decision-making and representation take place all along the chain, not necessarily in the hierarchical, prescripted order. This new state functions as a network, in which all nodes interact and are equally necessary for the performance of the state's functions. It is a state whose efficiency is defined in terms of its capacity to create and sustain networks – global, regional and local networks, and through these networks, to promote economic growth and develop new forms of social integration.

It is a state whose efficiency is defined in terms of its capacity to create and sustain networks – global, regional and local networks, and through these networks, to promote economic growth and develop new forms of social integration.

As I have argued here, knowledge is a very important element in this new global economy, and it is even more important in terms of a network state's role. Knowledge production plays a definitive role, both in creating the conditions for economic growth – attracting foreign capital and creating local capital – and in managing and compensating the disequalising effects of globalisation locally.

With the Internet and mobile phone technology and the private control of the medium, the monopoly of the state sector and information is clearly reduced. But the state still has a crucial role to play in creating the infrastructure to equalised access to such technology and in making the technology itself more widely available to economically marginalised groups.

In most countries schooling is still a state monopoly, at least, from a financial perspective. So even if it is privately run, it is financed by the state. Traditionally, schooling has been a selection mechanism. It also produces knowledge but its primary function is to decide who is going to get more and who is going to get less. That is what exams are about, that is what high school certification is about, that is what failing from university or finishing university is about. This has been a primary means to legitimate class differences by shifting class-consciousness to individual notions of success and failure.

In a new global environment, however, the selection function of the schools will have to be de-emphasised and the knowledge and skill production function has to be stressed. Making such a change is not a simple matter. The state will have to transform an entire school bureaucracy based on different conditions of work and different understandings of what it is doing. If the knowledge production system – the school system – is not transformed in this way, the very legitimacy of the state is at risk and the capacity of the state to sustain economic development in a global environment is also at risk. If people who are separated and alienated, who are no longer socialised, who no longer form their social collectivities around work, are not convinced that they have a reasonable chance to be incorporated into the world economy in some fashion, the nation-state really has not much left to do and it will become irrelevant.

The state must also be able to facilitate the creation of new communities and new identities around these communities. With knowledge at the centre of the network state and a global economy, it is likely that the new communities will be organised around continuous education institutions. Community identity will be created around the development of various forms of knowledge in these institutions, including self-knowledge – by that I mean ethnic and religious identities and gender identities.

Near Pretoria, there is a community built around a private school. This is not a township community. It is a very wealthy community, built around an elite school. The community has a wall around it, and it is organised around this good school. For years, people have organised themselves as communities around universities. More than before, with high-tech production, the universities are the centre of both production and residency. The highest paid labour in high-tech communities lives near the university that spawned the high-tech parks, and the workers live far away from such knowledge centres. These notions of community go from the very lowest level of schooling all the way to the highest level. In helping to define communities, the state has to consider the renewal of knowledge throughout workers' entire lives, including from a very young age, all the way to senior citizenship.

The state cannot survive for long without legitimacy. People must feel some degree of allegiance to the state, or state control will become synonymous with dictatorship. The betrayal of national interests, the rise of media politics and its close associate the politics of scandal, all contribute to undermine the legitimacy of the nation-state. Its strategy to escape de-legitimation is two-pronged: it strives to stimulate economic growth, national employment and domestic consumption; and, simultaneously, it decentralises political responsibility by increasing local/regional autonomy.

Security ultimately translates into economic growth and improving living standards.

For most people in the world, fully aware of what is going on, and ready to stay home, the critical matter is personal security. Security ultimately translates into economic growth and improving living standards. In this sense, even social inequality is not a major issue. If people see their lives improving, they will not be ready to lose what they have only to correct the injustice of the rich getting richer. So, steady improvement of living standards for the large majority of the population, via informational productivity and globalisation-induced economic growth, is the main axis for building state legitimacy. I am not saying this will work. I am simply observing that this is a widespread state practice, and is, in fact, the only option once the choice has been made to adapt to the rules of global financial markets. In addition, redistribution through welfare, pensions, taxation and other efforts to equalise income, whenever and wherever possible, would increase legitimacy. But this is an afterthought for the network state. Redistribution is only implemented under substantial pressure from social movements.

I have argued that knowledge production and distribution is becoming a primary form of both stimulating economic growth, as it has been traditionally but even more so in a global economy, and of reincorporating disaggregated, individualised workers into a sense of society and community. In that sense, state legitimacy will increasingly depend on the state's ability to deliver knowledge and information efficiently to a diverse population.

At the same time, the legitimacy of the nation-state and its capacity to enforce the underlying rules and regulation of national market economies through democratic means and smoothly running political apparatuses, as well as to support a well-developed knowledge and market information system, are important to global finance capital.

References

Carnoy, M (2000) *Sustaining the New Economy: Work, Family and Community in the Information Age.* Cambridge: Harvard University Press.

Poulantzas, N (1980) *State, Power, Socialism.* London: New Left Books.

Saxenian, AL (1994) *Regional Advantage: Culture and Competition in Silicon Valley and Route 128.* Cambridge: Harvard University Press.

Martin Carnoy is a Professor of Education and Economics at Stanford University. After graduating from Caltech with a BS in electrical engineering and the University of Chicago with Ph.D. in economics, he worked at The Brookings Institution for four years, writing on Latin American trade and development. In 1969 he came to the School of Education at Stanford where he helped build the International and Comparative Education Programme he currently chairs.

shiv visvanathan

The grand sociology of Manuel Castells

Introduction

The Information Age is a record of one of the master narratives of the 20th century. In fact, Manuel Castells chronicles the one idea that has survived the 20th century.

The last century has been a strange one. There is a sense of premature closure about it. The 20th century had died of an entropy of ideas by the nineties. All its heroes and ideas faded prematurely. The Bolshevik Revolution had run its course. Castro sounded stale. Mao was dead. The great debates of planning were over. Che Guevara was an advertising pin-up. Glasnost was over. The great movements of nationalism and its leaders – Nkrumah, Nasser, Nehru – sounded stale or moth-eaten.

In fact, there is a sense of irony, of strange laughter, when Castells says that the hero, the agency of the 21st century is not the state, nor the non-governmental organisation, nor organisations like the party and the trade union, but the network. Castells' work reminds one of Eugene Marais' *The Soul of the White Ant* (1937). The reader discovers that the individual is not the termite but the entire termite mound itself. The network is a new kind of collective – fluid, amoeboid, totally unlike those earlier agencies of the 20th century, the party, the nation-state, the proletariat.

There is something Tolstoyan in the sheer monumentality of the Castells *œuvre*. A blurb writer could dub the three volumes *War and Peace in the Network Society*. There is an enormity, a range to the work. But along with the monumentality and the self-disciplined objectivity, there is a sense of the protean, the mobile. For Castells, Procrustes and Proteus have to be captured simultaneously and separately. It is this many-sided shiftingness that makes Castells' work a monumental one, where he has to capture both the whole and the synecdochal part. How does Castells tackle this problem? He does it by showing that the nature of the narratives of dominance have changed.

Within the comparative sociology of development, the Weberian narratives have been dominant. The usual question asked is, how did the West become dominant? This exercise is generally broken down to, why did capitalism first emerge in the West? or, why did science not emerge in China? The basic narratives from Weber to Needham split the narrative between the West and the rest of us.

Underlying these grand narratives is a periodisation of societies into tribal, agricultural, industrial and the service economies. This sequence of stages is seen as the trajectory of the West and is then packaged as a theory of development, a sequence of stages that the 'rest' must undergo. Those that fail to conform are confined to 'the dustbin of history', given the fact that it is the West that writes such histories. The narratives that explain why the West succeeded are elaborated in the writings of David Landes (1998) and Andre Gunder Frank (1998). Accompanying them is the question, why has the Third World failed? This is caught in the outpourings of the great industry of academics from the Harvard Institute for International Development, the Institute of Development Studies or their epigoni.

Castells breaks away from the frozen geometry of the West versus the rest, or the immobility of the centre–periphery model. The cartography of the network society eludes these standard geographies of power. The fluidity of the network society is such that peripheries exist within the centre and that the Schumpetarian explosions of innovation can mushroom anywhere, as Taiwan, Japan or the Asian Tigers have shown within limits.

The 20th century world of citizens is different from the emerging world of netizens.

The totemic relation to place is elusive. The nature of finance and multinational capital is such that it can uproot itself and locate itself anywhere. It is like a game of musical chairs where the players and the chairs are moving and even the music changes. But disembedding the network society from the standard cartographies of power is not quite enough. The hegemony of the new atlas loses its fixity of territory, the sheer physicality one associated with old travelogues of power embodied in colonial anthropology, orientalism or 19th century ideas of political economy. The network is virtual. Many of the old categories of work, labour, value do not apply easily. Gandhi and Marx seem jaded in this simulated world. The 20th century world of citizens is different from the emerging world of netizens. The old continents were discovered. The map did not exhaust the diversity of territory. The old Cartesians could say, like Columbus, the map is not territory. But the network society appears to be an invention. Map easily redraws territory and reinvents it. Huge sectors of place get transformed into indifferent space in a manner of minutes. The network as the impending future recreates itself. It appears both parthenogenetic and also able to cannibalise itself. But beyond such biological breathlessness, there is a physicality to it, a history and most of all, a framework of politics, we need to question and explore.

My article focuses on the politics of Castells' work narrowing itself to two questions: How does Castells locate his network/information society within a politics of knowledge? How does Castells' network society stand as a fragment of the democratic imagination? The essay plays hedgehog to Castells' fox.

The Castellian narrative is also a political script. At one level, it is a grand story and at another, it is an open script inviting us to enact our part in our own way. How does Castells elaborate the network society as a rule game? Because if we don't understand the rule game, we might at best be third- or fourth-rate players. The question before us is do we play the game, or do we challenge the rules of the game? We are immediately faced with questions such as, what should the Fourth World do? What role can South Africa play? Does India have a role or is its almost total absence from these giant narratives an erasure, an amnesia, an absentmindedness? How do we challenge the grammar of the net society?

The first kind of politics can be effective but reactive. It is like the choice of a set of bit players training or aspiring for bigger parts. It is the choice of many states and people aspiring to replicate Silicon Valleys or imitate Bill Gates. Such a strategy leaves too many of us as extras or bit players. The second strategy needs to understand, master or even change the rule game. This statement is made with the belief that every individual is a philosopher and that as philosophers, citizens can change bits of the world and themselves.

The politics of knowledge vs the politics of information

I would like to repeat a story which, like other stories, I have told often. A few years ago I was delivering a paper on alternative energy systems. During the course of the presentation, I observed how philosophy of science as a discourse had emerged from the grassroots movements in India rather than from the academe. These feminist, ecological and tribal groups realised that it was not just a question of good or bad science but of the axiomatics of science as knowledge. And in this context I used the word 'epistemology'. A leading development expert who was assigned to comment on my paper asked, 'Why do you use the word "epistemology", the World Bank president can't understand it?' And I answered, 'That's why.' But the reason was more than that moment of perversity. The movements in India and their narrators realised that science as a rule game must be challenged or reworked and thus epistemology, that is, rules or methods for the making of knowledge, becomes crucial.

We have to ask what is Castells' theory of knowledge. What is his conception of the politics of knowledge? Following Thomas Kuhn (1970), he refers to the 'information technology paradigm'. Kuhn's notion of the paradigm is more intellectualist and internalist, less open to the socio-economic dynamics of ideas. Castells' idea of the paradigm is techno-economic. But in exploring Castells' idea of the paradigm which borrows more from Christopher Freeman (1982) and Carlotta Perez (1983) and contrasting it with the classical Kuhnean idea, one discovers some fatal differences. Castells in a footnote follows Daniel Bell's (1976) affable definition of knowledge as 'a set of organised statements of facts and ideas, presenting a reasoned judgement or an experimental result, which is transmitted to others through some communication medium in some systematic form', and then follows Porat's (1977) operational definition of information as 'data that has been organised and communicated'. Because of Castells' preoccupation with information, there is a strange silence about knowledge. Castells' network society is sociology of the informational paradigm without sociology of knowledge or a theory of knowledge. Castells is brilliant on the socio-technical nature of the paradigm but is less sensitive on the politics of the paradigm itself.

There is a politics of knowledge which is present in Kuhn's idea of the paradigm. Paradigms in the Kuhnian sense have a many layered density. They function as myths, metaphors, methods, models, techniques. Yet they are woven together into a tight architectonic, a unity which determines what is relevant and irrelevant, what one can see and not see, what one can say and not say or even be heard. A paradigm in its everydayness is an entire civics of knowledge blind to other alternatives. Whatever diversities exist, exist within the monoculture, the hegemonic reign of the paradigm. The dominant paradigm has no place for defeated knowledges or alternative theories of knowledge.

Castells' work has no explicit theory of knowledge or the varieties of knowledge. He takes the nature of modern science for granted. His information technology paradigm is really only a revamped but playful transfer of technology model with a place for finance capital and criminality. As a result, Castells' network society is the gigantic civics of the transfer of technology paradigm, embodying a new relation between map and territory. What it lacks is a politics of knowledge and a politics of competing theories of knowledge. Castells' paradigm would see alternative epistemologies as 'noise'. For example, Africa is compulsively a part of the Fourth World as a result of the failure of development. But apart from the breakdown of the state and the growth of a predatory elite, the failure might be a result of the models of science applied to it. It is often argued that African models of farming might embody different notions of community and science. It is this community of expertise that the official application of development might have destroyed. Within such a framework, African agriculture and systems of healing might be alternative paradigms, elusive and elliptical to current models of science. Viewed in this way, the Fourth World becomes not a void or a black box but an alternative list of diversities, possibilities, epistemologies.

Within this context, one is reminded of the botanist Wes Jackson's observations. Both in his *Altars of Unhewn Stone* (1987) and in personal conversations, Jackson made the comment that he was often puzzled that America was called a 'high information society' and as a corollary Africa and India would be 'low information societies'. Jackson claimed that he was puzzled that America was treated as a high information society when it had reduced its varieties of apples from 160 to five. Jackson observes:

> Though conventional wisdom holds that we are in the midst of an informational explosion, more careful consideration must surely convince us that the opposite is true. Think of all that has happened to the world since 1935. Few dispute that there is less biological information. Species extinction at the rate of one thousand species a year or so, especially in the tropics, coupled with the genetic truncation of major crops, undeniably is a major loss of biological information. (Jackson 1987: 11)

Jackson adds that 'species extinction and genetic narrowing of crops aside, the loss of cultural information due to the depopulation of our rural areas is greater than all the information accumulated by science and technology in the same period'. Jackson's notion of information is not a disembedded one. He observes:

> Farm families who practised traditions associated with planting, tending, harvesting and storing ... gathered information, much of it unconsciously from the time they were infants: in the farm household, in the farm community, and in the barns and fields. They heard and told stories about relatives and community members who did something funny or were caught in some kind of tragedy. From these stories they

> learned basic lessons of agronomy. Much of that information has already disappeared and continues to disappear as farmers leave the land. It is the kind of information that has been hard won over the millennia, from the time agriculture began. It is valuable because much of it is turned to the harvest of contemporary sunlight, the kind of information we need now and in the future on the land. ...
>
> A friend of mine, a distinguished professor in a major university, is terribly alarmed about species extinction in the tropics. He is a leader in the fight to save rain forests everywhere. As a person who has joined the fight to preserve the biota of the planet, he gives numerous talks each year about the problems of overpopulation, resource depletion, and pollution. He heads the library committee for his university and is much impressed with the 'knowledge explosion', how much we now know, and how much better educated graduate students are now than they were when he was a student. As do most Americans, he sees Silicon Valley and the computer industry as representing an expansion of knowledge. When I suggested that there is less total cultural information in the United States today than fifty years ago, he did not agree. I was thinking about the cultural information just mentioned, the information that has left the countryside, the kind of information that is the necessary basis for a sustainable or sunshine agriculture. (Jackson 1987: 12)

The definition of knowledge is thus crucial to the debate. To define knowledge as formal, abstractable knowledge is to impoverish knowledge and to deny the existence of tacit knowledges, embodied knowledges, alternative knowledges. It is this wider epistemological politics of knowledge that is missing in Castells' work. The danger is that knowledge might soon be rewritten to suit the paradigm. As a result that which cannot be reprogrammed for the network ceases to be knowledge. Castells' core work avoids this issue though he is sensitive to it when he discusses the Japanese experience in his reference to the importance of tacit knowledge in the Japanese work organisation.

Castells cites information science and biotechnology as the two basic sites of innovation. Castells devotes roughly five pages to biotechnology despite the paradigmatic statistic accorded to it. If Castells had considered the nature of knowledge formation, especially of science, he would have been more critical about the antiseptic nature of information. Castells celebrates the idea of virtual knowledge but he does not consider knowledge either within the history of science or the political economy of modern technology.

The idea of virtual knowledge and the amoeboid flexibility of networks, the sense of unboundedness, gives knowledge a sense of a contemporary commons, a sense of accessibility, of freedom of innovation. But the way in which scientific knowledge is constructed needs to be understood. The construction and possession of knowledge has a politics and history Castells ignores in his disembodied civics of information.

Modern scientific knowledge is both disembodied and disembedded. This disembedding stems from the objectification and splitting of observer and observed present in the development of the linear perspective. Science in relation to the 'other' operated through three techniques: monoculturism, reductionism and appropriation through patenting, dismissal or virtualisation.

Consider a prospective dialogue between science as 'information' and knowledges from other systems. History has shown that science is a hegemonic form of knowledge that proceeds by splitting knowledge between self and other, by reductionism and by museumising other forms of knowledge as defeated, archaic forms of knowledge. Modern science as a system has veered towards monoculturalism where other forms of knowledge are seen as superstitious or archaic knowledges. This process of disembedding is supplemented through processes of 'patenting' as appropriation of forms of knowledge. The history of patenting often verges on piracy when it comes to biodiversity. There is little to choose between plant hunters and gene hunters. Patenting in the United States recognises only knowledge that is recognised within the 'eminent domain'. A patent is officially recognisable knowledge and a lot of traditional knowledge is not even recognised as knowledge, condemned as it is as being archaic, defeated or localised. The work of Cary Fowler (1988) and Susan George (1976) has shown that patenting and biopiracy have been literally synonymous. The process of treating knowledge as virtual as in the human genome project adds to the process of disembedding, disembodying and dispossessing. This process has been chronicled repeatedly so as to require little description here.

Modern science as a system has veered towards monocultur-alism where other forms of knowledge are seen as superstitious or archaic knowledges.

What is seen as information is a reduction of knowledge to bits or bytes which can be appropriated, transferred, patented. All living cultures are Silicon Valleys of information in their own right. But by locating information as capitalised, valorised in terms of modernity, Castells is blinded to alternative ideas of livelihood, knowledge and even different notions of the future. It is this blindness about knowledge that blinds Castells to the possible futures for Africa or South Asia. He black-boxes the latter and converts the former into a black hole. This is digital ethnocentrism at its best. In Castells' world there is no mention of a dialogue of knowledges or even an idea of cognitive justice. We define cognitive justice as the right of many forms of knowledge to exist because all such knowledge is seen as partial and complementary or because it contains incommensurable insights. By being insensitive to the fate of different knowledges and their link to livelihood, lifestyles and forms of life, Castells becomes a mere cheerleader of the latest form of research and development management as a model for a wider politics.

The politics of time and the politics of democracy

Manuel Castells' celebration of the Information Age is around certain kinds of time. If Braudel's (1996) classic study of the Mediterranean celebrated the long duree, Castells celebrates the space-time compression and also the interplay between instantaneous and glacial time. In fact, Castells is more interesting on time than on space. His reflections on collectivisation as a violation of notions of peasant time is fascinating. The clash between peasant Christian time and Stalinist Stakhanovite time gives this period a different kind of poignancy. Yet, it is this very politics of time that makes his book a deeply problematic one. If industrial society faced the disembodiment of clock time, the network society needs a new anthropology for instantaneous time. As Castells observes:

> Industrial machinism brought the chronometer to the assembly lines of Fordist and Leninist factories almost at the same moment. Long distance travel in the West became organised by the late nineteenth century around Greenwich Mean Time, as the materialisation of the hegemony of the British Empire. While, half a century later, the constitution of the Soviet Union was marked by the organisation of an immense territory around Moscow Time, with time zones arbitrarily decided by the bureaucrats' convenience without proportion to geographical distance. (Castells 1996: 432)

Thus time became a means of organising and representing conquest. Yet time is also the repository of resistance. Castells adds that 'the first act of defiance of the Baltic Republics during Gorbachev's perestroika was to vote for the adoption of Finland's time zone as the official time in their territories'.

But the network society goes beyond linear, irreversible time, predictable time. It desequences this linear time, and creates an instantaneous or eternal time. For the first time markets operate on real time. Capital shuttles back and forth between different economies in a matter of hours, minutes and seconds. Both the time of life cycles and the timetables of mass production, rhythmicity both biological and social, are rendered irrelevant. Even old age and death have lost their ritual quality. Old age becomes a bricolage of people including early retirees, average retirees, able elders, disabled elders, shuffling age sets into a variety of combinations. Even media events lose their internal chronological rhythm, becoming a culture of undifferentiated temporality. As Castells notes, elimination of sequencing creates undifferentiated time which is tantamount to eternity. The anthropology of this disembodied digitalised time is fascinating. Castells becomes an anthropological McLuhan but without the literary exuberance. But this dissociationism between time as a marker and the varieties of lived time prompts one to ask two sets of questions. Does Castells really escape the cosmologies of Christian western time or is he silent about it? Is the apocalyptic time of nuclearism or the Christian sense of entropic ending embodied in the heat death of thermodynamics absent or unstated? Castells' information society enacts by default one of the oldest myths of the western scientific regime – the myth of the perpetual machine. In fact this has been one of the great underlying myths of modern science – the search for the eternal machine, without friction, not bound to the laws of scale. Modern science has two metaphors or models of entropy: the energetic and the informational. By ignoring the energetics, the ideas of thermodynamics, Castells' informational society evades what Frank Kermode calls 'the sense of ending'. The network society operates like an 'isolated system', where death or pollution is still an externality or an embodiment of the 'Fourth World'.

If industrial society operated between the time of Taylorism and Roethlisberger time, which is the time of communities, informality, goldbricking and everyday resistance, the network society moves between instant time and glacial time. Glacial time is a concept Castells borrows from Lash and Urry (1994). Glacial time is time that is long term and evolutionary. For Castells, it is the time of the ecological movements. For Castells ecological thinking considers the relations between humanity and nature in the long run. It helps create a new biological identity, the identity and unity of the species as a whole. Yet he is also clear that the glacial time of ecology is not a mystical or Luddite notion, it is a search for a delicate ecological equilibrium by 'a science-based movement'. The success of the environmental movement lay in fact in its serious ability to master the new conditions of communication. The electronic dramaturgy of Greenpeace, Food First, Friends of the Earth and The Rainforest Action Network bears testimony to the Castellian thesis. Yet Castells' reading, while brilliant, is eventually ethnocentric. It talks of a world which has access to TV and it also reads the environmental movement as scientific and as an attempt to restore nature as an artifice. But the issue is not one of communion with nature, it is a battle for survival.

Ecology is a subversive movement because 'it runs at right angles to science'. It is a search for new epistemologies for science, new frameworks for diversity beyond the museumisation of modern science, a museumisation that made western science smell of 'death and formaldehyde'. Ecology is not merely the search for renewal but a way to avoid the genocidal impulse of obsolescent time, the time of erasure, amnesia and forgetting. Ecology is also an attempt not just to promote grassroots democracy with its ideas of participation and consensus but to confront one of the great issues of modern democracy: the opposition between expert and layman. It seeks to show that scientific controversies need forms of resolution beyond standard scientific models. For example, the current debate on diversity of Vavilov Zones and the World Trade Organisation is not about species identity but about the incredible nature of agriculture as a corpus of inventions. What it seeks to diversify is not variety but the diversity of knowledge systems. It is not a search for information but an attempt to create a commons of information, a commons which seeks diversity but not exclusion. Nowhere in Castells is there a reference to a search for the commons. Such ecology highlights the fact that current ideas of property, rights, official science are inadequate to create a sense of species unity or survival. What we face in ecology is not so much glacial or geological time, but a haemorrhaging of nature and cultures in historical time. The rate of species loss, the decline of soils, the disappearance of skills, the loss of memory, are occurring at speeds which would fascinate a Paul Virilio (1998).

Ecology is also an attempt not just to promote grassroots democracy with its ideas of participation and consensus but to confront one of the great issues of modern democracy: the opposition between expert and layman.

Castells locates South Asia and Africa outside his paradigmatic ecology. What he fails to do is to confront the instantaneous time of finance capital and the evolutionary time of the ecologists. If he did he would realise that desequencing of instantaneous time is genocidal. What Castells' notion of time lacks is an anthropology of differentiated times and an attempt to link and counterpose ecological time to network time. Because he uses time as a measure and as a marker he can celebrate digital time and the nanosecond, but he cannot dialogue network time and the times of the Fourth World.

Castells is superb in his anthropological listings of instant time or desequenced time. He talks of split second capital transactions, flexitime enterprises, the blurring of the life cycle, instant wars and virtual time. Somehow for Castells the Fourth World (for all his sensitivity) becomes the failed time, the obsolescent time, the museumised or genocidal time of the network society. The recovery of the Fourth World needs notions of time beyond the limited anthropology of this world. It needs body time, lived time, the time of grief, mourning, memory, entropic time, the time of dwelling, apocalyptic time. It needs a variety of lived times beyond the semiotic times of biology, machine and cyberspace. It needs not only a glossary of times but an interlinking and dialogue of these variety of times. Net time is not the celebration of the eternal because it has no sense of the cosmic. There is about the network society a sense of necrophilic time, amnesiacal time, the time of nuclearism, the genocidal time of obsolescence and instant wars. If a network is a ganglion of connections, then the net society is an impoverished connection of time. I would like to suggest an interesting exercise. What one needs to probe is the notions of pathology, health, normalcy of the network society. A full anthropology of the network society needs to explore not just the parallel and hyphenated time of criminality but the time of health. How does net time affect notions of health, psychiatry, the ideas of grief, memory, generations, recovery? What Castells sketches in his observations on time and collectivisation he must develop for the 'lived time' of network society. Does net time elude evolutionary time and what is the relation between them?

There is about the network society a sense of necrophilic time, amnesiacal time, the time of nuclearism, the genocidal time of obsolescence and instant wars.

Unfortunately Castells spatialises time. Corporate time is the domain of instant time, ecological time is the time of the movements and of large parts of civil society. But what Castells does is raise a fascinating link between citizenship, time and democracy.

Citizenship is a cartography of available spaces and times. Theories of citizenship are located generally on the accepted time of modernity. One has to reach modernity to be a full citizen. Development as a project creates the inclined plane of progress so tribals, peasants and other forms of marginalised time can climb up to the space of citizenship.

Castells creates a tabloid of times but he fails to link it to the democratic imagination. How does one locate the time of obsolescent people in a Castellian world? Are they pure noise? Or is Castells arguing that tribal time, peasant time, defeated time have all to accommodate and be assimilated to the time of finance capital? The relation between time and capital is clear but the implications of the varieties of time for democracy are truncated. Such a theory of information society does not understand how its antiseptic nature can eventually be genocidal. People can be triaged out of history or the future because they don't belong to the time of corporations. Castells is brilliant on the time of Stakhanovites or the imperialism of Greenwich time. But he does not work out the full consequences of instant time and its hegemony. Only this time, genocide will look like a 'pert' chart or a well-dressed transfer of technology model. What Castells fails to understand is that ethnicity is not merely about identity but about the right to different forms of lived time which include both multiculturalism and diversity, not just as texts in a syllabus but as part of an active constitution in a contemporary world.

One could dialogue with Castells on a range of issues from the nature of cyberactivism to the role of the nation-state, to the question of civil society in South Asia or the moral fabric of a network society. But I will stick to the above two issues and end with a more generalised response to the triptych of books.

Conclusion

CH Waddington (1948), in an essay on the scientific method, set out his guidelines for evaluating a scientific theory or hypothesis. Firstly, one looks for the truth of the theory, its empirical validity. Secondly, one explores the range of issues it covers and the aesthetic power of the theory. Is it beautiful? Is it attractive? Is it persuasive? Waddington's third criteria was fruitfulness, the array of possibilities a theory offers in renewing new questions and domains. Manuel Castells' is a work that will be evaluated across this impersonal grid of scholarship.

However, my reaction to Castells is a trifle more personal. When you wade through his book, it is like exploring a territory and you feel a range of emotions as you struggle through and with it. First you arm-wrestle with the sheer enormity of the book, its pythonesque muscularity which seems to swallow you. The range of nations, case studies, the volume of statistics, awe one. You begin with jottings on an old sheet of paper and then, realising its idiotic inadequacy, you buy a notepad, two notepads, in fact, and start your mapping of the book. A walk becomes a hike becomes an adventure. The *flâneur* acquires thick-soled boots and a collection of well-worked pencils. Your relation to the book also changes from labour to play. One internalises the idioms, the ideas. One moves from arm-wrestling to Chinese checkers. One hops and skips over a few pieces, invents a few moves and games, plays with small possibilities. Then one internalises more of the book and it becomes a dialogue, a quarrel. You argue with the author, nod familiarly at certain points. Overall a book becomes a small symphony, the author orchestrating mounds of data and the individuality of different sections. One hears the power of it, one ponders the silences. The work is now the author's and one's own.

Castells' is not a great classic, but it has classic dimensions. It reminds one of the great civilisational histories. Castells' network society is on the broad line of Norbert Elias (1982) and Braudel's work, possessing the same obsessions, the same sense of a new world being created. Braudel has an obsession with a varieties of trade, winds and storms. He names each one of them, creating a geo-ecology of the area. Castells' preoccupation with crime or the behaviour of the net creates that same supple set of nuances for a techno-economic world. There is a sense of grandeur of scale, of a new continent being invented. To use the hyperbolic narrative of Jacques Arlandis:

> The Internet is a virtual continent, the seventh continent where you may soon be able to install everything that exists in real continents, but without the constraints of materiality: libraries, then shops, soon production plants, newspapers, cinema studios, hospitals, judges-policemen, hotels, astrologers, places of leisure and entertainment. Within this continent, empty of real inhabitants, a huge business will develop between virtual agents of a pure and perfect market economy ... (Arlandis 2000: 214)

One needs a personal salute to the triptych of books. My essay is more a personal review rather than a policy narrative. My encounter is not complete but Castells has produced a handbook, a travel narrative, a mega-irritant for thought and action. I feel a bit like the oysters described by Walter D Mignolo.

> In the early 1950s, biologists pulled a dozen oysters out of New Haven harbour and shipped them a thousand miles away to Northwestern University, inland, to a different time zone. The oysters were kept in the same water but in total darkness. The biologists tied fine threads to the shells to monitor movements. In the beginning the oysters remained snug in their home time despite the displacement. After four weeks of recording and analysing the data, the biologists realised that the shells had adapted to the rhythm of the tidal cycle in Illinois. The oysters were still behaving as if there was an ocean in that location. (Mignolo 2000: 238)

In the beginning I was like that oyster, snug in my own time, and then transported into the world of net. Yet I now feel a bit different. My mind responds to the time of net and yet my mind is also resonating the time of Narmada, Orissa and Delhi. I feel persuaded by the power of Castells. Yet I am captive to the politics of my place, my world, my location. I feel an ambivalence and an attraction and also a deep need to quarrel with the book. This, I have tried to capture.

References

Arlandis, J (2000) 'The "triad" and the cyberworld', in ER Larreta (ed.) *Time in the Making and Possible Futures.* Rio de Janeiro: Unesco/Educam.

Bell, D (1976) *The Coming of Post-Industrial Society: A Venture in Social Forecasting.* New York: Basic Books.

Braudel, F (S Reynolds, translator) (1996) *The Mediterranean and the Mediterranean in the Age of Philip II.* California: University of California Press.

Castells, M (1996) *The Information Age: Economy, Society and Culture. Volume 1: The Rise of the Network Society.* Oxford: Blackwell.

Elias, N (1982) *Power and Civility: The Civilising Process.* Oxford: Blackwell.

Fowler, C, E Lachkovis, P Mooney and H Shand (1988) 'The laws of life: another development and the new biotechnologies', *Development Dialogue,* Nos 1–2.

Frank, AG (1998) *Reorient: Global Economy in the Asian Age.* Berkeley: University of California Press.

Freeman, C (1982) *The Economics of Industrial Innovation.* London: Pinter.

George, S (1976) *How the Other Half Dies.* London: Harmondsworth.Freeman, C (1982) *The Economics of Industrial Innovation.* London: Pinter.

Jackson, W (1987) *Altars of Unhewn Stone.* North Point Press.

Kuhn, T (1970) *The Structure of Scientific Revolutions.* Chicago: University of Chicago Press.

Landes, D (1998) *The Wealth and Poverty of Nations.* New York: WW Norton.

Lash, S and J Urry (1994) *Economies of Signs and Space.* London: Sage Publications.

Marais, EN (1937) *The Soul of the White Ant.* London: Methuen.

Mignolo, WD (2000) 'Coloniality at large: time and the colonial difference', in ER Larreta (ed.) *Time in the Making and Possible Futures.* Rio de Janeiro: Unesco/Educam.

Perez, C (1983) 'Structural change and the assimilation of new technologies in the economic and social systems,' *Futures,* 15: 357–375.

Porat, M (1977) *The Information Economy: Definition and Measurement.* Washington DC: US Department of Commerce, Office of Telecommunications.

Waddington, CH (1948) *The Scientific Attitude.* Harmondsworth: Penguin.

Virilio, P. Der Derian J (ed.) (1998) *The Virilio Reader.* Oxford: Blackwell.

Shiv Visvanathan is a Senior Fellow at the Centre for the Study of Developing Societies in Delhi, India. An anthropologist and human rights researcher, his work has explored the question of alternatives as a dialogue between the West and India. A particular concern of his is demystifying modern science as a legitimising category for organised violence and exploitation.

charles soludo

Disputing Castellian globalisation for Africa

Introduction

Globalisation, however defined, is real, and Castells has illuminated the character and ramifications of this phenomenon in a masterly way.

Industrial capitalism and national policies have broken down and in their place are a new economy, a networked society and state – all centred around informational capitalism. This new economy has brought tremendous benefits across the globe but with it also an unspeakable human toll – in the form of what Castells calls the 'black holes of informational capitalism' (Castells 1998: 161). Castells observes that more than half of humanity, including sub-Saharan Africa (hereafter referred to as Africa), is locked up in this seemingly inescapable black hole. And Castells also argues that this phenomenon is both unstoppable and unsustainable, but leaves open the question of what to do.

For Africa, Castells simply reinforces the 'impossibility theorem' rooted on a now familiar stereotypical fatalism and hopelessness. Africa is caught up in a vicious web of social exclusion, poverty, technological backwardness, deficient institutions, and so on, and Castells cannot see how it can escape these throes and be an active participant in the global economy. We challenge both the account and the conclusion. Our thesis is that the 'black hole' of globalisation is not destiny for Africa. Being unsustainable, globalisation's trajectory needs to change. But it requires a rethinking of the institution of multilateralism, as well as consciousness and organisation on the part of Africans to do what is necessary to escape the script already written for it by unfettered globalisation.

In this paper I summarise what globalisation means for Africa from Castells' perspective. Then, I seek to widen the Castellian lenses regarding Africa's future, and argue that while globalisation is inevitable, its form is not destiny.

How Castells sees Africa in a globalisation context

On facts and their implications, Castells' is a fair narrative. It is true that Africa has been basically bypassed by the globalisation phenomenon and is increasingly marginalised. In economic terms, sub-Saharan Africa with 600 million people is merely the size of Belgium (ten million people), accounting for less than two per cent of world trade (less than half that of Hong Kong), and with about 40 per cent of its population living in absolute poverty. Africa remains the world's daunting development challenge.

On why Africa is where it is, there is no shortage of debate, but Castells' contribution is the attempt to link the characteristics of informational capitalism with the rise of inequality, social polarisation, poverty and misery in most of the world, including Africa. He argues that 'globalisation proceeds selectively, including and excluding segments of economies and societies in and out of the networks of information, wealth and power, that characterise the new, dominant system' (Castells 1998: 162). An understanding of Africa's trap in the Castells black hole of globalisation can therefore be better understood within the context of a historical progression of globalisation. His explanations can be grouped into three sets of interrelated factors: the fractured integration of the region into the global economy; the maladjustment of Africa under the structural adjustment programme; and the politicisation of ethnicity and failed leadership which is partly a consequence of globalisation pressures.

The first factor is the region's unique economic history – the precolonial primitive economy and slavery; the European concoctions that turned into the bifurcated, fragile, largely unviable African states; the nature of the economy handed over to the natives at independence and its fractured integration into the global capitalist system; and the ravages of the Cold War politics that created and sustained dictatorships, demolished popular democratic movements and escalated the militarisation of African states to the unbearable burden of gigantic defence budgets and aid dependence. On the basis of these, Castells reckons that 'Africa got off to a bad start' in the 1960s:

> The lack of a national basis for these new African nation-states, a basis that in other latitudes was usually made up of shared geography, history and culture, is a fundamental difference between Africa and the Asian Pacific, with the exception of Indonesia, in the differential fate of their development processes. (Castells 1998: 111)

Then came the 1970s with a major crisis in the global capitalist system and with it, the collapse of Africa's development model. By the end of the 1970s, Africa needed a major bail-out from foreign lenders and international institutions. But the prescribed remedies aggravated, rather than solved, the problem.

The failure of structural adjustment programmes thus constitutes the second set of factors. According to Castells:

> In the 1980s, the burden of the debt and the structural adjustment programmes, imposed as a condition for international lending, disarticulated economies, impoverished societies and destabilised states. It triggered, in the 1990s, the incorporation of some miniscule sectors of some countries into global capitalism, as well as the chaotic de-linking of most people and most territories from the global economy ... Structural adjustment programmes, advised/imposed by the International Monetary Fund and the World Bank, aggravated social conditions while failing to make the economies dynamic. They focused on downsizing the state and stimulating primary commodity exports. This latter goal, in general terms, is a losing bet in today's technological and economic environment; and in specific terms an unrealistic proposition when confronted with persistent agricultural protectionism in Organisation for Economic Co-operation and Development markets. (Castells 1998: 113)

Third, the politicisation of ethnicity and the predatory behavior of the African elites/leaders made matters worse. Given the seemingly forced marriages of disparate ethnic groups into African nation-states, it is not surprising that, in the face of pervasive poverty, such fractionalisation was easily politicised as a basis for economic survival. Deepening poverty and the end of the Cold War (together with the decline in financial aid from trusted allies) intensified ethnic rivalries and civil strife and wars. Castells also links this 'domestic' aspect to 'external forces'. According to him:

> This perverted political system has been historically produced, and is structurally maintained by the European/American powers, and by the fragmented incorporation of Africa into global capitalist networks. It is precisely this selective articulation of elites and valuable assets, together with the social exclusion of most people and the economic devaluation of most natural resources, that is specific to the newest expression of Africa's tragedy. (Castells 1998: 128)

The consequences of the foregoing for Africa, according to Castells, have been deepened poverty and social exclusion, institutional disintegration, widespread violence and civil wars. African states engage in the political economy of begging, while the diminished resources from the formal economy force large sections of the population (including the political leaders, bureaucrats and business people) to engage in 'large-scale illicit trade, including joint ventures with various partners in the global criminal economy' (Castells 1998: 114). Drug and human trafficking, advance fee fraud, massive brain drain, were all aspects of the responses to the new economy. Broadly interpreted, Castells sees Africa as one of the locations badly hurt by globalisation, and its response has been mostly in terms of integration into the booming global criminal economy as well as financial and human capital flight. Put differently, a Fourth World has emerged, made up of multiple black holes of social exclusion throughout the world, and Africa is the fulcrum of this new world. Again, very few people would dispute this characterisation.

On where Africa goes from here, Castells offers little help. In fact, he cannot see how Africa can escape from the descent into the black hole. Africa, in his estimation, belongs to 'those regions of society from which, statistically speaking, there is no escape from the pain and destruction inflicted on the human condition for those who, in one way or another, enter these social landscapes'. First, Castells argues that 'technological dependency and technological underdevelopment, in a period of accelerated technological change in the rest of the world, make it literally impossible for Africa to compete internationally either in manufacturing or in advanced services' (Castells 1998: 95). The disinformation of Africa at the dawn of the Information Age is interpreted by Castells as perhaps the most lasting wound inflicted on the continent by new patterns of dependency. Each leap forward in technological change leaves Africa further behind. Second, 'the crisis of the nation-state, and of the institutions of civil society constructed around it during the industrial era, undermines institutional capacity to correct social imbalances derived from unrestricted market logic'. Third, Castells cannot see how South Africa can play the role of a growth pole to lift the rest of the continent. This is essentially because South Africa has its own mountain of problems and risks of being capsized by the ocean waves of globalisation. Furthermore, years of relative isolation under apartheid ensured very few linkages with the economies of the southern African sub-region. Thus, Africa seems doomed into the vicious circle of social exclusion in this Castellian characterisation.

Each leap forward in technological change leaves Africa further behind.

Castells may be right

What is scary is that the facts and even insights from the endogenous growth theory give indications that Castells might be right. Africa has 33 of the 48 least developed countries in the world, and 18 of the 20 poorest countries are in Africa. In about 30 years, hardly any African country (except the diamond-rich Botswana) has graduated out of the least developed country status. Rather, more countries continue to join the club. In a world of globalisation, the scope for tapping into technological development and catching up might be great, but so also are the constraints posed by the daunting initial conditions. Endogenous growth theory teaches us that initial conditions matter, and that path dependence is valid. Most of the African countries (especially the least developed countries) might be too poor and too fragile to lay even the foundations for sustainable take-off or be able to tap into global informational capitalism. And these are the countries being continuously impoverished by the asymmetries of globalisation. An important feature of the current form of globalisation is that it allows valuable, productive assets (financial capital and high-skilled labour) to be mobile across national economies while the populations/labour are confined to geographic boundaries.

An important feature of the current form of globalisation is that it allows valuable, productive assets (financial capital and high-skilled labour) to be mobile across national economies while the populations/labour are confined to geographic boundaries.

Thus, these highly impoverished countries continue to experience the worst forms of human and material capital flight. Collier and Gunning (1999) estimate that the private agents in Africa hold about 40 per cent of their wealth abroad (compared to about three per cent for Asians), while other researchers reckon that about 30 000 skilled African professionals migrate to the West every year. In this world, Africa's efforts at savings or higher skill development constitute a subsidy to the West. The consequence is multiple equilibria in the global economy – localised traps exist in some regions (characterised by vicious circles) while a virtuous circle exists in other locations with an ever-prosperous 'new economy'. Furthermore, some diseases have now become African in character and magnitude – malaria, HIV/Aids, tuberculosis – while Africa needs specific technological developments to cater to its peculiar tropical environment. With nearly 50 per cent of the population living in absolute poverty, a growth rate of five per cent of gross domestic product is required just to prevent the number of poor people from increasing, and an annual growth rate of more than seven per cent is needed to significantly reduce poverty in the longer run. Even with the East Asian efficiency levels, this would require an investment rate of about 30 per cent, a large number compared with the average savings rate of 13 per cent in the 1990s. In a world of declining foreign aid, Castells may well be right that the script already written for Africa under the present form of globalisation as the world's destitute region is true.

Escaping Castells' black hole

Philosophers, it is said, have interpreted the world – but the problem is to change it. Castells has done precisely the same. The master narrator, Castells, has interpreted the complex phenomenon of informational capitalism. But the world, especially those locked up in his black hole, is still waiting for clues as to what can be done to change it. Here lies the greatest weakness of Castells. His only clue is simply to assert that something can be done, but he leaves open the specifics. In his words:

> Everywhere, they are growing in number, and increasing in visibility, as the selective triage of informational capitalism, and the political breakdown of the welfare state, intensify social exclusion. In the current historical context, the rise of the Fourth World is inseparable from the rise of informational, global capitalism ... Whatever the reason, for these territories, and for the people trapped in them, a downward spiral of poverty, then dereliction, finally irrelevance, operates until or unless a countervailing force, including people's revolt against their condition, reverses the trend. This is unless there is a change in the laws that govern the universe of informational capitalism, since, unlike cosmic forces, purposive human action can change the rules of social structure, including those inducing social exclusion. (Castells 1998: 162–165)

The above is both a statement of facts and a call for action. Unfortunately, for a three-volume work (covering over 1 000 pages), the above are the only clues that Castells provides on the way forward.

Castells' message of doom for Africa can be right only on his own terms – a static analysis of the facts as they are today, and a *ceteris paribus* assumption about the future. In a world where human beings simply stand arms akimbo and watch the invisible (unstoppable?) hands of globalisation wheel their destiny, Castells' prediction of doom for Africa might be right. But such a *ceteris paribus* presumption is both atheoretical and ahistorical.

First, the same endogenous growth theory that predicts path dependence also admits of the cumulative and virtuous effects of shocks. Economies trapped in low-equilibrium levels could be liberated by some positive shocks, which push them above the minimum threshold for self-sustaining development. That is why policies matter, and resources matter. Here, Castells ignores the current momentum for reforms – political and economic – taking place in the region, both at the national levels and within subregional integration schemes. He is probably wrong in not seeing the potential dynamic interrelationships between the South African economy and the economies of East and southern Africa. With South Africa in a free trade agreement with Europe as well as the Southern African Development Community region in Africa, the new European Union–Africa Caribbean Pacific (EU–ACP) Agreement (Lome V), the United States Africa Growth and Opportunity Act, re-thinking of the aid relationships, and so on, Castells fails to see the potential dynamic effects.

Second, the history of humanity has shown previously destitute locations turn into harbingers of modern civilisation. In the 1940s and 1950s, most economists gave the Asians no chance of success (on account of their culture and lack of natural resources). Today, the dynamics of the growth process is different. So also can and should the future dynamics of globalisation change.

Thus, an important argument is that while the phenomenon of globalisation is inevitable, perhaps unstoppable, its form and character are subject to change.

Thus, an important argument is that while the phenomenon of globalisation is inevitable, perhaps unstoppable, its form and character are subject to change. Since the present form of globalisation serves fewer of the world's population (and is thus unsustainable), the form can be tamed by 'purposive human action' since the present form is not the result of an invisible hand but was consciously woven by human actions. This is not the same thing as stopping globalisation, nor does it mean halting innovation. The various redistributive programmes and social insurance mechanisms introduced to carry everyone along at the national levels in the industrial capitalist countries did not amount to stopping capitalism. An analogy here would be the globalisation of the lesson long learnt at the national levels, namely that growth is not sustainable without equity. What is sorely missing under the present global framework is that we have a global market but without the appropriate global governance structure to properly mediate conflicts, resolve market failures, and devise and implement social insurance mechanisms to carry every location along. In essence, the disjuncture of the globalising market structure *vis-á-vis* the politics of resource allocation (restricted to national boundaries) creates tensions and unsustainable consequences that can only be mediated through reformed multilateral arrangements.

A paradox of much of the analysis of globalisation is that while most analysts recognise the unsuitability of the current multilateral arrangements to deal with it, the intellectual debate is often limited to tinkering at the margins on what nations should do, and perhaps one or two marginal reforms of the existing multilateral arrangements. The presumption is that the world may lack the political will to act in the desired direction. Two objections can be raised to this mindset. First, the unproven calculation of possible political resistance should not stop us from the normative thinking about what should be. Second, this theory of the political impossibility of change in the current form of globalisation is not valid. Fundamentally, it assumes myopia on the part of otherwise rational agents – that is, not able to intertemporally maximise their benefits under given constraints. The current beneficiaries of globalisation know, as Castells argues, that the system is not sustainable, and they are rational enough not to wait for the 'revolt' predicted by Castells to materialise before they can act to maximise their long-term interests.

Recent developments bear out the above arguments. In large measure, the intellectual climate is beginning to change, perhaps in contradiction of Castells. The United States bi-partisan Report on the Bretton Woods institutions and debt (Meltzer Commission Report 1999) is the clearest demonstration that not only is there new thinking but even a potential political will to act differently. The recent EU–ACP (Lome V) Agreement and the United States Africa Growth and Opportunity Act are a tacit agreement that Africa needs measured special and differential treatment. The challenge is to co-ordinate these disparate initiatives into coherent and consistent strategy, and deepen thinking on what the specifics of the new multilateral arrangements should be. The Meltzer Report, together with various submissions by non-governmental organisations and other United Nations agencies on how to reform the current trading and financial arrangements, constitute important bold steps. There are important ideas emerging on how to mobilise appropriate levels of mandatory transfers (as grants, not loans) to the poorest regions of the world to make them profitable investment sites, as well as to provide international public goods – vaccines for localised diseases such as malaria, HIV/Aids and tuberculosis, finance research and develop/adapt technologies to specific environmental conditions, provide education and health, and link these economies to the information super-highways (see Soludo 2000; Sachs 2000).

The central point is that unlike the Castells description of what is, there is a need to co-ordinate the disparate but important ideas that are emerging and which proactively think about what can be done.

Whatever is the outcome of the multilateral reforms, it is evident that in the medium term, the nation-state would continue to be the dominant centre of actions. Africans on their part need a new consciousness and organisation to deal properly with the new phenomenon. The old responses based on protests would not go far, although Africans need to work in coalition with other partners globally to press for changes in the global rules of the game that hurt them. But the fact remains that it is difficult to see how a small, poor country can prosper without tapping into the global pool of finance, trade, information and technology. There is no prize for isolationism. The question is not whether Africa should integrate or not, but to integrate into what, when, and how? Already, Africa has integrated deeply into the global system, albeit at the wrong end of the stick (aid dependence, capital flight, brain drain). A challenge now is to reverse this form of integration. This requires deepening many of the reforms already under way in many countries and sub-regions – to create favourable environments for enterprise to flourish. It also requires explicit national ideology and vision anchored on entrepreneurship, outward-orientation, equity and competitiveness. Furthermore, it requires national and sub-regional arrangements to deal with the adjustment costs associated with the integration process – especially threats to jobs and restructuring of investments.

Conclusion

The Seattle fiasco that halted the World Trade Organisation meeting and the Prague and Washington protests are increasing reminders that the internationalisation of non-governmental organisations is emerging to occupy a vacuum left by the rather obsolete multilateral arrangements to respond to globalisation. Such protests will not go away. Though the different groups of protesters have different, often conflicting interests, a perceived common enemy – globalisation and the institutions perceived to be behind it – unites them. These protesters might also ironically be the fulfilment of Castells' prediction of 'violent revolts' to change things. Increasingly, the non-governmental organisations serve notice that the world will not simply let things be directed by the invisible hands of the markets. People will intervene visibly.

References

Castells, M (1998) *The Information Age: Economy, Society and Culture. Volume 3: End of Millennium.* Oxford: Blackwell.

Collier, P and JW Gunning (1999) 'Explaining Africa's economic performance', *Journal of Economic Literature.*

Meltzer Commission Report (1999) Websites: http://phantom-x.gsia.cmu.edu/IFIAC/USMain.html or http://csf.Colorado.edu/roper/if/Meltzer-commission-mar00/

Sachs, J (2000) 'A new map of the world', *The Economist,* 24 June.

Soludo, C (2000) 'Globalisation tax as remedy to underdevelopment traps and ineffective aid'. Forthcoming in Conference Proceedings of the 12th Annual World Bank Conference on Development Economics.

Charles C Soludo is Professor of Economics at the University of Nigeria, Nsukka, and Executive Director of the African Institute for Applied Economics, Enugu, Nigeria. His teaching and research interests are in the areas of macroeconomic theory, econometrics, international trade and industrial competitiveness, public finance and fiscal policy, and development economics. He has been a visiting professor at Swarthmore College, a Smuts Research Fellow at the University of Cambridge, a visiting scholar at the University of Oxford, UK and a visiting fellow at The Brookings Institution in Washington. He has consulted extensively for many international organisations including the World Bank, IMF, UNCTAD, USAID, UNECA, UN-Secretariat; IDRC Canada; etc. as well as for the Federal Government of Nigeria.

stephen gelb

Globalisation, the state and macroeconomics[1]

Introduction

Does globalisation render national states powerless? When the globalisation process began to be analysed in the late 1980s, a major impetus in formulating – 'naming' – the concept was the debate about the roles of, and relationship between, 'the state' and 'the market'. Protagonists in this debate shared the assumption that the issue could be understood as 'states versus markets', that is, the two concepts were alternatives rather than complements. As markets for finance, goods and (some categories of) labour increasingly transcended national boundaries and became globalised, the process was widely understood to signal the eclipse by 'the market' of 'the state', a victory reluctantly conceded by some, and celebrated by others.

Discussion of globalisation has continued to be tied closely to notions of a weak (national) state even though, a decade or more later, the paradigm of state versus market seems disarmingly simplistic. Manuel Castells' richly-textured three-volume work, *The Information Age: Economy, Society and Culture*, certainly has no truck with this bipolar approach to the state–market debate. The dominant motif in Castells' work is the network, which he applies *inter alia* to both market and state in the globalised economy, and which is incompatible with the opposition between two self-enclosed social domains implicit in the state-*versus*-market paradigm.

But in wholeheartedly asserting that globalisation represents a fundamentally new phenomenon, with different features from 'nationally-based' capitalism(s), Castells displaces the complexities of state–market interaction, relocating them to the supranational level – since the market is global, the state must be global too. Castells reiterates the common view that the state, at the national level, is 'powerless': his main discussion of the issue is entitled 'A Powerless State?'[2] (1997: 243).

Castells suggests that, as a result of globalisation, national states are 'adrift': the developmental state has 'sunk' and is a 'captive of its anchoring in national shores' (1998: 213). The starting point for his general argument about the fate of the national state is his view of macroeconomic policy: 'individual nation-states are losing and will lose control over fundamental elements of their [macro and other] economic policies'. This 'loss of control' over macroeconomic policy is the outcome of increasing financial and currency market interdependence, with the G3 – the United States, Germany and Japan – at the centre:

> All other currencies have become linked to this triangle of wealth. ... [If] the exchange rate is systemically interdependent, so are, or will be, monetary policies. And if monetary policies are somehow harmonised, at a supranational level, so are, or will be, prime interest rates and ultimately budgetary policies. (Castells 1997: 245)

And later:

> The nation-state is increasingly powerless in controlling monetary policy, deciding its budget, organising production and trade, collecting its corporate taxes, and fulfilling its commitments to providing social benefits. In sum, it has lost most of its economic power, albeit it still has some regulatory power. (Castells 1997: 254)

Underlying these views is Castells' notion that state power can be understood as 'control' or 'instrumental capacity' (1997: 244). He implies that the state had complete control over various activities within the nation-state, including, in particular, macroeconomic policy, and is now losing that degree of control. This comes close to what I would see as a 'total' view of power, but Castells applies it generally to industrial capitalist states.[3]

In this paper, I argue firstly that this conception of state power as control is inadequate – the conception of power must be qualified. Secondly, I argue that under all circumstances, including globalisation, states are forced to make choices amongst the various desiderata of macroeconomic policy, since all cannot be achieved. Globalisation certainly creates considerable pressure on the state to choose a particular subset of the possible options, but states still have some freedom of manoeuvre. Finally, combining a more nuanced conception of state power with a more appropriate view of macroeconomic policy choice, shows that the macro policy regime – interdependent exchange rates and monetary policy harmonisation – which Castells suggests reflects state weakness, in fact is chosen under certain circumstances by strong states as well, precisely because their strength enables them to exploit this arrangement to support domestic growth.

The nature of state power

Let me elaborate a different view of state power, based upon the view that power is not just a zero-sum game between state and society. An increase in the state's power does not imply less power in society. Power also derives from co-operation and collaboration between the state and society, or elements within society. In other words, we need to think about 'power with' as being different from 'power over'. Strong states are able to take advantage of this positive-sum possibility.

This leads to a distinction between the despotic power of the state and its infrastructural power (Mann 1986; Gelb 1998a). Despotism is the power of the state to act over society, in other words, to issue instructions and to expect that the instructions and orders will be carried out. This kind of power needs to be distinguished from the ability of the state to ensure that those instructions in fact are executed. For the latter, the state requires infrastructural power, embodied in links with society (or more precisely, with organisations and institutions in society) which enable the state to penetrate society and ensure that its needs and objectives are actually met. Infrastructural power is power 'with' or 'through' society, rather than power 'over' society. This type of power is reflected in the density of the networks between the state and society, and is a key index of the state's strength.[4]

Infrastructural power can be categorised as follows:

- penetrative links enable the state to communicate and engage with society to ensure its objectives are carried out
- extractive links enable the state to obtain resources from society for its own purposes
- collaborative links are negotiated relationships between state and society enhancing the capacities of both.

Some of these points can be illustrated by the East Asian 'developmental state', which has a very high level of infrastructural power, in the sense of capacity in the areas referred to. The East Asian state is based on promoting development as the principle of legitimacy (Campos and Root 1996). Castells highlights this point (1998: 276), but doesn't emphasise sufficiently some other key features. The first is state leadership over social classes, especially the capacity to dominate and penetrate capital. This was due to the fact that all social classes in Taiwan and Korea were very weak at the time of economic take-off. This was partly a result of land reforms, which ended the power of the landed classes. Since urban industry remained immature, the business classes were also relatively weak. As a result, the state was able to provide leadership for national economic development which it saw as necessary for its own survival in the face of external threats (from politically successful Communist regimes).

State leadership of national economic development involved it defining the strategy, but using business as the chief implementing agents. The state provided financial subsidies to business to encourage production in the sectors it had identified as strategic, but also used a principle of 'reciprocity', imposing (production and especially export) performance criteria on those businesses – if those weren't met, financial support was withdrawn, and strict discipline imposed (Amsden 1989). This critical feature derived from the ability of the state to provide leadership over weak social classes. In its leadership of national development, the state built close collaborative links with producers, involving on-going interaction in business and industry councils about which industries to promote, how to promote them, how to move into new export markets and so on (Cheng et al. 1999). If reciprocity reflects penetrative infrastructural links as discussed above, then the business councils can be seen as reflecting collaborative links (Weiss 1999).

Another key feature of the East Asian structure was shared growth, with very high levels of distributional equity comparatively. An important basis for this was the use of 'wealth-sharing mechanisms', asset distributions which provided the poor with access to potential ongoing income streams, if they made appropriate use of the assets, which included land, housing, education and rural infrastructure. One dimension of these mechanisms was that they involved more than simply one-off transfers from the state; instead, on-going service provision in the context of these mechanisms linked the state with rural peasants and with urban working classes, that is, established infrastructural power in relation to these non-elites (You 1999; Campos and Root 1996).

Macroeconomic choices

Moving on to the macroeconomic issues, I noted above that the state cannot achieve all its desired macroeconomic objectives, but needs to make choices. A common conceptualisation is to think about a 'trilemma' in an open economy. There are three desired macroeconomic objectives:

- full capital mobility, the movement of finance in and out of the economy
- fixed exchange rates
- monetary autonomy, the use of monetary (interest rate) policy to achieve domestic growth.

A standard macroeconomic result is that it is not possible to have all three of these at once. All policy regimes require choosing only two of the three (hence 'trilemma'), not just in the world of globalisation, but in economies operating in any international environment (Obstfeld 1998; Rodrik 2000).[5]

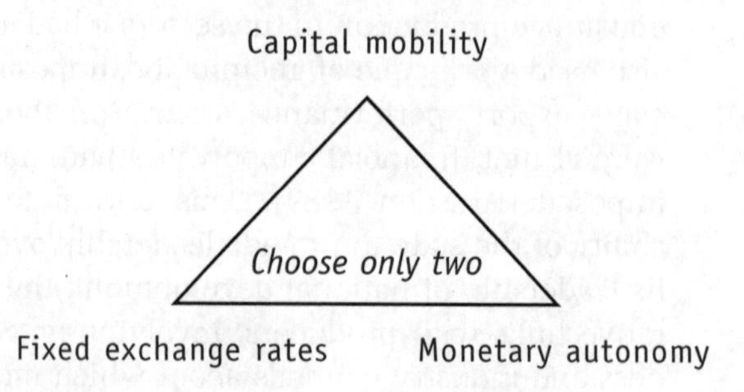

FIGURE 1: The open economy trilemma – making choices

What is the logic behind this trilemma? If exchange rates were fixed with the capital account open (free capital flows), interest rates would be forced to match those in the rest of the world closely – otherwise capital will flow out to higher interest rate regimes. In other words, under these conditions, monetary policy is not autonomous. If the capital account were then closed, but the exchange rate kept fixed, the authorities could reduce interest rates, as capital could not leave in response – monetary autonomy would then exist. If, on the other hand, capital mobility were maintained, an independent monetary policy which lowered interest rates would lead to pressure for a currency depreciation as capital flowed out, in other words, fixed exchange rates would have to be abandoned.[6] Only two of the three alternatives are possible.

The implications for economic growth are significant. With fixed exchange rates and low interest rates (monetary autonomy) to encourage domestic investment, high levels of domestic savings are needed, as well as large foreign exchange reserves based on exports. Without exports, capital mobility could result in economic growth hitting a balance of payments constraint. In other words, a foreign exchange crisis will lead to pressure for exchange rate devaluation to discourage imports and encourage exports. In addition, interest rates may have to be raised to discourage imports by choking off growth. The result is a stop–go cycle of economic growth, if there are insufficient domestic savings and forex reserves. Without the latter, the economy must attract steady foreign investment inflows, requiring of course capital mobility, or the possibility of autonomous outflows. This then requires abandoning the fixed exchange rate or increasing interest rates.

The point though is that choices must be made, amongst options that are all to some degree unhappy. The macroeconomic policy regime can't have everything at once. Of course, the trilemma is a stylised version of the choices. In reality countries are able to locate themselves somewhere within the triangle of Figure 1, not necessarily only at the corners. But looking at the stark choices helps to understand the trade-offs.

The East Asian developmental states rejected capital mobility, choosing the other two options. Fixed exchange rates were an important support for export competitiveness, particularly in stabilising exporters' expectations and reducing their risk. Monetary autonomy, the ability to move interest rates up and down, was critical to the state providing financial support to firms, to encourage and assist their move into export markets. But there were a number of essential economic conditions which enabled those countries to resolve the trilemma in the way they did.

The first condition was very high domestic savings rates, resulting in part from strong economic growth, but also a strong savings response to growth. Average Asian savings rates in the late 1980s were 31 per cent of gross domestic product, compared with around 22 per cent in Latin America at the same time, reflecting the relative growth performance of the two regions (Reisen 1996). Savings rates in South Africa were 16,4 per cent on average, between 1994 and 1997, reflecting a pallid growth performance, but also implying continued dependence on capital inflows to sustain even the low rate achieved.

Secondly, the East Asian economies had rising exports, on the basis of the state–business relations discussed above. Thirdly, they were assisted in very important ways, particularly in the early stages of growth in the 1960s, by non-market capital inflows, aid linked to geo-political issues at the time. Capital mobility was not essential in part because finance was already flowing in which eased any potential balance of payments difficulties, and supported growth. Finally, fiscal pressure in East Asia was restrained, in part because high growth was shared across the society in relatively equitable fashion, reducing pressures on the fiscus for redistribution.

It is interesting that although the East Asian crisis had in 1997–1998 pushed growth rates in the region well below zero, in 1999 and (expected for) 2000, there has been a return to very high positive growth. Korea grew at nine per cent in 1999 and is expected to reach seven per cent in 2000. Investment increased by

48 per cent in 1999 over 1998. This suggests the developmental state was not destroyed by the East Asian crisis – the institutional arrangements and processes linking state and society remain in place, and enabled a strongly export-led recovery, tied also to the devaluation of the currencies which was part of the crisis itself.

One of the factors that led to the crisis was the opening up of the capital markets, without abandoning either fixed exchange rates or monetary autonomy, in other words, an attempt to evade the trilemma. Something had to give, and eventually it was the exchange rate. The opening of capital markets was not handled well, in particular, there was not strong regulation by the national state in those countries. But it is interesting that with the exception of Malaysia, there has been no retreat from capital mobility, but rather moves to enhance financial regulation.

Globalisation, the trilemma and the state

This leads to globalisation's impact on the state. Globalisation changes the specific macroeconomic constraints faced by the state, rather than introducing constraints for the first time. In particular, the state is under pressure to choose capital mobility in resolving the trilemma, leaving it with one other option between fixed exchange rates and monetary autonomy.

Is capital mobility unavoidable? Firstly, if national capital is in a sense over-developed for the domestic market, it is very difficult to avoid: once domestic firms have grown beyond a certain size, it is very difficult in a globalised world economy to try to restrict them to the national economy. The East Asian experience is again instructive. The liberalisation of the Korean capital account from the late 1980s was pushed very hard not only by foreign firms wishing to enter, but also by Korean business wishing to expand outwards, in particular the conglomerates which have dominated Korean development. This is in contrast to Taiwan, where firm size is much smaller on average. Taiwanese firms began investing internationally at an early stage, and there was little pressure for full capital account liberalisation during the 1990s. In Singapore, the state pushed Singaporean business to invest more internationally, to enhance the state's own international growth project (Woo 1991; Wade 1999; Wade and Veneroso 1998; Weiss 1999).

A second point is that global capital wants to come in once an economy reaches a certain level of development. As noted, this was important in Korea: the knocking at, indeed the battering down of, the door of Korean controls on inward direct investment, particularly by foreign, mainly United States, financial institutions during the 1990s (Wade 1999). If there are market opportunities, there will be pressure which is very difficult to withstand. Limits on capital flows are possible, as Malaysia's 1998 reintroduction of controls indicates. Some countries – Chile being the best example – have found it desirable to introduce limits on short-term inflows of capital during the 1990s, as strong inflows threatened to appreciate the currency and hit exports. The ability to regulate inflows depended in part on high domestic savings, close to East Asian levels of 30 per cent in the early 1990s, as well as high forex reserves and exports (Agosin et al. 1994).

... it may be possible to shun capital flow liberalisation if you have no capital shortage domestically.

In other words, it may be possible to shun capital flow liberalisation if you have no capital shortage domestically. The political balance will depend in part on the relative pressures from foreign capital to invest inwardly and from domestic capital to exit. In Chile, the equation was tilted strongly towards the former in the early 1990s, but after the Mexican and East Asian crises of the mid-1990s, the withering of portfolio investor interest in all 'emerging markets' raised Chilean concerns about adequate capital supply and the controls were rolled back. Maintaining the combination of fixed exchange rates and monetary autonomy raised the risk of marginalisation, as illustrated in Figure 2 on page 68.

The state's need for deficit financing can also be a critical variable in opening the capital account. The greater this latter need, the more the state can be subjected to pressure to allow capital mobility, which then puts it in the position of seeking financing from the global, rather than domestic, capital market.

In assessing the political pressures to liberalise the capital account, it is important to note also that there is a differential cost to exiting for capital of different types. The exit option is often thought to be one that business can always exercise, but productive investors cannot simply uproot costlessly. Financial capital is in a different position, with easier exit (Frieden 1991). Therefore, the relative composition of potential capital inflow and outflow – direct versus indirect (portfolio) investment – is also a determinant of the political pressure on the state. The greater the preponderance of potential portfolio capital flows in both directions, the greater the pressure on the state to liberalise. Since portfolio flows are to some degree a function of the level of sophistication of the domestic financial system, the latter is an important index of susceptibility to pressures to allow free capital mobility.

Once a state has accepted capital mobility, its challenge is to develop new mechanisms and relations of power with global capitalism, that is, new infrastructural capacity with an international character. It must achieve 'credibility' with investors to encourage capital inflows. But more importantly, it must develop bargaining power with potential and actual foreign investors and indeed domestic investors who are becoming global. The state's role is to regulate not only the terms of entry and exit for capital but more importantly the activities of global capital within the national market, with the objective of achieving growth. Developing these new capacities takes time, and is not something that can be put in place overnight. Furthermore, the process is not necessarily successful – it is self-evident that merely introducing capital mobility is not sufficient for economic growth. If the state is able to develop new infrastructural capacities, the result is an internationalised state, or a state with international infrastructure power. This is an enhancement of the national state, not necessarily its diminution.

Once the state has opted for capital mobility, should fixed exchange rates or monetary autonomy be the other pole of the trilemma? The second choice is shaped in part by the availability of international linkages, but the primary influence is the state's existing infrastructural power, which has a primarily national character. Each possibility leads to a different kind of state. The combination of capital mobility with fixed exchange rates leads to what could be called a 'subaltern state' within the global system, while the combination of capital mobility and independent monetary policy produces an 'open regionalist' state. This is illustrated in Figure 2.

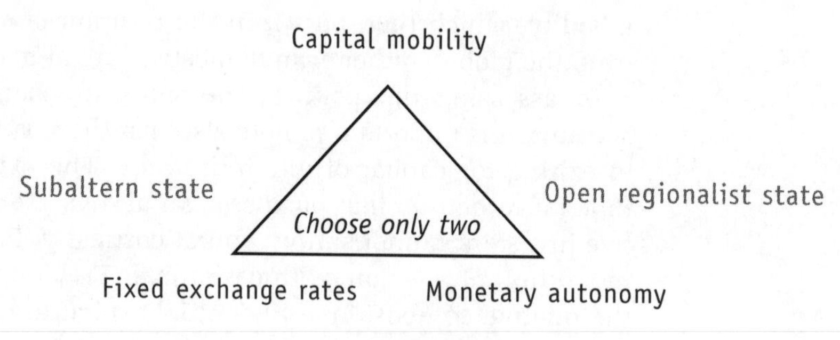

FIGURE 2: The open economy trilemma and the state

What do these labels mean? The 'subaltern state' option is likely to be chosen by states with either very weak or very strong infrastructural power. Very weak states are those without significant links to society – Honduras or El Salvador in Central America, and most of sub-Saharan Africa – or states which are unable to resolve very high levels of social conflict – Argentina in the late 1980s, where social conflict was reflected in an inflation rate of around 4 000 per cent. Very strong states are the East Asian developmental states like Korea and Taiwan, or the smaller European states like Holland or Belgium, which have also opted for open capital markets with fixed exchange rates.

States at both ends of the spectrum choose to use the external discipline of a fixed exchange rate to impose burden-sharing amongst domestic groups of the costs of adjustment to the rules of the global game and other international shifts. For weak states, the fixed exchange rate substitutes for the state's own lack of capacity to lead a national economic development process.

In 1990, Argentina tied its peso to the United States dollar at an exchange rate inscribed explicitly in the constitution as one to one. This raised enormously the cost of a devaluation or revaluation, forcing groups in society to accept price levels as determined by the fixed exchange rate, and bringing inflation down to single digit levels in a few years. In effect, Argentina recognised its inability, because of state weakness, to manage monetary autonomy, and opted instead for the other two poles of the trilemma. To manage capital mobility, it 'borrowed' credibility from the United States, in particular from the Federal Reserve, to demonstrate to international investors the total commitment to low inflation. Weak states in several smaller Latin economies have also seen this route as viable during the 1990s, and one or two (Ecuador, El Salvador) have gone even further, abandoning their own currency entirely and simply using dollars for all domestic transactions. Such 'dollarisation' has been debated in Argentina. But in late 2000, notwithstanding a decade of relative success for the macroeconomic policy regime, the economy hovered on the brink of financial crisis. The fixed exchange rate requires sustained capital inflows, but foreign investors threatened to withdraw in the face of incomplete fiscal reforms, illustrating that macroeconomic policy alone cannot substitute for, nor strengthen, a weak state.

A fixed exchange rate helps to underpin the domestic financial market, as well as exports, reducing the risk of investment.

Why would strong states opt for 'subaltern' status? A fixed exchange rate helps to underpin the domestic financial market, as well as exports, reducing the risk of investment. Stable political equilibrium in countries like Holland or Belgium has rested upon domestic burden-sharing of adjustment to shocks from the international economy, negotiated between the state and social interest groups. A fixed exchange rate enables this balance to be maintained over time (Katzenstein 1985).

The other alternative in the trilemma under globalisation is the combination of capital mobility and monetary autonomy which

I have labelled the 'open regionalist' state. Interest rate (monetary) policy is used for domestic political objectives, supporting specific groups in society. This is a preferable option for states with 'intermediate' infrastructural power, neither very weak nor very strong. To succeed, these states must have sufficient infrastructural capacity to use interest rate policy to support domestic economic growth and to offset as far as possible the domestic impact of exchange rate volatility. The existence of some links with society enables these states to contain inflationary pressures (at least to moderate levels), but distributional conflict remains at levels which are too high to co-exist with a fixed exchange rate in the face of periodic external shocks.

These 'intermediate' states attempt to build credibility in relation to international investors, rather than borrow it. To do so, they use domestic institutions and processes such as an independent central bank and fiscal discipline, to offset fears of an exchange rate depreciation, which is the big risk for global capital operating within the domestic economy, that is internationally oriented capital which may be based domestically or abroad. The key actors within global capital are financial investors and exporters, who are less tied to domestic economic conditions and would indeed prefer a fixed exchange rate. Instead of the latter, these states focus on building multiple international alliances as a way of reducing risk for global capital within the domestic economy, by opening new markets and stabilising flows of goods and money. The focus on multiple international alliances leads to the label 'open regionalism'.

In comparing 'subaltern' with 'open regionalist' states, it is illuminating to consider the differing approaches of the Dutch and Canadian states. Dutch society reflects a high degree of co-operation amongst groups and individuals, and an emphasis on conflict resolution, which underpins a strong state. Within the European Union, Holland has adopted a subaltern position, fixing its currency to the Deutschmark, and subsequently adopting the Euro. In this environment, the Dutch economy has prospered during the 1990s. Like Holland, Canada's economy is dominated by a much more powerful neighbour. But relative to the Dutch state, the Canadian state is weak, riven by conflict between social groups across several divides, including national and regional as well as socio-economic. The Canadian state has adopted a position much closer to open regionalism, allowing its exchange rate to float against the United States dollar, and entering the North American Free Trade Agreement with the United States and Mexico, but pursuing other bilateral and multilateral relationships at the same time.

What the above has shown is that combining a fairly simple macroeconomic model with a more nuanced view of state power demonstrates that the national state retains a central role in economic policy, a very different conclusion from Castells'. While it is true that states which are already very weak are forced into a fixed exchange rate regime which keeps them basically powerless over economic policy, many strong states enter such regimes voluntarily because they provide the appropriate context for them to sustain and reinforce that strength. And a third group of states are able to choose to retain a significant degree of control over domestic economic policy.

South Africa, democratic transition and state power[7]

Some of the arguments in the previous section can be illustrated by reference to South Africa's transition. The apartheid state's infrastructural power involved extensive penetrative links with both white and black society. This protected the state from being overthrown by military and political force, and helped to produce a negotiated transition. But the apartheid state was unable to establish infrastructural power in relation to black civil society which began to emerge from the late 1970s. Instead linkages grew between the latter – including trade unions, community organisations, the women's movement and so on – and sectors of white civil society (including business and professional associations and the nascent non-governmental organisation sector) which also began to press for democratisation. Throughout the 1980s, there was increasing interdependency between these civil society groupings, and by 1989, there was broad support for a negotiated transition which avoided the costs of either a violent revolution or the reinforcement of racial authoritarianism.

From 1985, after the 'Rubicon' speech by then-President PW Botha, a 'financial blockade' was imposed by international portfolio investors, and capital outflows were required to repay debt. Forced to run a surplus on the current account of the balance of payments, economic growth had to be cut off because it depended on imports of capital equipment and intermediate goods. Within four years, this situation had pushed South African business to support democratisation as a necessary – if not sufficient – condition for restoring global links and the resumption of capital inflows.

The two processes described here were central in the unbanning of political organisations and the formal start of transitional negotiations in 1990. During the four years of constitutional negotiations, the African National Congress (ANC) leadership – if not the organisation in its entirety – came to recognise that economic growth required a leading role for private sector investment, both domestic and international capital. This led to what I have called an 'implicit bargain' between the ANC leadership and the private sector – in exchange for continued support from business for democratisation, the next government (that is, the ANC) would open up the economy (Gelb 1998b). In the terms of the trilemma, South Africa would opt for capital mobility as one of its two poles.

The newly democratic South African state was weak – the apartheid state whose institutional structure it inherited did not have infrastructural linkages with key social groupings, as indicated. The long duration of the transition – effectively from the 1970s – meant that the state's links with society had become attenuated. Nonetheless, the transition meant that socio-economic conflict levels had abated somewhat, and there was a sense of co-operation towards the democratic state. This is not to suggest that competing or conflicting social interests had disappeared, or that there were no economic problems, but socio-economic conflict was at historically low levels.

... the negotiation period demonstrated a very high capacity for domestic conflict management, both at the political level to achieve a new constitution, and in relation to socio-economic issues ...

An important issue was that the negotiation period demonstrated a very high capacity for domestic conflict management, both at the political level to achieve a new constitution, and in relation to socio-economic issues, with the emergence of the National Economic Forum and lower level fora during the period.

There were two somewhat contradictory policy thrusts that the democratic state had to address. The first involved building linkages with key new political constituencies, in particular the black middle class which was very important right from the start, as well as the urban black working class, given the critical contribution of the trade unions to the transition. Secondly, the 'implicit bargain' with capital implied that the state moved to re-establish global economic linkages and began to build international infrastructural power, to support South African capital trying to establish itself in the global arena.

The need to combine a focus on domestically oriented constituencies with opening up to global capital flows led South Africa inevitably towards what I have characterised above as an open regionalist state. Firstly, macroeconomic institutions and policy aimed to build credibility with international investors. For example, a key step towards credibility was inscribing Reserve Bank independence in the interim constitution in 1994, as agreed in the constitutional negotiations. Secondly, there is unambiguous leadership from the fiscal authorities in determining economic policy as reflected in the Growth, Employment and Redistribution (Gear) policy, which as it has unfolded, has focused fairly directly on achieving fiscal deficit targets. Thirdly, inflation targeting, a collaborative process between the Reserve Bank and the Treasury, is an additional step towards international credibility.

The second process the state has undertaken is to establish multiple international economic alliances. These include agreements concluded or in discussion with the Southern African Development Community, the European Union and the Mercosur countries in Latin America, and initial explorations with India. South Africa is trying to take a leadership role in an array of multilateral fora, including all three Bretton Woods institutions, as well as in Africa and the G77 non-aligned movement.

Since late 1999, monetary policy has moved towards greater autonomy. Under the previous monetary policy regime, in a sense a continuation of the apartheid era, the focus had been on stable nominal exchange rates, fixed if possible. The new Reserve Bank Governor has indicated the intention to use interest rate policy to address domestic issues, rather than simply to respond to currency shifts. As expressed in the Gear statement (but not implemented before late 1999), the aim now appears to be a stable real exchange rate to support export competitiveness, with inflation to be addressed via the new inflation targeting regime. An interesting reshaping of the social organisation of capital across racial lines is occurring, with the move towards merger between the South African Chamber of Business and the National African Chamber of Commerce. These groups are oriented to the domestic economy, towards import competition and non-tradable services, and oppose the reduction of inflation to very low levels, because of the impact that a very restrictive anti-inflation policy would have on economic growth and their investment possibilities. On the other hand, those groups that are more externally oriented, such as exporters in the mining and other primary sectors as well as financial institutions, are insistent on inflation targets being met, that is, a range of three to six per cent by 2002.

Industrial policy also reflects an attempt to maintain a somewhat contradictory equilibrium between domestic and global orientations. The three key objectives of industrial policy have been identified as promoting small and medium size enterprises (generally oriented to the domestic market), black economic empowerment (again a domestic political objective), and encouraging inward foreign direct investment.

Conclusion

The South African state is heavily engaged in bilateral and multilateral interactions aimed at building its international infrastructure and securing the conditions for profitability for global capital. Democratic, globalising South Africa has experienced two foreign exchange crises, in 1996 and 1998 – three if we count the rand's collapse in 2000 – all the result of investor confidence collapses. At the same time, its domestically oriented infrastructural power remains inadequate, with domestic firms citing social problems such as crime and unemployment as significant obstacles to investment and expressing high levels of alienation from government, while urban black classes express dissatisfaction with the pace of policy reform in their favour. Are we to conclude that Castells is correct, and the national state has been rendered powerless by globalisation?

An ironic but illuminating comment on both the importance of globalisation to the state, as well as the importance of the state to globalisation, was Manuel Castells' departure for a four-hour visit to Durban on the first afternoon of the Pretoria workshop, despite his being the 'star' of the show. The purpose of his trip? To meet with President Thabo Mbeki, who was there for the World Economic Forum's (WEF) annual southern Africa jamboree. Mbeki is a busy man, but himself found it worthwhile spending three full days with the WEF 'cosmocrats', as the new global ruling class have recently been dubbed (Micklethwait and Wooldridge 2000). And Manuel Castells found it worthwhile to make the effort to meet the leader of what is after all not a major player, but a fairly small state on the global stage.

... national states remain, as they have always been under capitalism, the main agents integrating national economies into international markets.

This paper has argued that national states remain, as they have always been under capitalism, the main agents integrating national economies into international markets. This is unlikely to change while factor mobility is still imperfect, that is, until there is completely free movement of labour as well as productive capital across national borders. Until then, the substantial national differences in factor markets are likely to persist.

What the era of globalisation has done is to raise the demands and pressures on national states considerably, because states are forced to respond to the needs of a very powerful ruling class – global capital – which transcends the domain of any individual national state. In trying to meet these pressures, states which are already strong will do well and become stronger, whereas those that are weak (even where weakness is the result of new, unconsolidated political institutions) might be unable to break into the 'virtuous circle' leading to a stronger state. Globalisation is thus not likely to render all national states 'powerless', but rather to promote growing inequality amongst states, just as it promotes growing inequality amongst individuals within and across national borders.

Notes

1 The views expressed in this paper are personal, and should not be attributed to any organisation or institution.

2 Note the qualifying question mark.

3 The same view is illustrated in Castells' discussion of the media: 'Control of information and entertainment, and through them, of opinions and images has historically been the anchoring tool of state power' (1997: 254). Governments today, he argues, have influence but not power over the media and over, therefore, opinions and images. In my view, democratic industrial states never had this form of control over the media, particularly not the press, but also other media, although authoritarian states did.

4 It is interesting that the notion of networks and a networked state arises in the context not just of the state under globalisation (as Castells suggests), but also in the context of a range of earlier capitalist eras.

5 This was first shown by 1999 Nobellist Robert Mundell in 1961.

6 These results can be illustrated with a simple supply-demand analysis of the foreign exchange and money markets.

7 This section draws heavily on Gelb (1998a; 1998b; 1999).

References

Agosin, M, JR Fuentes and L Letelier (1994) 'Chile: the origins and consequences of external capital', in JA Ocampo and R Steiner (eds), *Foreign Capital in Latin America*. Washington: Inter-American Development Bank.

Amsden, A (1989) *Asia's Next Giant: South Korea and Late Industrialisation*. Oxford: Oxford University Press.

Campos JE and H Root (1996) *The Key to the East Asian Miracle: Making Shared Growth Credible*. Washington: Brookings Institution.

Castells, M (1997) *The Information Age: Economy, Society and Culture. Volume 2: The Power of Identity*. Oxford: Blackwell.

Castells, M (1998) *The Information Age: Economy, Society and Culture. Volume 3: End of Millennium*. Oxford: Blackwell.

Cheng, T, S Haggard and D Kang (1999) 'Institutions and growth in Korea and Taiwan: the bureaucracy' in Y Akyuz (ed.) *East Asian Development: New Perspectives.* London: Frank Cass.

Frieden, J (1991) 'Invested interests: the politics of national economic policies in a world of global finance', *International Organisation,* 45(4).

Gelb, S (1998a) 'Consolidating democracy: the state and the transition from apartheid.' Conference on Democracy and the Political Economy of Reform, Cape Town.

Gelb, S (1998b) 'The politics of macroeconomic reform in South Africa.' Conference on Democracy and the Political Economy of Reform, Cape Town.

Gelb, S (1999) 'Sustaining the nation: economic growth, people and the environment', in G Maharaj (ed.), *Between Unity and Diversity: South Africa and the National Question.* Cape Town: David Philip Publishers.

Katzenstein, P (1985) *Small States in World Markets: Industrial Policy in Europe.* Cornell University Press.

Mann, M (1986) 'The autonomous power of the state: its origins, mechanisms and results', in JA Hall (ed.), *States in History.* Oxford: Basil Blackwell.

Micklethwait, J and A Wooldridge (2000) *A Future Perfect: The Challenge and Hidden Promise of Globalisation.* London: Heinemann.

Obstfeld, M (1998) 'The global capital market: benefactor or menace?', *Journal of Economic Perspectives,* 12(4), Fall.

Reisen, H (1996) 'The management of capital flows: lessons from Latin America and Asia', in R Hausmann and H Reisen (eds) *Securing Stability and Growth in Latin America: Policy Issues and Policies for Shock-Prone Economies.* Paris: Organisation for Economic Co-operation and Development.

Rodrik, D (2000) 'How far will international economic integration go?', *Journal of Economic Perspectives,* 14(1), Winter.

Wade, R and F Veneroso (1998) 'The Asian crisis: the high-debt model versus the Wall Street–Treasury–IMF complex', *New Left Review,* 228.

Wade, R (1999) 'The Asian debt-and-development crisis of 1997–?: causes and consequences', *World Development,* 26(8).

Weiss, L (1999) 'Managed openness: beyond neoliberal globalism', *New Left Review,* 238.

Woo, JE (1991) *Race to the Swift: State and Finance in Korean Industrialisation.* Columbia University Press.

You, JI (1999) 'Income distribution and growth in East Asia', in Y Akyuz (ed.), *East Asian Development: New Perspectives.* London: Frank Cass.

Stephen Gelb is an economist at the Development Bank of Southern Africa. He has taught economics and political science at universities in South Africa, the United States of America and Canada. He was active in the Canadian anti-apartheid movement, and before 1994, assisted the Congress of South African Trade Unions and the African National Congress to develop economic policies. Since 1994, he has been a policy consultant for many government and public sector organisations in South Africa, including the Office of the President.

joel netshitenzhe

Black holes, or green fields of opportunity?

South Africa's transition and globalisation

South Africa's transition has been accompanied by intense international interest. In part, this is because we were and still are grappling with issues, including race relations, which are pertinent to social relations across the globe. There is a sense too in which the solidarity that we mustered in the last decade of apartheid rule reflected aspects of a globalising world – such as the media images, sanctions by financial and other institutions, and the swelling tide of a civil society-based global anti-apartheid movement.

South Africans are now struggling with the application of theoretical generalisations in what we believe is a very complex transition. Such complexity arises out of a number of objective and subjective realities, and I will refer to some of them.

Firstly, we have to manage a transition that requires detours. We had to go the route of reconciliation, normally referred to as reconciliation amongst races. In reality, given the social permutations in South African society, this was and is also reconciliation amongst classes.

The danger arising out of this is that the idiom of 'miracle' can lead to the co-option of the agenda of transformation. We are tempted to bask in the glory of world acclaim, to the extent that necessary action against inequality and poverty tends to be seen as rocking the boat. Theoretically, the danger does exist of rationalising inaction, and even elevating compromise to the level of principle.

The second reality is that, inasmuch as transformers seek to be as creative as possible in advancing the national democratic project, so do those who, on a global scale, devise creative means of resistance against transformation. The issue here is not only in relation to the objective problems of globalisation but also many specific problems including, in my own assessment, the manner in which financial markets operate as judges, jurors, executioners.

Objectively, through their actions, financial market-players can beggar whole economies. There are many instances, from our own experience, where direct or indirect action in financial markets can result in bizarre developments. One instance in this regard occurred after a very successful 1996 visit by then-President Nelson Mandela to the United Kingdom, where he interacted with government, business people, media and other opinion-makers. At the end of the visit, before his departure to France, the rand plummeted and no one really understood the cause. Later, it was established that some South Africans had started deliberately peddling rumours at the London Stock Exchange that the then-Governor of the Reserve Bank was about to resign.

Subjectively, the daily dose of market analysis can also have that effect. Pessimism within a well-endowed community, which is not at ease with change, does feed upon itself to create a negative impact.

In making these observations, one is not condemning markets *per se*. We do recognise their value as a critical part of allocative capital and do accept the proposition that, in the long run, strong fundamentals can withstand irrational movements – but at what cost! The central point is that, in addition to the problems of normal speculation, the markets are susceptible to subjective manipulation.

The third complication in South Africa's transition arises out of the superstructural elements of globalisation, which complicate our national democratic project.

We seek to create a new state under conditions in which the integrity and legitimacy of the state is globally under attack, precipitating what one can refer to as the 'cynicalisation of politics'.

Further, we seek to build a South African nation in a situation in which there are strong centrifugal tendencies of narrow identity, but also extra-national centripetal tendencies of globalisation. To trivialise the latter, in such a situation, how do you mould a youngster whose heroes are Tupac Shakur and Snoop Doggy Dog into a South African?

It is in this context that we find Castells' writings useful as tools to understand the nature and manifestation of globalisation. We do not view the writings as an immutable system of knowledge, but as aids in separating the wood from the trees, in a phenomenon that can overwhelm by sheer dint of detail.

The role of the state

However, what one finds lacking in the writings is explicit reflection on the question: where to? The impression created is that we should seek ways to ameliorate the conditions of the poor in a system that doesn't burst asunder, 'the expropriators are not expropriated'.

An interesting observation has been made about the middle classes in the United States who have invested massively in the financial markets. A profound market crash, it is argued, could result in mass revolt and a fundamental restructuring of the capitalist system.

Others argue that capitalism is a powerful system with inner strength for regeneration and will therefore exist in perpetuity. In this regard, the argument that Margaret Thatcher and Ronald Reagan engineered a specific form of globalisation could be turned on its head: they were a convenient product of the phase of incipient globalisation. Similarly, the social democratic parties dominant in Europe today are a convenient product of this phase of globalisation, to smooth over the rough edges of global capitalism's rapacious licence.

One is not proposing that the outcome of global capitalism's tensions will be either of these two opposites. The reality could be a synthesis in-between. But the central issue is that without explicit reflection on the question, where to?, descriptive sociology can become an exercise in fruitless shadowboxing.

It is in this context that one approaches the challenges facing the South African state. In his writings, Castells outlines the impact of globalisation on the state – its integrity, legitimacy and autonomy. As South Africans, we are grappling with these problems: in brief, what role, currently, the state can and should play.

How then do we characterise the South African state?

... the state is not an autonomous entity perched outside the polity it has to manage and regulate. It is a product of specific historical dynamics.

We proceed from the premise that the state is not an autonomous entity perched outside the polity it has to manage and regulate. It is a product of specific historical dynamics. The state thus emerges as a concentrated expression of attempts to resolve these contradictions. Ours is the product of the national liberation struggle; and the classes and strata which brought about this change seek to build a state that will serve their interests.

But the transformation project can also change the practitioners themselves, with the danger of 'social distance' developing between those who operate in government and the people whom they represent, and even their colleagues in the extra-parliamentary terrain. To borrow from some of Castells' categories, we need to integrate identities: the legitimising identity, the resistance identity and the project identity, to ensure particularly that the latter two view the state, together with this legitimising identity being constructed, as an instrument that they can use for purposes of transformation.

On the other hand, those operating in the state should help to reinforce this legitimising role. Often, we equate popular causes with organs of civil society. There is no law that decrees that political activity and political institutions should operate in an unpopular fashion. There is nothing that prevents parliament from truly becoming a tribune of the people; or government from constant interaction with the people.

The South African state also has to manage many primary contradictions – reconciliation is an attempt at addressing these. At the secondary level, there are the two tendencies of globalisation: improvement of conditions for already skilled workers; and pauperisation of the majority as a result of changes in the workplace (more outsourcing, casual labour), as well as unemployment. It would be remiss if the state concerned itself only with the interests of employed and 'established' workers.

In a situation of transition, there is also the danger of the emergence of a parallel state, in terms of private security companies, intelligence structures and so on. To deal with all these challenges, the new state relies on the Constitution and Bill of Rights, transparency, openness and the rule of law. In many respects, ours is still a state in transition.

Does the state have a role to play in the economy? From Castells' writings we learn that whatever the social project, the strength of a state as an instrument of coercion and cohesion derives from its legitimacy. A critical element in this is ensuring that the ideas of the social project, of its mission, become the dominant ideas in society.

One of the immediate challenges in South Africa is to forge national consensus around the understanding that the kind of disparity prevalent here is unsustainable; that it is in the interests even of the upper classes that there should be transformation.

As such, the relationship between state and capital will permanently be that of unity and struggle. Unity in that there are many things that could be pursued in partnership: capital wants profit; we want the creation of jobs, technology transfer and so on. There is much common ground. But there is also struggle: the state regulates the operations of capital, introduces labour legislation, forms of taxation, and so on, which constrain unbridled profit-making.

The state relates to capital by taking into account its various categories:

- fiscal capital: resources in the hands of the state and the power of leverage and licensing
- state capital: public enterprises wholly or partly owned by the state
- social capital: trade union funds, stokvels and other forms of community funds
- institutional capital, such as pension funds
- the mass of private capital.

A special category related to all the above is allocative capital. What possibilities are there to regulate financial markets? How do we regulate the operation of banks to ensure that the extension of credit meets the objectives of transformation including extension of credit to small and medium enterprises? What kind of strength should state-lending institutions such as the Land Bank and the Development Bank have?

Given these categories and others, what balance should be struck among the competing interests of financial markets and institutions, export-oriented industries, and the bulk of internally focused manufacturing and service enterprises? An examination of the preferences of each of these sectors and even sub-sectors within them on issues such as the value of the currency and interest rates demonstrates that, even in this sphere, the state has to manage secondary contradictions. As with the secondary contradiction between employed and unemployed workers, the state should pursue what it believes is in the national interest.

In other words, the state is not a helpless entity in relation to capital. Even under conditions of globalisation it has direct and indirect leverage on the employment of capital; and it has to strike the correct balance among competing interests. It also has to act jointly with others regarding areas that it cannot regulate alone, such as the trade regime and portfolio capital flows.

Globalisation and Africa

These opportunities and constraints facing South Africa should be viewed against the backdrop of our geography: South Africa will never succeed as an island of excellence in a sea of failure and despondency. As such, the project of the African Renaissance is a matter of selfish interest on our part.

Does Africa – Castells' so-called 'black hole' of exclusion – have any hope? Marx and Engels, in the *Communist Manifesto,* approach earlier internationalisation differently:

> Modern industry has established the world market, for which the discovery of America paved the way. This market has given an immense development to commerce, to navigation, to communication by land. This development has in its turn, reacted on the extension of industry; and in proportion, as industry, commerce, navigation and the railways extended, in the same proportion, the bourgeoisie developed, increased its capital and pushed into the background every class handed down from the Middle Ages.

> The need of a constantly expanding market for its products chases the bourgeoisie over the whole surface of the globe. It must nestle everywhere, settle everywhere, establish connections everywhere.
>
> In place of the old local and national seclusion and self-sufficiency, we have intercourse in every direction, universal interdependence of nations. And as in material, so also in intellectual production. The intellectual creations of individual nations become common property. National one-sidedness and narrow-mindedness become more and more impossible ... [This system] compels all nations, on the pain of extinction, to adopt the bourgeoisie mode of production; it compels them to introduce what it calls civilisation into their midst, that is, to become bourgeois themselves. In one word, it creates a world after its own image. (Marx and Engels 1971: 37)

Of course, qualitative changes have happened over the years. Castells identifies today's attributes aptly: a system that works as a unit in real time on a planetary scale. The problem, I suppose, is about his absolute categories of exclusion and inclusion. I believe that there are objective conditions for the excluded to penetrate the glass ceiling.

For a start, if indeed, as Castells says, productivity in the developed world is outstripping consumption and that labour conditions are seen as a serious impediment to profitability, is Africa not virgin territory for expansion, both as a market and an investment destination? The Africa Telecom Conference held some two years ago is one good example of potential partnerships between African governments and the global private sector, where precisely because of under-development, you have immense opportunities for mutually beneficial relations.

Secondly, if the collapse of the Soviet Union and the end of the Cold War has undercut the platform for blind support to dictators, doesn't this create a possibility for partnership across the board for democracy and development? Africa is often counselled to follow the example of south-east Asia and, to an extent, Latin America – on such issues as human resource development, savings, interest rates and role of financial institutions – to leap-frog various stages of development. This is genuine and good advice! But what is often left unsaid is the issue of the Cold War dividend that East Asia reaped: massively assisted because some of these countries were seen as bastions against revolutionary upheavals. In other words, there is a logic of strategic political self-interest, and in this instance, it should be based on democracy and basic human values.

Thirdly, the shrinking of time and space in terms of visual media, disease, migration, global environmental degradation and so on, turns into a common interest the resolution of Africa's conflicts and epidemics, and the maintenance of its environmental endowments as one of the lungs of the whole planet. At the psycho-political level, South Africa's liberation has created a better environment for a more objective African self-appraisal, for the emergence of stronger civil society and a new corps of leaders.

A new world agenda and Africa

Recent global market crashes and collective resistance to an outdated set of models have created a new level of discourse on global economics, the emergent so-called 'post-Washington consensus'. Matters such as the role of the state, importance of indicators such as low budget deficits and low inflation are being reexamined. So are searching questions being posed around the architecture of the Bretton Woods institutions.

To extract maximum benefit from its comparative advantage, Africa should also identify, cultivate and build alliances across the globe, including mass democratic organisations, on issues such as these.

Africa also needs to take advantage of movement towards new world governance in politics. The recent Gallup Poll (Millennium Survey) conducted by the Secretary General of the United Nations to prepare the Millennium Report (Annan 2000) is an example of the nascent potential. Combined with democratisation of, and equitable representation in, such institutions, a new paradigm for the common good of humanity can emerge.

Added to this is the combined pressure for intra-state good governance in politics, economics and social issues that goes with the serious steps towards regional integration in regions such as southern Africa. Further, the campaign for debt relief has brought into bold relief the responsibility of Africa proactively to address issues of prudent, sustainable and people-centred utilisation of resources.

All these, I believe, augur well for a new world agenda in partnership with Africa, for globalisation in the interests of the majority. The question is whether Africa is prepared to seize the moment.

One of the most critical problems is the brittleness of the African state, and we need to develop theory beyond slogans around democracy. How does the world assist in reinforcing the integrity of the African state? How do we deal with the kind of conflicts that lead to the common ruin of the contenders, as in the Democratic Republic of Congo, Somalia and Angola? If in the past, pursuit of self-interest on the part of the West meant blind support for the so-called rebels in some of these conflicts, what alternatives are there today?

Underpinning these conflicts is the violent accumulation of resources by leaders of the contending parties. Can such accumulation be legitimised on condition that those benefiting from it accept the state's integrity - pay tax, agree to disarmament and leave politics? After all, many of today's hallowed financial and other multinational institutions do have a similar background! The challenge in the case of these conflicts, and in view of the brittleness of the African state, is to find an exit point from the vicious cycle and thus institute a new and sustainable legality.

Conclusion

There are numerous difficulties and disadvantages attached to globalisation. Most of them are objective phenomena and others depend on the ingenuity of the role-players. But even the objective phenomena can be changed in the long run. The challenge is whether we are able to mobilise for the kind of globalisation that serves the interests of humanity.

Therefore, strictly speaking, there is no 'black hole' of despair; but green fields of opportunity. That is Africa: that is what the continent should convince the world about.

References

Annan, K (2000) *We the Peoples: The Role of the United Nations in the Twenty-First Century.* New York: United Nations.

Marx, K and F Engels (1971) *The Communist Manifesto.* Moscow: Progress Publishers.

Joel Netshitenzhe was appointed Chief Executive Officer of the Government Communication and Information System (GCIS) in 1998. From 1994 he was Head of Communications in the President's Office. He left South Africa in 1976 while studying at the University of Natal (Medical School) and joined the African National Congress (ANC). After receiving military training he worked in the ANC's Department of Information and Publicity and was editor of the ANC journal, *Mayibuye,* for over 10 years. In 1990 he was part of the ANC's constitutional negotiating team. A member of the ANC National Executive Committee from 1991 to date, he has an M.Sc., Financial Economics and a Post-graduate Diploma in Economic Principles from the University of London and a Diploma, Social Sciences from the Institute of Social Sciences, Moscow.

ebrahim patel

Shaping or submitting to the global economy?

I would like to start by commenting on Castells' theory of the new economy, or what we loosely refer to as globalisation, and end with Carnoy's comments on the state. Globalisation is clearly an engine of incredible economic growth but at the same time it is also an engine of incredible social inequities. Globalisation combines the hardened logic of economic competitiveness with an incomparably more flexible means of accumulation – and in the process, the world within which social engagement takes place (that is, both the world of enterprises and the world of workers) is transformed substantially. It is evident that globalisation shares many characteristics with that other key moment of economic transformation, the Industrial Revolution. It also has major differences. The most vivid images of the early days of the Industrial Revolution are of smokestack industries and of Dickens describing the social conditions of work. Social exclusion and economic instability as factory production starts root themselves in society, and the trauma and transformation are all images that in some or other way we can tie to globalisation.

At a level of very broad simplification, the Industrial Revolution collectivised work out of individual labour where artisans were brought into factory production on an ever-increasing scale. What globalisation is partly doing is individualising work, which leads to a rise in the precariousness of work. Whereas the Industrial Revolution brought in its wake some form (always just some form) of permanent employment, globalisation brings precariousness.

I qualify by saying that there is a tendency to individualisation because even in the period of advanced globalisation today, massive industrial complexes are being set up in Vietnam and China. For example, shoe factories making Nike shoes employ eight or nine thousand workers in one complex. So there are both these tendencies, but there is clearly a greater individualisation of work.

The workplace is undergoing tremendous change. On the one hand there is a geographic change with manufacturing shifting from developed to developing countries, with most consumption still trapped in developed countries. There is also an organisational shift with the growth of non-standard employment. Here I refer to flexibility, decentralised management (that is not a technical but a political shift) in production, part-time and temporary work, and customised production.

But in addition to the growth of non-standard employment, sub-contracting has increased in South Africa and elsewhere on the continent, and indeed more broadly. Through sub-contracting companies have shed what they call their non-core work and have defined their core work in ever more precise and narrow ways. Multinational enterprises are now no longer the sprawling, massive employers of labour. Instead they are the head of a network of economic activities, often small and medium enterprises with a value chain that is more complex, more interrelated. The same goes for the informal sector. The separation between the formal sector and the informal sector has been destroyed and the value chain finds the cheapest place that it can source anywhere.

In its wake this has brought disguised employment relationships and real, new employment relationships both living side by side. In some cases in South Africa large numbers of people have been legally reclassified as independent contractors, doing exactly the same work but the contract of employment – the legal basis – has changed. Triangular employment relationships have also become much more important.

Even though Castells says that labour remains at the centre of the new economy, I contend that the action has moved from industrial relations to more complex financial instruments and sophisticated marketing strategies. This is where the creative energy of modern capital is going.

Enterprise is now part of this network of interrelated economic and commercial organisations. This has been done partly to improve productivity, reduce costs and increase flexibility. The question of productivity and cost represents one of the core dilemmas for the new economy.

The Industrial Revolution, via a long period of economic crises, social organisation and struggle engagement by human beings, had its more socially destructive effects tamed by the rise in industrialised countries of the wealthy estate and of course, all over the world, by the trade union movement, finding its organisational base in manufacturing and mining. In industrialised societies, a careful balance of power was established, sometimes referred to as a partnership between labour and capital, that ensured a rising industrial wage and a rising social wage. Many developing countries sought to emulate this pattern, this model of development. What globalisation or the new economy has done is that it has shifted this balance. There has been a fundamental shift characterised by increased mobility of capital and by the individualisation of the workforce.

The mobility of capital has been the economic basis for the internationalisation of production.

The mobility of capital has been the economic basis for the internationalisation of production. The flows of capital are more rapid, easier, less regulated but the mobility of goods are also a proxy for the mobility of capital. As tariff barriers came down, sourcing became internationalised. And of course, quite fundamentally, and perhaps over-commented on, has been the technological basis to this – the Internet, the new communication technologies.

The mobility of capital has manifested itself in two consequences. The first one is the decreased power of national regulation. Companies are able to evade new rules or laws by simply moving offshore. Second, the state receives fewer resources from corporate taxation and progressive taxation, and from tariff duties. So the state is weakened in two ways: you take out its teeth, its ability to bite, and you take away its hands, its ability to reach out and assist.

From the view of organised labour, the power of corporations is clearly greater relative to the workforce and relative to governments than it was 15 or 30 years ago. The consequences for corporations have been quite profound. The nation-state and organised labour have been the relative losers. We've lost, in relative terms, because both the state and trade unions became locked into a specific form of economic organisation. Although the national economy had international links it was national in character and it became displaced with the growth of the new form of economic organisation. The global economy had networks of supplies and customers that were more sophisticated.

In summary the profound changes at the workplace, the cost productivity issue, the massively increased mobility of capital, together with the weakened political and industrial organisation in society, pose new challenges for the new economy for all of us.

The first challenge is the inherent instability of the system. This is not a new attempt to repackage the inherent crisis but clearly there is a set of anecdotal evidence that shows problems in the global economy. The South East Asian crisis; Malaysia's attempt to buck that crisis; the Bretton Woods' fight between the World Bank and the International Monetary Fund; the huge public tiff over who created these Asian crises; Stieglitz, previously Chief Economist of the World Bank, attacking the Washington consensus; Ravi Kanbu, the leader of the World Development Report for the World Bank, deciding in a blaze of publicity to announce his resignation because Larry Summers allegedly tried to interfere with the content of the World Development Report when it sought to argue stronger redistribution and less obsession with simply arguing pro-growth policies; George Soros doing his famous book on the crisis of capitalism. So these fissures, these debates, these contradictions are emerging within advanced capitalism.

But perhaps more fundamentally there is the economic challenge. As costs come down and productivity rises, the tools to manage the expansion of aggregate demand to absorb what is coming out of the new economy are not available. Bear in mind, a lot of the production shifts to people who are paid less, not all of it, but a lot of it. So the wages that slosh around in the global economy, able to buy goods and services, are not as easily directed by collective bargaining in the new economy as they were in the old economy. Fiscal policies and monetary policies are now more constrained by good practice internationally but the tools to manage the synchronisation between expanding supply and increasing demand are now missing.

There are also challenges from outside the economic logic. Seattle is a key and defining moment of this. But Seattle is just the media event. It is the massive unrest, strikes, loss of production all over the world, the less commented strikes in South Africa where for example four million workers out of a workforce of eight million went on strike in May 2000 over issues around job creation. Recently in Nigeria, a big strike took place against a policy by government over the petrol price that was created by external pressures. The big strikes in Brazil, Korea and France; the shop-floor activism in the United States – these are certainly getting a bit more media attention. I can mention more of these, for example the environmental struggles, but they are all unconnected nodes of opposition.

... the economy is a set of connected nodes which Castells calls the network.

So the economy is a set of connected nodes which Castells calls the network. The struggles are unconnected nodes, struggling against a similar phenomenon but separated. The question and the dilemma for us at a level of policy is, how does the state and the trade union movement, as two of the instruments that have been relative losers, respond to the mobility of capital, to new networks of work and to the individualisation of work? That is the challenge. At one simple and almost sloganistic level we can say that the state and social organisation have to become global in focus and shift their organisational basis. If you can conceive of a value chain that stretches from the head office of a multinational corporation in New York into the informal sector in Indonesia which has a series of interconnected customer supplier relations that co-operate for production, the question is, what is the network of governance that can match that? The G7 is one attempt. The G77 is a very different attempt. Regionalisation – the European Union, the Southern African Development Community, Mercosur – are all attempts to manage both the economic and the social dimensions of this.

But there is also the question of a new organisation of workers which reflects the new forms of work and humanises it. When the first wave of the new economy hit them, trade unions said: hey, this is temporary, this is bad, we must oppose it, we must resist it. Very little attention went into organising it – not because unions were reluctant to organise people who were working, but because at an early stage it wasn't evident that this was a trend that was going to continue into the future. Rather it was perceived as a dip, that with a bit of resistance, one could change.

So, how does one start to organise around the new forms of work? It requires a seminar of its own so I'm just going to give heads of arguments rather than the detail. Firstly, trade unions will have to rediscover their role in the skill enhancement of workers. Ironically, in the Industrial Revolution, trade unions found their initial monopoly power through the training nexus. Now, more and more unions are seeing human resource development as a major area of their work, their time, their resources, their people.

Secondly, there is the question of social security, of fighting for things that are global and not linked to where you work at a given point. Thirdly, the issue of political representation and the challenge of individual services: can workers who are no longer life-long Toyota workers be life-long National Union of Metalworkers members? Can they have permanent membership of an organisation even though they may not work permanently for one corporation? And can that organisation represent their views and their interests wherever they may work? Does one only organise around the current employment relationship or should one start to organise around the skill that workers are able to contribute in the economy? In Europe there is a rich and long history of organising unemployed workers who were previous members of the union. In Italy there is the interesting tradition of organising pensioners, people who were members of the union. In both those categories people remain members of the trade union, which is why it's so hard to compare membership figures. So the question is, can we learn something from that non-workplace form of organisation, which we can start to bring into the new complex ways in which trade unions will have to organise?

Who are the bargaining partners? This has become more complex. In the new networked complex there is a global bargaining partner and there's an anonymous bargaining partner with interconnected forms of economic activity. Codes of conduct (which ironically unions were not very keen on initially) may pose an interesting model of how wider collective bargaining engagement can be conducted with more than one bargaining partner. On the other hand, because codes of conduct try to deal with the customer–supplier relationship, they can so easily cut across into the supplier network relationships. The current, very big, campaign at universities in the United States against sweatshop labour and the fight against Nike, is one issue on which labour and non-governmental organisations may well find a lot of common cause.

Codes of conduct ... may pose an interesting model of how wider collective bargaining engagement can be conducted with more than one bargaining partner.

Let me conclude with a reflection on a recent meeting of the International Labour Conference of the International Labour Organisation (ILO) that I attended. I would like to make four points about the ILO that I think illustrate the question of the state.

The first one is the new framework for policy called Decent Work endorsed by the ILO last year. The framework seeks to combine the quantitative and qualitative challenges of employment. It states that the goal of the global economy is good employment and full employment, and sets forth a range of ideas and mechanisms of how to develop that. Amartya Sen, the previous Nobel Economics winner, addressed the International Labour Conference last year and made an interesting comment about decent work as an appropriate framework, not just for the ILO but for global society.

Secondly, Burma has recently been accused of contravening a Convention of the ILO, namely the Forced Labour Convention. Through two laws, the Village Act and the Towns Act, women, children and men were basically captured and pressed into forced labour. Since the ILO was founded in 1919, despite major violations of worker rights, it has never used sanctions. For the first time this year, on a vote, it invoked Article 33 of its Constitution (although it will suspend it for about five or six months). Article 33 says that because Burma uses forced labour in its economy, the global community should be morally obliged to take action against Burma and it is now spelling out what that action is.

So this is a groundbreaking shift for the ILO. It shows one element of the level of global co-ordinated efforts to promote fair labour. But there is another spin to it. Many governments voted for that resolution because of Seattle and the pressure in the World Trade Organisation (WTO). The argument was that if the ILO is not shown to have teeth it would pave the way for the social clause to be argued at the WTO. So I think it brings those two dimensions together.

Thirdly, a conclusion was reached on human resource development. Workers, employers and government sat down to look at human resource development and decided to begin with the need to expand aggregate demand in the global economy and the need to promote collective bargaining as a means to distribute the outcome of economic activity. They decided that if there was going to be integrated economic and educational policies, these would require consideration of a new financial and social architecture for the global economy. The ILO is now committed to investigate this.

The final point I want to make is the vote on a Maternity Convention adopted at the ILO. This is a controversial convention which, in summary, for the first time broadens its scope beyond people in the formal sector. In its scope it seeks to cover the new forms of work and it seeks specifically to identify atypical dependent workers. So at a global level there is a recognition that there is a huge area of work growing in the dependent work sector, and if you're going to say something sensible about standards, you must also say something that can be applicable there.

I think that represents, in some ways, the governance responses. These are just three or four very anecdotal illustrations of governance responses that are required in order for human beings to shape the global economy, rather than submitting to the way in which the global economy functions.

Ebrahim Patel is the National Convenor for Organised Labour on the statutory civil society negotiating forum of the National Economic, Development and Labour Council. He is also General Secretary of the Southern African Clothing and Textile Workers' Union. He serves on the National Executive of the Congress of South African Trade Unions and is a commissioner on the Financial and Fiscal Commission. He is a member of the Council of the University of Cape Town and a trustee of the Bureau of Economic Research at the University of Stellenbosch. He serves on the Governing Body of the Commission of Conciliation, Mediation and Arbitration. He also serves on two international bodies, namely the executive committee of the International Textile Garment and Leather Workers' Federation, and the Governing Body of the International Labour Organisation.

andre kraak

Debating Castells and Carnoy on the network society

Introduction

This report provides an interpretative summary of the discussions that took place at the Gauteng two-day seminar led by Manuel Castells and Martin Carnoy on 22 and 23 June 2000. The report does not take the traditional form of workshop minutes. Rather, it deliberately focuses on one of the key issues that arose during the deliberations – that being the role of the nation-state during the era of globalisation.

In addition to covering this major issue, the report also highlights certain methodological concerns regarding Castells' notion of the network society. The discussion concludes with Castells giving an outline of his views on the way forward. He makes a very specific proposal for a 'Technological Marshall Plan' which he sees as a critical strategy for bringing the under-developed Third World back into the global economy on more equitable terms. In doing so, human capital formation is being privileged, for the first time, as a top priority in the economic development debate in South Africa.

Methodological issues

In structuring the report, it is useful to make a distinction between the methodological and political concerns that dominated the Gauteng debates. There was a general acceptance that Castells' trilogy constituted the 'finest piece of contemporary social analysis' at the turn of the century and that Castells was the 'first significant philosopher of cyberspace' (journal review comments).[1] However, this praise had the effect of dampening the academic engagement and criticism of Castells' methodological approach that one would have expected at a gathering of this kind. Much of the engagement was not methodological but political in nature. The next section will therefore raise some of the methodological issues that were implicit rather than explicit in the dialogue.

Globalisation as an all-pervasive, totalising narrative

Much of the literature on globalisation, particularly that which describes 'post-Fordism' and 'flexible specialisation', has been criticised for assuming an all-pervasive uniform transition to the new global economy. Although Castells' trilogy is monumental and provides a vast tract of evidence to back his main thesis, his work also suffers this methodological flaw. As Langa Zita, African National Congress Member of Parliament, pointed out in the debate, Castells makes a number of observations about what is happening in the advanced economies that are then generalised across the globe. The reality is a much more continuous process of change with forms of productive and social organisation continuing from the past into the present alongside the leading networks of innovation – both in the advanced and developing economies. Fordist, mass-producing manufacturing, low-skill labour intensive production and economic activity based on familial labour – to cite three examples – continue to exist alongside the new high-tech networked economic subsectors in both the advanced societies (for example, in Japan, the Asian Tigers and the United Kingdom) as well as in the developing world (for example, in South Africa, Brazil and India). The diffusion of the network society is more uneven than that described in Castells' trilogy. It does not totally displace old forms of social and economic organisation, but rather, co-exists alongside them with the network society becoming the new commanding heights of most advanced national economies.

This all-pervasive imagery of transition to the network society impacts on all the other debates which stem from Castells' work – for example, the question of whether individual nation-states have any other option but to succumb to the dictates of globalisation. However, if global incorporation is viewed as partial, the space for national action is wider.

Ignoring 'middle' society

Castells himself emphasises that it is only the core activities of the economy that are globalised. He lists these activities as financial markets; the information and communication technologies (ICTs) sector; international trade, particularly high value-added exports and the activities of multinational corporations; and lastly, the internationalisation of science and technology and human capital formation.

Castells also describes the disconnected – the structurally irrelevant – who reside in the Third and Fourth Worlds, and in the pockets of poverty in the advanced economies as well.

However, the core and periphery do not constitute the total society, for in between is surely middle society. Middle society constitutes the bulk of economically active citizens who are neither knowledge workers nor symbolic analysts (Robert Reich's

[1991] term) in the core sectors, nor are they economically irrelevant. They are not accounted for in the trilogy, although they probably constitute the majority of society. For countries such as South Africa, the stability and expansion of middle society is the paramount political goal. Jobs and security for these people lie in an expanded manufacturing sector, in a revitalisation of the mines and farms, in the state and in small and medium enterprise activity. Much of this economic activity and livelihood is a continuation and expansion of past economic forms.

Such a formulation poses the advance of globalisation and the agency of the state in a different light. It provides the state with an ongoing obligation to manage the national economic and social agenda, although with a far greater sensitivity to the needs and adaptations required by the world economy. In this formulation, the nation-state is less a captive; the political outlook is less bleak.

The triumph of empiricism

During the afternoon session of the first day of the workshop, Castells found himself 'being pushed into doing what I don't want to do and that is to propose a political vision for South Africa'. Castells had received two related criticisms of his methodology. The first was in response to his description of his work as being empirical, based on fourteen years of rigorous research, observation and theorisation. However, most participants wanted to know where Castells stood politically in relation to the socio-economic impact of globalisation. Charles Soludo, Professor of Economics in Nigeria, asked of Castells: 'Where do we go from here? What can be done at the national level and at the regional and multilateral levels?' Joel Netshitenzhe, Head of the South African Government Communications and Information System (GCIS), too asked of Castells: 'What one found lacking is the answer to the question: where to now?'

As Nico Cloete (the organiser of the seminar series) observed, this question resonated well with the new South African fixation for always wanting to read the political implications of a phenomenon and the associated programme of action to remedy the problem. Castells was resolute in the defence of his empirical work although, as may be seen in the conclusion to this chapter, by the end of his visit Castells appeared to have succumbed to South African pressures to spell out the political implications of his main thesis.

The second criticism came from Soludo and others, and had to do with the absence of history in Castells' treatment of the less developed countries of Africa. In particular, they believe he underplays the historical factors, such as the experiences of colonialism and post-colonialism, which substantially account for Africa's inability to meet the minimal conditions for participation in the new economy.

The role of the state in the era of globalisation

A central element of the Castells and Carnoy thesis on globalisation is their view that globalisation has precipitated the decline of the nation-state. This has occurred primarily because globalisation has rendered all national economies highly dependent upon the performance of their financial markets that are globally integrated. The state in these countries has therefore lost control over monetary policies and interest rates – key levers of national economic policy. In addition, these economic developments (according to Castells and Carnoy) are accompanied by other social changes that have accentuated the decline of the nation-state. They are:

- The decline of the social welfare system and its associated institutions and forms of social regulation – the demise of a protected labour market, minimum wage legislation, a consensual industrial relations system structured around a strongly organised union movement, and a social safety net including unemployment, health and other social benefits for the poor and sick.
- Changes in the labour market centred primarily on the rise of 'flexible labour' and the growth of part-time, self-employed, non-formal and other forms of temporary and outsourced employment.
- The demise of the nuclear family. Female labour now constitutes the greater part of this new, flexible labour force. These changes have had dramatic implications for the organised union movement, which has been predominantly male based. Male workers have in the past been the main source of income for the nuclear family.
- The failure of the educational apparatuses. Educational institutions, particularly schools, were characterised in the industrial era by processes of social selection, exclusion and regimented learning (what Carnoy calls 'warehousing'), rather than by the promotion of mass access and the accelerated development of human capital at all levels throughout life – which is what the new economy requires. As a response, more and more parents are losing faith in the public school and university system, seeking

private and alternative forms of educational provision outside of the state's control.

- Changes in class consciousness. Under Fordism (the industrial model of social organisation) workers' class consciousness was diluted through a consensus-seeking industrial relations system and then reincorporated into a new set of values arising from the workings of the nation-state and its key juridical, educational and social institutions. These new values included being a 'citizen', being a member of a 'nation', and benefiting from the protection of a common state. Under the new economy, these forms of national and class identity are falling away, with the social organisation of work today being highly differentiated and individualised:

> The effect of individualisation and differentiation is to separate workers from the 'permanent', full-time jobs in stable businesses that characterised post-World War II development ... The new transformation is dissolving the identity that workers developed with industrial organisations such as the corporation and the trade union. Workers are being individualised, separated from their 'traditional' identities built over more than a century and from their social networks that enabled them to find economic security. The 'job' and everything organised around the job – the group of work friends in the company, the after-work hangouts, the trade union – lose much of their social function. They are as 'permanently temporary' as the work itself. (Carnoy and Castells 1999: 15)

The above social institutions and social processes that formed the bedrock of the nation-state are now in decline. In the process, the nation-state has lost its legitimacy and power.

Gelb's disagreement with Castells' depiction of the state

Stephen Gelb, Senior Economist at the Development Bank of Southern Africa, took issue with Carnoy and Castells' portrayal of the state. At the heart of his disagreement was what he termed an inconsistency between two of Castells and Carnoy's main theses: on the one hand, their argument about the decline of the nation-state and its associated loss of power; and on the other hand, the critical role that they acknowledge was played by the developmental state in the economic success of the advanced economies and the newly industrialised 'Asian Giants'.

Gelb disagrees with the first thesis, that under the conditions of globalisation, the state has lost its power and is 'adrift'. He rejects this instrumentalist view that the state is about 'control' and 'coercive' power. Gelb posits an alternative conception that distinguishes between 'despotic' and 'infrastructural' power, the latter referring to the state's capacity to provide economic and political leadership over the productive classes and to promote 'development as a legitimacy principle'. Capitalist states have never really had true 'despotic' power and have always had to make key choices and compromises amongst a range of strategic objectives. The power of the state is derived less via despotic control and more through the key macroeconomic choices it makes, the social and technological infrastructure it lays out for development to take place, and the solidity of social partnerships it forges with other social classes. It is power derived with others through strategic collaboration, not power over others through coercion. Other features of this interpretation of state power are that it is penetrative – it needs to penetrate the grip on power of the ruling classes and provide them with strategic leadership. It is also defined by reciprocity: incentives for development are provided by the state to the capitalist classes, but are withdrawn if this development fails to take place – as was the case in the Pacific Rim countries. And finally, the benefits of growth are shared across the state and the ruling classes as well as other incorporated social strata. These are the key features of the 'developmental states' that emerged, for example, in the Pacific Rim region.

The power of the state is derived less via despotic control and more through the key macroeconomic choices it makes, the social and technological infrastructure it lays out for development to take place, and the solidity of social partnerships it forges with other social classes.

Gelb argues that one of the key choices that states have to make is in the monetary policy realm because not all monetary objectives can be met simultaneously. He calls this the policy 'trilemma'. The key monetary objectives are capital mobility, fixed exchange rates and monetary autonomy. Only two of these can be attained simultaneously, and the choices made play a constitutive role in shaping the character of the state and the national economy. In short, Gelb argues that the state has a critical role to play in enabling the national economy to engage the global economy on successful terms. Some of these related conditions include attaining a high level of domestic savings, increasing the levels of direct domestic investment, increasing exports, benefiting from international aid flows, and lastly, ensuring domestic restraint and a small fiscal deficit.

In reply, Castells suggested that his work and that of Gelb differed only in terminology and that states were not powerless in the face of globalisation. The strategic macroeconomic and other choices highlighted by Gelb were critical in shaping the role of the state. However, there was much disagreement amongst the participants, particularly the economists in the audience, about the exact relationship between the levels of domestic savings, the degree of capital mobility, and their relationship to direct domestic investment and economic growth. This is the terrain where the state and its choices clearly play a major 'agency' role.

Participant responses

South African participants were most 'agitated' to respond to the debate on the nation-state and its contemporary role. This has probably to do with the fact that South Africa has only recently attained the status of 'democratic state', with many citizens holding high expectations for its consolidation as a strong developmental state. This places South Africa in a unique position with much of the (mainly developed) world currently witnessing the gradual diminution of the state and its loss of legitimacy.

South African participants were particularly driven to respond to much of Carnoy's input, who spoke of the naïvety of Third World strategies which sought to stay outside the loop of globalisation or which lent undue weight to globalisation's unsustainability, hoping for its eventual demise. Carnoy had argued, 'We should not build a political strategy around the notion of globalisation's unsustainability. This would be a big error.' He did not advocate incorporation on any terms, but merely 'described its reality and the inevitability of incorporation'. We should not 'deny the existence of this powerful politico-economic force'. Similarly, Castells stressed the 'need to join the global networks. Self-reliance was not an option.'

Speakers from the floor such as Karl Von Holdt (of the National Labour and Economic Development Institute) and Hein Marais (a writer and analyst) were strongly opposed to the idea of accommodation with globalisation. They were not convinced of the notion of the decline of the nation-state. The weakening of the state was not inevitable and unstoppable but rather a result of neoliberal policies such as Growth, Employment and Redistribution (Gear), which were stripping the South African state of its key assets and capabilities. They believed that key social institutions such as the progressive trade union movement still had currency. And they demanded that Carnoy and Castells articulate a political strategy or programme of action that defined an appropriate way forward for the Third World.

Von Holdt asked whether the state could resist and reshape the terms of its incorporation within globalisation. Would a multi-state oppositional movement have an impact? What were the prospects of the new social movements emerging across the world opposed to the globalisation agenda – for example, the anti-World Trade

Organisation Seattle-style protests? Building on the notions of another participant, Shiv Visvanathan (Professor at the Centre for the Study of Developing Societies in India), regarding cultural resistance, were there not local as well as global strategies, both pre-modern and modernising resources (such as trade unions), strategies within and outside of the nation-state, that could be mobilised to shape the terms of engagement with globalisation? Von Holdt was adamant that he was not articulating isolationism. Forms of resistance to globalisation did not preclude engaging with globalisation but had to be on terms more beneficial to developing societies.

The South African government's view on the agency of the state

The Head of the South African GCIS, Joel Netshitenzhe, argued that the new democratic state in South Africa had a critical agency or developmental function, but that this capacity needed to be understood against the background of its fragile and incomplete transition from the previous apartheid regime to the current democratic era. This fragility arises from the political compromises made, most significantly, the reconciliation of both race and class relations that underpinned the settlement in 1990. This compromise has limited the new state's powers to act decisively. South Africa's re-entry into the global economy has also weakened the new state primarily because of the power of financial markets and their 'susceptibility to subjective manipulation'.

However, the democratic state is being viewed by the new political dispensation, according to Netshitenzhe, as the vehicle for a substantial national democratic project of transformation. Elements of this transformation include:

- A legitimising function whereby the state leads the process of social transformation and its personnel remain true to the task – avoiding the 'danger of social distance developing between those who operate in the state and government, and the people whom they are supposed to represent'.
- A unifying role. 'The state has to manage the primary contradictions that emerge from this phase of social development, particularly the processes of inclusion and exclusion described by Castells. The state must ensure that its relations with capital are those of both unity and struggle – unity in the sense that there are many things that can be pursued in partnership, and in struggle

because the state also seeks to regulate the operations of capital and the market.'

- A development role. There are huge resources in the hands of the state – fiscal or state capital – that can be deployed for socio-economic programmes, for improving the quality of life and for the building of infrastructure. The state also has the power 'to leverage investment through procurement, through incentive prescribed assets, public–private partnerships and licensing'. In short, the state has access to a wide variety of capital: fiscal capital (taxation), state capital (public enterprises), social capital (trade union funds, pension funds) and allocative capital (the regulation of the allocation of private capital).

Netshitenzhe summed up his response to the debate about the state by arguing as follows:

> The state is therefore not a helpless entity in relation to capital. Even under the conditions of globalisation it has direct and indirect leverage on the employment of capital. Of course, this will be tempered by all the realities of globalisation but this does not subtract from the principle. It merely affects the extent, the timing and the articulation of the intentions. ... Most of the objective difficulties facing the state can be changed, but they require an accurate reading of the balance of forces that will define the tactics to be adopted at each stage of the transformation. ... Objective circumstances are not carved in stone. Any balance of forces is dynamic, influenced by changing endogenous and exogenous factors. That's the challenge we face.

Castells concedes that the state has a key role

As was first highlighted by Gelb, there was an interesting and ongoing inconsistency in Carnoy and Castells' arguments that was picked up at the seminar. On the one hand, they maintain that globalisation occurs at the expense of the nation-state, but on the other hand, they concede that the stabilising role of the state is ongoing and beneficial to global capital:

> The legitimacy of the nation-state and its capacity to enforce the underlying rules and regulation of national market economies through democratic means and smoothly running political apparatuses, as well as to support a well-developed market information system, are important to global finance capital ... Global

> capital's 'co-dependence' on smoothly functioning civil-political societies offsets some of the decline in national autonomy we have described. (Carnoy and Castells 1999: 32–33)

In addition, Castells writes that an educated labour force – a critical ingredient of the informational economy – also requires 'good health, decent housing, psychological stability, cultural fulfilment' – the key attributes of the traditional welfare state. Castells acknowledges this by writing that 'welfare states, minus their bureaucratic undercutting and wasteful civil service perks, could be sources of productivity rather than budgetary burdens' (Castells 1998: 17). The provision of these benefits is dependent on the restructuring pathways chosen by nation-states in adapting to the dictates of globalisation – the neo-liberal 'cost-lowering' model, or the more social democratic 'productivity enhancing model' (Castells 1998: 17).

In the Gauteng discussions, Carnoy and Castells conceded that different state models led to different social policies and institutional arrangements that have a differential impact on the quality of life. Castells noted the important role of state policies 'in shaping the engagement with globalisation, but restricted within the context of possibility'. Left-leaning governments across the world (for example, Jospin in France and Cardoso in Brazil) are trying to adopt policies that simultaneously modernise the economy yet continue to maintain key social institutions and programmes that benefit the people. In response to a question regarding African states, Castells suggested that these states were in many cases 'rotten, corrupted and subject to acute problems such as clientelism'. These countries still needed the 'social revolutions that occurred elsewhere in the world in earlier centuries to transform governmental apparatuses into effective nation-states'.

In response to a question regarding African states, Castells suggested that these states were in many cases 'rotten, corrupted and subject to acute problems such as clientelism'.

The overall impression of the debate on the state was that its alleged 'decline' had been overly exaggerated with the reality being far less dramatic than that predicted by Castells. Globalisation is not a great epochal rupture from one social system to another. There is a far higher degree of continuity from one social structure (industrialism) to the other (informationalism) than is usually accounted for in the literature. The state is still a pivotal institution in the life of national economies, although its interventionist role in the economy has shifted in the advanced economies from that of being a bureaucratic Keynesian welfare state heavily involved in production and state enterprise, to a state that is 'less bureaucratic, less involved in production, more efficient, incentivising and wise; a state that focuses on building key infrastructural capacity such as ICTs, and high-level human capital formation; a state that has the capacity to facilitate and function within information networks' (synthesised comments from both Castells and Carnoy).

Changes in Castells' original thesis: an emerging new 'vision'

As indicated earlier, a significant development occurred during the Gauteng seminar between the position initially taken by Castells – to avoid describing the forms of political engagement that was required in the Third World – to the position he finally adopted at the end of his visit where he began to specify some of the central determinants of a political response to the exclusionary effects of globalisation.

Cloete engineered some of this shift by suggesting that Castells did not merely describe and theorise the characteristics of the new economy and its associated social structure. Castells also provided an implicit critique of globalisation by suggesting that it was shaped by fundamental contradictions and was unsustainable in the long term. Both Castells and Carnoy in their writings highlight the failure of existing social and cultural institutions in providing legitimacy for the nation-state. Both scholars in their dialogues with participants spoke of the new politics that was beginning to emerge worldwide in opposition to globalisation. They highlighted a number of factors that can be identified as causal determinants in the changing political landscape occurring globally. These included the emergence of new forms of resistance to the inequalities generated by globalisation and its unsustainable patterns of development; the changing nature of work and employment; and a loss of faith amongst the citizenry that the state represented 'government by the people for the people'.

The unsustainability of the new economy

Castells describes the central characteristic of the network society as its being simultaneously creative (in terms of continuous innovation) and destructive (in terms of its exclusionary effects). The network society is riddled with in-built contradictions, the most explosive being the volatility of financial markets and the problems of over-production (increases in worldwide productivity are faster than those of worldwide consumption). He predicted that a combination of a downturn in both the business cycle and financial markets could lead to an economic plunge not seen since the Wall Street crash of the late 1920s and 1930s. A more contemporary crash would be exaggerated by the fact that many United States and European households have large slices of their family income invested in stock markets. A severe plunge would be devastating across all social classes. Joel Netshitenzhe reminded the seminar that when Fidel Castro addressed South Africa's Parliament in 1998, he warned that when such a crash of the financial markets occurred, it 'would lead to a massive revolt and a fundamental restructuring of the capitalist system'.

Two trajectories for globalisation's future development were sketched by Castells. One was based on 'trickle-down' theory, in which the time frame for growth would be at least 20 years before benefits began to accrue to the underclasses. Such a time frame was too slow and would be socially explosive. The other trajectory was one characterised by survival economies, disconnected from the major flows of capital and trade, with people surviving on a minimal subsistence mode. Castells argued that it would be 'naïve of global capital to assume that it can exclude two thirds of humankind indefinitely'. This opened the way for a new third alternative.

The failure of existing social and cultural institutions

In developing his theory of the new politics, Castells cites a United Nations (UN) report recently released by the Secretary General, Kofi Annan, that reviews the role of the UN in the new millennium. One of the report's observations is about the loss of legitimacy by the nation-state across the globe. The report cites a Gallup International poll (the Millennium Survey) of 57 000 adults in 60 countries spread across six continents – the largest international survey of public opinion ever. The findings on the 'image' of the state and of politics are very revealing. According to this report:

> in most countries a majority said their elections were free and fair, but as many as two thirds of all respondents felt that their country, nevertheless, was not governed by the will of the people. Even in the world's oldest democracies many citizens expressed their deep dissatisfaction. (Annan 2000: 15–16)

Castells and Carnoy suggest that there are a number of causal factors in this decline of confidence in the legitimacy of the state and its associated social and cultural institutions. The key factor has been the collapse of the conditions necessary for social incorporation in the transition from 'industrialism' to the 'network society'. A number of social institutions associated with the period of industrialism – the nuclear family, the public school, the trade union and regulated and secure labour market conditions – have lost their social utility. For example, the social conditions that underpinned male dominance in the labour market have all but collapsed with female workers proving to be much more adaptable.

As highlighted earlier, the new forms of work organisation individualise and differentiate workers amongst themselves without any meaningful ideological reconnection to a particular social identity. The new flexible workers remain alienated as part-time, temporary, outsourced, self-employed workers without a meaningful new social identity.

Castells and Carnoy warn that the decline in the influence of the nation-state over the most marginalised segments in society – those who have difficulty accessing knowledge and who have the least formal education – pushes these dispossessed segments to:

> seek refuge in new and more exclusive collectives. These collectives help develop self-knowledge and self-confidence. They can provide community and therefore a sense of belonging. These new identities – whether religious or ethnic, regional or local – are antidotes to the complexity and harshness of the global market as the judge of a person's worth. (Carnoy and Castells 1999: 20)

The plurality of emergent identities poses a major challenge to the traditionally unifying role of the nation-state.

These new identities exist in sharp contrast to the sharing of cultural codes that the modern state was able to build upon. Castells argues that if these codes are not shared within society, society will begin to degenerate into isolated communities. The challenge of the new state is to build bridges between these cultural codes in a highly plural world. Carnoy warned that in the absence of these ties, society would be highly unstable especially during severe economic downturns.

The 'new politics'

The 'new politics' thesis was received with scepticism during the Gauteng seminar. The majority of participants were doubtful of the extent to which the South African citizenry had pluralised into this myriad of multiple identities. It was suggested repeatedly by participants that the democratic state, the trade union movement and nuclear family structure in South Africa had not yet outlived their unifying social purposes. Participants were also sceptical about the absence of any critique in the works of Castells and Carnoy of this new identity politics. Was this a pre-given process of social transition that was unstoppable?

Reluctantly (as a result of this kind of South African questioning and pressure), Castells and Carnoy began to construct an outline of the possible forms of an engagement with globalisation and its new identity politics. Five key areas of political action were identified in the discussion. These were:

- the rise of new progressive social movements
- the transformation of international institutions
- multilateral political and economic solidarity
- a 'Technological Marshall Plan'
- the primacy of ICTs, and human capital formation.

Each of these elements will now be briefly discussed.

New social movements

Carnoy and Castells both argue that the new social movements and initiatives that are emerging in response to the global are forming around 'the local' – a decentring of power to regions, localities, non-governmental organisations (NGOs) and so forth. It entails a shift from representation through the nation-state to representation across a diversity of localised constituencies and institutional forms – be they the revitalisation of devolved power in regional governments and municipalities, or through the increased activities of NGOs, some of whom provide services previously offered by the nation-state. Citizens now identify with these new institutions, shifting power, responsibility and legitimacy away from the central state. 'Legitimacy through decentralisation and citizen participation in NGOs seems to be the new frontier of the state in the twenty-first century' (Carnoy and Castells 1999: 31).

Transformed international institutions

The second key change in the political character of global society is occurring through the rethinking and restructuring of the role of the world's key international institutions – the United Nations, the World Bank, the International Monetary Fund and the World Trade Organisation. All of these bodies – in differing degrees – are recognising a number of changed elements in the character of international relations. Castells cited regularly from the findings of the UN study referred to earlier. The findings included the following:

- Globalisation presents an unsustainable model of development. As the UN Secretary General's Millennium Report indicates:

  > for many people, globalisation has come to mean greater vulnerability to unfamiliar and unpredictable forces that can bring economic instability and social dislocation, sometimes at lightening speed. ... Even in the most powerful countries, people wonder who is in charge, worry for their jobs and fear their voices are drowned out in globalisation's sweep. (Annan 2000: 10)

- There is now a recognition that a broad global compact is needed. 'Rich countries must further open their markets to poor countries' products, must provide deeper and faster debt relief, and must give more and better focused development assistance' (Annan 2000: 3).
- Existing international institutions must change their modus operandi.:

  > We must adapt international institutions, through which states govern together, to the realities of the new era. We must form coalitions for change, often with partners well beyond the precincts of officialdom ... These [reformed] institutions must serve as an arena for states to co-operate with non-state actors, including global companies. In many cases they need to be complemented by less formal policy networks, which can respond quickly to the changing global agenda ... To survive and thrive, a global economy must have a more solid foundation in shared values and institutional practices – it must advance broader, and more inclusive, social purposes. (Annan 2000: 2, 7, 9)

- The most dramatic changes will have to come with the Bretton Woods institutions. As the Millennium Report suggests:

  > our post-war institutions were built for an international world, but we now live in a global world ... [The] post-war institutional arrangements were premised on a world made up of separate national economies, engaged in external transactions, conducted at arm's length. Globalisation contradicts each of these expectations.

  The calls for a new financial architecture which attempts to regulate global financial markets and reduce Third World debt are now insistent across the globe – from Seattle, United States to Okinawa, Japan.
- Multilateral action. Castells argues that governments are increasingly agreeing to join together in shared programmes of global development. Soludo agrees, maintaining that Third World coun-

tries need to form regional economic blocs with open borders so as to unleash maximum economic co-operation. The UN is calling for a 'broad global compact', which would see co-operation between governments, corporations, non-profit foundations and NGOs around key development issues, particularly ICTs and human capital formation in the developing countries.

Joel Netshitenzhe of GCIS is optimistic about the possibilities thrown up by this new global political environment:

> One reflection of this tendency towards improving global governance [is something] that Africa can take advantage of. And there's of course also a developing willingness on the part of countries of the South and Africa in particular, to pool sovereignty without which it wouldn't be possible for us to assert ourselves in this world. All these, I believe, augur well for a new world agenda, for globalisation in the interests of the excluded. The question, as I've said, is whether we are prepared and able to seize the moment through our own behaviour and the manner in which we engage with the developed world.

A 'Technological Marshall Plan'

One of Castells' strongest political recommendations was his call for a 'Technological Marshall Plan' – a programme of First World intervention in Third World 'info-development' on the same gigantic scale as that which occurred during the original Marshall Plan intended for the post-war reconstruction of West Germany. Castells' main rationale for this plan is the need to implement a strategy of development aimed at modernising Third World information technology infrastructure and human capital formation on the basis of massive Western governmental, multinational and NGO aid. In addition to building ICT infrastructure, this intervention would also trigger a classical Keynesian stimulus of demand and lead to associated forms of industrial and economic development. Many of these ideas were presented as a keynote address at the Economic and Social Council of the United Nations, New York, delivered by Castells on 12 May 2000. In this speech Castells defends such a gigantic action on the basis of a model for growth which he calls 'info-development' (reprinted in this volume as Section Three Chapter 1).

This is a theory of economic 'leap-frogging' – a strategy whereby developing nations can use the new information technologies to leap beyond the difficult steps and constraints of traditional models of industrial development, particularly the requirements of economies of scale and low-cost mass production. The new technologies are more adaptable and can be more pervasive in a developing context. The only problem is breaking through the vicious cycle of deprivation where developing nations remain excluded because they do not have, as Soludo put it, the minimum threshold of information technology infrastructure and human capital to kick-start this strategy.

The 'Technological Marshall Plan' is ultimately a strategy about helping the Third World join the network society, joining a series of nodes interconnected with other production locales in the world. As Castells warns, if we fail to join up, we face 'structural irrelevance' in the future.

The primacy of ICTs and human capital formation

The cornerstone of Castells' idea of a 'Technological Marshall Plan' is the development of ICTs and human capital formation. Castells argues that 'human resources are critical'. Human resource development is the 'essential infrastructure, without which technology means nothing. The new economy is a people-based economy. This means education' (Castells 2000: 4).

Castells' observation about the importance of education is significant as he would have been part of the devastating critique of neo-classical economic theories of human capital articulated in the early 1970s. These critiques argued that education was powerless to alter the fundamental class location and labour market trajectories of working-class learners. It was also argued that there was no clear correlation between educational improvements and economic growth. In a significant turn-around in this debate, Carnoy and Castells are now admitting that education and human resource development do matter to a great degree in terms of economic growth:

The old school of thought centred around the notion of human capital is fully vindicated. To invest in education is a productive investment. An educated labour force is a source of productivity (Castells 1998: 16).

The key difference, of course, between the debates of the early 1970s and the current period is that capitalist progress in the 1960s and 1970s was premised on cheap labour and low-cost raw materials, with education a fairly insignificant determinant of profitability. In sharp contrast, productivity and profitability today are entirely reliant on the total labour force being educated, trained and innovative – with cost being a secondary factor.

Conclusion

The dialogue with Castells and Carnoy was inspiring for most participants in the Gauteng seminar. It was a difficult journey to acknowledge all the obstacles that lie ahead for a developing country such as South Africa. But it was also an inspiring journey, certainly for educators present at the deliberations, in that for the first time in the economic development debate in South Africa, human resource development and human capital formation have been placed at the top of the list of development priorities. This makes the transformation of schools and universities into high-quality institutions a more pressing social priority than ever before.

Notes

1 See journal review comments at http://www.chet.org.za/CastellsReviews.html

References

Annan, K (2000) *We the Peoples: The Role of the United Nations in the Twenty-First Century.* New York: United Nations.

Carnoy, M and M Castells (1999) 'Globalisation, the knowledge society, and the network state: Poulantzas at the millennium.' International Conference on Nicos Poulantzas, Athens, Greece.

Castells, M (1998) 'Possibilities for development in the Information Age: information technology, globalisation and social development.' Paper prepared for the UN Research Institute for Social Development, Geneva.

Castells, M (2000) 'Information technology and global development.' Keynote address at the Economic and Social Council of the United Nations, New York, 12 May. Reprinted in this volume as Section Three Chapter 1.

Reich, R (1991) *The Work of Nations.* New York: Random House.

Andre Kraak is Research Director at the Human Sciences Research Council. He was previously Co-ordinator of the M.Phil. Programme in the School of Government at the University of the Western Cape (UWC). Before that he was Academic Planning Officer at UWC and also lectured in the Comparative Education Department. He completed his doctorate on education and training policy options for South Africa at UWC and has acted as a policy consultant on education and training for government and public sector organisations.

section two

the net and the self

2

> Identity ... is the construction of meaning, the meaning of actions by social actors on the basis of social attributes.

manuel castells

Growing identity organically

If you look at society from the point of view of the social actor, at South Africa from the point of view of people, instead of looking at it from the point of view of structure, I cannot think of a more important issue than identity, identity's meaning. Meaning is what makes you live: everything else only makes you survive.

When it comes to identity, the cultural context, the social context and the political context are decisive. I think I can say something not only about the theoretical but about the personal too, about feeling myself a Catalan, which for the last 500 years or so has been an oppressed identity. We are getting it back at last. I feel that the way to address this issue of identity in a country such as South Africa is in the context of Africa. I read a number of studies on African identity in order to write my book. I didn't understand the specifics but I understood the importance of 'African identity'.

Let me start with a few general considerations before coming to the heart of the matter, which is really trying to explain how I see what's happening in terms of the process of historical construction and reconstruction. I will approach it by examining the issue of European identity and then see how we can connect to the issues that you raise here.

First of all, if someone asked me to summarise in one word what my trilogy is about, I would say it's not really about information technology. It's about the contradictory interaction inherent in the process of building a network society with people. It's about a society's technology, its institutions, its culture, building a society that embraces the entire world in a very differential way. Therefore the process of homogenisation seems to me like the great march of industrialism in the 19th and 20th centuries under its two versions, capitalism and statism.

On the other hand, my trilogy is also about the resistance, orientation and shaping of this process by people rooted in their specific meanings which generally are considered to be identities. However, don't think only of identity as ethnicity or religion. It is also people resisting or reorganising or shaping the process in terms of their personal identities. It's both things. If my book dwelt mainly on ethnic, national, religious and gender identities, it's because that's what I was seeing, empirically. But these are not the only possible identities people can have. As you well know, in many developed countries people are not so much approaching the future with this kind of collective identity as they are building their own identities. Some people in California, for example, have decided to be Buddhist or Ecobuddhist. That's their right, and why not?

That's what I try to summarise by referring to the dialectic between the net and the self as the central dialectic of our world. It is not the inexorable march of a structure led by information technology. Rather it's the explosion and the contradiction between people deciding to be themselves on the one side, and the transformative system on the other.

In between, institutions of the industrial era, including the state, are shaken. They are not disappearing, but they don't know what to do in all of this. They try to interpret the oracles of global financial markets. I think it's significant that everybody – including presidents and prime ministers – starts the day with CNN Financial News.

So, what is identity? Identity for me is the construction of meaning, the meaning of actions by social actors on the basis of social attributes. This very important topic has been polluted lately by all kinds of postmodern vagaries, and I will not go into that because I think the best thing one can do with postmodern theories is to be silent about them. Identity, as with everything in this world, is not made out of words or feelings or moods. It is made material, as everything else is, with the works of history and experience. We can discuss how this experience is perceived, transformed, rearranged – but the point is, identity which is not rooted in experience is fantasy, not identity.

Identity works on the materials of experience, experience that is historical and can be collective and/or individual.

Identity works on the materials of experience, experience that is historical and can be collective and/or individual. Certainly anyone can invent his or her own identity, but it will be a very weak identity. In other words, a state can decide, 'This is going to be your identity: I am going to enforce this identity on you, I am going to create the Inquisition and you will be Catholic or tortured,' and then if you insist on this for enough centuries, those who survive will become Catholic. So yes, identity can be built artificially. But it only becomes a material force and a material source of meaning when it has been enforced enough over time and in the depths of people's bodies and souls. Then it becomes an experience. That's why personally I don't like state-enforced identities very much because there's always an element of absolute coercion. But still, the possibility does exist of building identity through the state.

We always start in history with some kind of identity.

However, there's no such a thing as an empty cultural space. We always start in history with some kind of identity. People, from the very moment they exist, have meaning – and this meaning comes from something and this something is a shared experience. Some people add in the biological aspect of it. I don't, because as we know, any rewiring of the brain that takes place, not only on the biological basis but on the relationship between this biological basis and people's experiences, already produces differences. For example, studies with twins show that, after a few months, they are already different. So it's really the interaction and experience that makes people's minds, individually and collectively.

In the modern age, national states, very insecure creations at their origin, have tended to try to eliminate all the existing identities, not only to superimpose an identity, but to impose a new identity based on the political definition of identity. The ultimate example here is the French Revolution which has been the matrix or touchstone for most western intellectuals; it liberated individuals but exterminated identities. When the French Revolution came to power, only 13 per cent of people in France spoke French, the language of the Franks, not the rest of the nation. Most people were Catholic, the Church was the main institution in their lives. All this had to be eradicated to create the new universal citizen, a good French citizen who would be equal, free, fraternal and ready to fight throughout the world to expand the new notion of freedom and to civilise the rest of the world, particularly the rest of the European countries, and most particularly Spain. Spain fought desperately against the French Napoleonic invasion and since then, for at least a hundred years, the progressive Spanish intellectuals were totally delegitimised in Spain as *afrancesados* ('French-like'). This divided the countries internally amongst themselves, between those people who were seen as 'foreigners' who wanted to impose something foreign on our lives, and 'us', those who fought against the French Revolution.

In fact, although the French Revolution tried to exterminate identities by force, that was an unfinished task in France. By the end of the 19th century there were still many identities and particularly, the whole thing about Catholicism and all these backward notions, that there was a God and there was something other than the state, were still a widely diffused way of existence. What really did the job was the Third Republic school system under the leadership of Jules Ferry, who decided that everybody had to go to the state school or to the schools chartered by the state, under which they could learn exactly the same thing across the entire country under the same conditions with the same exams, because that was 'progress'. In this way everybody was inculcated with exactly the same ideology. Now you can understand why, in the 1990s, there was such outrage in France when some Muslim girls decided to go to school wearing the chador and they were expelled, because the notion here was that the school had no other values than the values of the state. The values of society are going to be the values that the state decides.

That was a remarkable accomplishment. France is probably the only country in the world that really exterminated all identities other than the French identity, with the exception of Corsica and maybe the Basque identity as a reflection of what is happening across the Spanish border. Of course, there are still a few Bretons, and a few Occitans, and a few Alsacians, but, by and large, they are part of the folk. There is really not much of an Occitan identity these days. There are some disgruntled Occitan intellectuals, but at the grassroots level there is no strong identity other than the French identity (which is now becoming more complicated because you've got the French soccer team who is now mainly Arab and black). So then the French model became the most effective model in building the citizen identity. This is an identity which is abstracted from any other historical group except the state, the democratic state. Therefore, good progressive values, which I personally share and many of you certainly share – freedom, democracy, representativeness – are part of individual identity conceived of as citizen of the state. So it's between you and the state. You are French, because the French state tells you that you are French, and trains you and raises you to be French. And then from being French, you develop your other secondary identities. But first of all, you are French.

... good progressive values – freedom, democracy, representativeness – are part of individual identity conceived of as citizen of the state.

In my book (Castells 1997), I describe at length how the Soviet state tried to build a new identity on the basis of the Soviet state. In that sense, the two major systems, and the two major theories that have dominated the industrial era, are capitalism and statism. But frankly, in 1789, there was not much capitalism in France. The French Revolution made capitalism; capitalism did not make the French Revolution. So it's really liberalism on the one hand and Marxism on the other hand that we need to consider here. Now, the Soviets and Lenin thought a lot about the national question. Why? Because they had a national problem. But the ideology, what became the Marxist/Leninist ideology, also started from the same principle as liberalism, that a new society had to be created out of the ruins of the past. Therefore in both cases, it was a rationalistic matrix, the triumph of reason. During the French Revolution the church in Paris known today as La Madeleine was the Temple of Reason, where the Goddess of Reason was worshipped.

The Soviet Revolution also had this notion of eliminating the irrational remnants, the vestiges of history, and rebuilding everything on the basis of a 'new man', who would be the avant-garde of the New World. You have to start, according to the matrix, by creating this new personality. The matrix of the Soviet culture was the negation of historical identities.

On the other hand, the Soviets had the problem that they were building the new society, the new revolution, amidst an incredible variety of historically and linguistically rooted identities. How do you handle that? There were, as you know, tremendous debates which I am not going to repeat here because Neville Alexander has discussed them very clearly in his paper. The main thing I want to say is that the Soviets tried something better than the French Revolution – at least on paper. At the same time they also decided to exterminate an entire people by sending them to concentration camps. But the intellectual project was a powerful one: you have to combine, on the one hand, religious and ethnic groups, often but not always expressed in linguistic terms; and on the other, territorial identity, and try to mix the two. So everybody in the Soviet Union had to have a stamp in his or her identity card that said you are a Jew, you are Russian, you are Armenian, and so on. It's stamped in your identity card, just in case you didn't know. That's very different from the French model.

A number of territories were declared republics. Some of them were republics of the Soviet Union, some of them republics of Russia, and in these republics there would be a predominant ethnic identity – predominant because Stalin decided that it was predominant, not because that ethnic group was numerically predominant. Even today the majority of the population of most of these republics is not the ethnicity of the republic. So every identity was given a piece of the state in a given territory and accordingly assigned an identity in the identity card.

This piece of the state, that is a given territory, had also some kind of linguistic privilege. In other words, in these areas there was a public policy of 'affirmative action' based on ethnicity. The net result of it was that some identities were privileged on the basis of their formal integration in the state, while the rights of identities as a collective expression of autonomy from the state were ferociously repressed. In other words, it was the moulding of historically produced identity, within what the state decided would be the identity. This led on the one hand to the inability of identities to express themselves autonomously, but on the other hand, led also to preserving enough segments of existence of the identity amongst the members of the state so that at the moment when there could be an expression of this identity, it took the form of territorial separation from the state.

The matrix notion was that the Soviet people would emerge as a new identity through the work of education over the long term.

The matrix notion was that the Soviet people would emerge as a new identity through the work of education over the long term. Again, it was a more intelligent scheme than that of the French Revolution but the ultimate notion was that all these residual vestiges of religion, ethnicity and nationality would be phased out and merged in this extraordinary development of the new Soviet man that would expand throughout the world and the whole planet.

So there were these two elements. There was the same rationalist project in the long term, and simultaneously, the opportunistic Stalin decision: 'let's give these people something because otherwise we will not be able to control them'. Ultimately, the experiment collapsed, there never was a Soviet man, and pieces of the state became the platforms of identity, became the launching platform for the disintegration of the Soviet Union. The ironic thing with Russia, by the way, is that it was the Russian nationalist movement led by Yeltsin that finally destroyed the project.

Now, beyond these two projects, there have been other experiments. Generally the most successful experiment for handling the new expression of identity in the modern context is considered to be the Spanish experiment of the late 1970s to the present: the rebuilding of the Spanish state to acknowledge the diversity of the Spanish nationalities, in spite of the continuing tension afflicting the Basque country. The Spanish Constitution in 1978 states in the second article, that Spain is a nation of nationalities, a contradiction in terms. Well, that means the recognition of the multinational character of the state, and at the same time, the army watching over the Spanish nation. So we have a Spanish nation of nationalities and everybody takes whatever they want from this.

Which means that if you are going to develop a constitution in any country, ambiguity is fundamental. Constitutions should always be ambivalent because they should evolve with societies and with political conflicts. That's why the American constitution is not a constitution, it's a series of amendments that actually made the American constitution a flexible constitution.

In my understanding of the African experience, there are two key things to consider. Firstly, states were decomposed through colonisation and people of different cultures were forced together, creating artificial provinces – artificial in the sense that they were not rooted in history. The Berlin Treaty of 1884–1885 was sealed with people sitting in a room in Berlin and saying, 'Here is a river. You take that side of the river and I'll take this side of the river.' Sometimes it was not even a river. They didn't even know the geography. And this totally artificial map, even more artificial than the French state or the Spanish state, was then transformed into countries after independence. Therefore, there was no relationship whatsoever between historically rooted identity and the nation-states of Africa, including South Africa.

... there was no relationship whatsoever between historically rooted identity and the nation-states of Africa ...

The second key point is that the multi-ethnic, multicultural, multi-religious, multi-tribal and some people would say multinational nation-states were created as apparatuses for the main source of accumulation in Africa. The African economy was then constructed by the accumulation of wealth through the state and by the state, in tandem with the national representatives of capital. This state-form then organised ethnicity as the key source of clientelism to support power systems and private accumulation. I don't think you in South Africa were so different from the others. Here, two particular tribes (the Afrikaners and the Anglos) got together to accumulate for themselves, excluding the others. So it's not so different from Nigeria or the Ivory Coast.

These discussions that we are having have a great deal of political prescience for South Africa. You are building a state as you are building a new society. If you aren't building a state, you're in big trouble, because states have to have some kind of relationship to a society. If you change society, if you dramatically change the fundamental cleavages in society, you have to change the state. And how to change the state and how to relate that to the whole notion of the politics of identity is the central issue.

Therefore, let me try to relate to this process in which you are trying to construct a new state which accommodates identities and at the same time, is able to function as a nation-state. You need a nation-state, certainly, because it's the only tool we have to relate collectively to the process of globalisation, and to other states. So any talk about the disappearance of the state is simply senseless. But which kind of a state and how it's connected to the global economy, to other states, to society, is the question. By the way, it's to society, not to civil society. If you want, we can discuss civil society: it's fashionable to say 'civil society', rather than just to say 'society'. Civil society is a very different thing. It's a set of political and social apparatuses that link the state to society. That's what we have to establish from the very beginning. So 'civil society' means 'nice people'? Not necessarily. Civil society, for Gramsci, was the Church, the labor unions, the co-operatives, all forms of organisation and institutionalisation of people's relationships with the state (Buci-Glucksmann 1975). Civil society only exists in relationship to the state. This is why the relationship between the state and society is fundamental. How you establish this relationship in terms of a plural identity in which people really feel this identity, even in linguistic terms, that's the issue.

I'm going to illustrate this issue with the analysis of a historical context/process: what the European Union is thinking about this matter. Over the last six months I worked on this issue with the Portuguese presidency of the European Union. My assignment was to discuss and elaborate how to build a European identity. I tried to make it as non-ideological as possible. Here is the position.

Firstly, the European Union is one economy. The British still think that they have their own economy because they have the pound, but that's a matter of political opportunism. In a couple of years, at most, you will have the British pound linked to the Euro. You cannot merge the Frankfurt and London Stock Exchanges while having different currencies. So overall, there's one European central bank, one European currency, no tariffs, freedom of labour, freedom of capital. You have one economy.

Secondly, there is one European state. It's not made up of the European Commission. The European Commission is a bureaucracy which many people hate and mistrust, and it clearly has no power. The power is in the European Council of Ministers, chiefs of government of all the countries meeting every three months, making decisions to be executed by the European Commission. It works, as I describe in my book, as a network state. It's the only explicit network state so far. The others are implicit. So take the two countries I know best, France and Spain: 80 per cent of the legislation in France and Spain has to go for approval to the European Union. In that sense they are not sovereign states. Defence is taken care of by Nato. The European Union is trying to move to something else now, but there are no national armies any more.

The problem here is that on the one hand, you have this process of total integration. On the other hand, you have a process of increasing multi-ethnicity in most European countries through immigration and differential birth rates. Europe still thinks about most of the minorities as immigrants. But a growing proportion of them are not immigrants, they are people born in the countries and usually, citizens. I say 'usually' because Germany still has this notion that you can be born in Germany but if you have relations in Turkey, you remain Turk. Like Koreans in Japan from three generations, they are still Koreans. Germany is changing, but changing slowly. Overall, ten per cent of Germans at this point are foreign born. Through the differential birth rate, the projection in twenty years for the European Union as a whole is to have about one quarter of the population belonging to ethnic minorities. But this average then concentrates in some countries, and sometimes, in some cities. London, Frankfurt, Berlin and Paris are already largely multi-ethnic metropolises.

Now, this has not been accepted in the collective mind of Europeans. There is still a homogeneous Europe which is being invaded by immigrants. Bad news for this kind of mentality is that these people are there to stay and their numbers are going to be increasing. And such conditions create doubts about what's happening to our national identity. At the same time, everything that is instrumental is European. Opinion polls show two things. First of all, there's a class divide. Everyone who feels European is in the upper segments of society. Professionals and middle classes feel European. Workers don't feel European, and this is so in all the countries.

Secondly, when people are asked, 'Do you feel European?' and they answer, 'Yes, I feel very European,' what do you conclude from that? No one knows what it means to be European. The European Union has at last started thinking seriously about the matter. Why? In a democratic society, when everything is going relatively well, everybody is winning by the fact of being in the European Union. But there are going to be crises, everybody knows that. Financial markets may collapse. There are going to be tremendous crises of transition to the new technological order. At that point, the national reflexes of closing the borders will seem irresistible.

So the idea of decomposing the European Union, breaking it up, is not imaginable. It would, in any case, be an absolute catastrophe. Therefore, the main preoccupation is how to build a European identity. That's the task that I was mercilessly assigned. First of all, you don't proceed like Yeltsin, by floating ideas about what the new Russia might be about; how to find the new Russian identity. You don't do that. Secondly, it is not about ideology, it cannot be a discourse: 'We are Europeans.' Previously the only possible way in which we as Europeans could resonate it was on racist and xenophobic terms. Which always, in moments of European unity, was against Islam, was always against the Muslims. That was the thing, and Spain, for example, grew from fighting the Muslims.

So, how was I to approach my task? The only thing I could come up with was to find material mechanisms of the production of identity in which governments could take the initiative but not the planning. But how do you bring a new identity into being without indoctrination? Firstly, because it's not nice to indoctrinate people, but secondly, because it doesn't work, because it results in a weak identity. Catalan, German, all those strong identities, you put in a middle layer of imposed weak identity, and it doesn't stick. That's what's already been done, and has failed.

How then do you grow identities organically that mix with others without contradicting them, and create a canvas of cultural meaning which is shared through economy and experience? In other words, if identity shares experience, can we invent mechanisms which make the shared experience develop, though not through coercion?

Some of the mechanisms are the following:

- One, *shared education,* primarily through students moving around. We already have something called the Erasmus Programme whereby students can have a year on other campuses. But this should be a super-Erasmus. Sending students around Europe, to the great joy of their parents – imagine one year of vacation from your children, knowing that they are safe, well treated, in some remote village in Europe ... Then, integration of programmes at some levels. For instance, in history, most children in the world don't know much about the history of other countries.

- Two, *language teaching.* English is becoming the common language of Europe, but no one can say that because it would just break up the Union. But together with the dominant language and your own language, what matters is that you have some knowledge and some ability to relate to other languages. Technology can help because we are very, very close to good, automatic translation programmes. So the possibility of switching from Hungarian to Catalan, and back to the language of Europe, is getting closer and closer.

- Three, *media*. The media are being increasingly integrated in Europe on the basis of private satellite television, cable television and so on, which carry mainly American productions. But unlike what people think, it's not American imperialism *per se*, it's European incapacity to produce something better. I don't think American television is great: it's crap, but very well produced crap. If you propose bird-watching programmes rather than action movies, it's a losing proposition. In America, they have great public television, and nobody watches it. So the notion here is, can Europe help the development of multimedia groups in the model of the British Broadcasting Corporation: good television, highly competitive, which produces programmes which are not as bad as American television, but with similar technical quality?

- Four, the *Internet*. The Internet is really a major source of cultural diversity and cultural exchange. There are two languages which are growing the fastest in the European Internet, Dutch and Catalan, in terms of the number of Websites in both languages. But at the same time, in both cases, these people connect also to the people who connect to Internet Websites. So all kinds of channels of multicultural communication through the Internet are possible.

- Five, the *European labour market*. If you work together in other countries and on equal conditions – not as the Spanish and Portuguese immigrants did in Germany or France in the 1970s – then the sharing of work is also a sharing of experience. Now, the geographical mobility in the European Union is possible but it's extremely limited by the problems of housing, social security, transfer of your pension fund, transfer of your degrees, etc. So in other words, the building of identity cannot be separated from the building of a European labour market.

- Six, *voting rights according to residence,* including immigrants who are residents. This is something that is openly discussed in the Council.

- Seven, *naturalisation policy*. Dramatic changes are needed in naturalisation policy with European standards of naturalisation because otherwise it's completely ridiculous that you cannot be German if you are born a Turk in Germany.

- Eight, a *shared foreign policy,* built on the basis of what all the opinion polls say, that the only principle that is shared by most

Europeans is a human rights-led foreign policy, expressed through the United Nations. Foreign policy is still not a European Union-shared competence but it's coming fast.

- Nine, as a consequence of the previous, but perhaps the most controversial thing, is an *autonomous defence policy*. If Europe is going to be something different to the United States, it needs to have a European army - and that's a huge discussion in Europe and the United States.
- And ten, the *harmonisation of the welfare state* and a charter of human rights which should be enforced in the entire European Union, as a concrete expression of what it means to be European, and particularly, a charter of women's rights which Europe is moving towards quickly.

All this is based on two major principles. The first principle is the building of a new identity on the basis of an existing identity, neither contradicting nor eliminating it. The second principle is the material building of the identity through inducing shared experiences rather than through coercion from the state.

References

Buci-Glucksmann, C (1975) *Gramsci and the State*. London: Lawrence and Wishart.

Castells, M (1997) The *Information Age: Economy, Society and Culture. Volume 2: The Power of Identity*. Oxford: Blackwell.

neville alexander

The politics of identity in post-apartheid South Africa

Who is an African?

Max du Preez, one of South Africa's best-known journalists, wrote in *The Star* newspaper on 4 May 2000:

> In my whole life I have never felt so white and Afrikaans as I do now ... I never thought that my pale skin and the fact that I come from Afrikaner stock were the factors that essentially defined me as a human being. Of course these were the facts of my life; I was born with a light skin from Afrikaner parents, I had no choice in the matter ... But throughout my adult life I believed that being a member of my broader society and a native of South Africa and Africa was what was really important – 'white Afrikaner' merely described my tribe ...
>
> Five, six years into the 'New South Africa' I am forced back into the little box of white Afrikaner. When I reminded political leaders not to use the term African in a way that would exclude Africans with white and brown skins, a senior journalist called it 'baas-business' and wrote that I only wanted to be an African suddenly because I wanted to steal more of black people's land.

This entire article could serve as a kind of coincidental introduction to the second volume of Manuel Castells' formidable three-volume analysis of the Information Age. It not only illustrates one of Castells' key notions in regard to identity formation but at the same time raises the question which came to my mind as I busied myself with his fascinating work, that is, what does this say about the project(s) we have set out to realise in what we all assume to be a new historical community on the territory of the post-apartheid Republic of South Africa?

To avoid any misunderstanding, it is essential that I indicate the scope of my response to this empirical and analytical horn of plenty. Although I shall unavoidably refer to some of Castells' theoretical positions, especially in regard to the state and the transformation of the function of the state in the Information Age, my interest and, I make bold to say, that of most South Africans, is focused on the strategic political implications of his work. And, while I am generally concerned with the implications of his hypotheses and projections for identity politics, specifically for social identities, I shall confine myself to what in my view is the Gretchen question of South African politics, that is, the national question. This approach, clearly, cannot begin to do justice to the wealth of thought and information contained between the covers of Castells' second volume, *The Power of Identity* (1997). It is a task for which I am certainly not competent but I would be extremely pleased if this essay, together with other formal South African responses and ad hoc interventions help to give Manuel Castells himself some sense of where we are at in this country and on this continent, both of which, as I have learned, have hitherto not really strayed into his line of vision. Who knows: our discussions might even inspire him to include 'the hopeless continent' on the research agenda of his institute! No less a person than Lawrence Summers, the United States Treasury Secretary, speaking at the University of Pretoria in mid-June 2000, has stressed the importance of South Africa for the rest of the continent and for the global economy, and has wondered whether the convergence in the South African and continental economies will take an 'upwards' or 'downwards' course (*Cape Argus*, 20 June 2000).

Castells himself, it appears, has a pessimistic prognosis as far as this question is concerned. According to John Saul (2000), Castells, despite believing that South Africa has more of a chance than the rest of the continent to enter into the charmed circle of those countries that are technologically and economically *salonfähig*, could, like 'its ravaged neighbours', fall into 'the abyss of social exclusion'.

The national question: relevant positions

There are two main positions espoused by Castells which call into question assumptions we have cherished in South Africa and which constitute the basis of the pivotal political project of the New South Africa. Stated simply, these are, firstly, his view that nations, or nationalities, ethnic and other historically evolved social groups, precede states and that such 'nations' and 'states' have nothing directly to do with one another. Secondly, there is his view that it is virtually impossible for states to give rise to nations. In respect of the first set of propositions, his own words are as follows: 'Nations are, historically and analytically, entities independent from the state ... nations, and nation-states, are not historically limited to the modern nation-state as constituted in Europe in the two hundred years following the French Revolution' (Castells 1997: 30).

With this latter proposition, we concur without any reservation.[1] We also concur with the corollary that it is not ethnicity, religion, language or territory as such, but 'shared experience', that gives rise to nations and nationalist movements. However, in so far as the formulation is intended as a critique of the ideas of Hobsbawm (1990), Gellner (1983) and Anderson (1983), among others (see Castells 1997: 29), I think it does not do justice to the subtlety and insight of Anderson at least. The latter's 'imagined communities' are in no way to be equated with Gellner's use of the term 'invented' in the meaning of 'fabricated', that is, falsely made or manipulated by self-seeking elites. Indeed, Anderson (1983: 15) explicitly criticises Gellner for the particular construction he places on the term 'invention'.[2] As will become evident presently, my defence of Anderson is occasioned by the fundamental significance which his reading of the origins and spread of nationalism has had for the 'nation building' project in South Africa.

To the extent that the statement: 'nations are, historically and analytically, entities independent from the state' refers to the modern bourgeois state, there cannot be much argument either (see Castells' elaboration of the point at 1997: 31–32). However, it ought to be clear that the development of 'nationalities', 'ethnic groups' and the like in pre-capitalist social formations was in most cases indeed the result of state building (dynasties, national monarchies, empires, even chiefdoms in a much earlier period).[3] Initially, I thought that I may be misunderstanding the point being made by the author. However, on reading his reflections on the question of identity in the former Soviet Union, I wondered whether there is not a fundamental issue at stake here, one with which South Africans have a special reason for engaging. His view that the emerging Soviet identity was a fragile one, which could not withstand the shocks of economic stagnation, is obviously correct, given the resurgence of ethnic passions and conflicts in the aftermath of the collapse of communism. On the other hand, there is no doubt that he over-generalises when he infers from the history of the Soviet Union that:

> While *sovetskii narod* was not necessarily a failing identity project, it disintegrated before it could settle in the minds and lives of the people of the Soviet Union. Thus, *the Soviet experience belies the theory according to which the state can construct national identity by itself.* The most powerful state, using the most comprehensive ideological apparatus in history for more than seven decades, failed in recombining historical materials and projected myths into the making of a new identity. Communities may be imagined, but not necessarily believed. (Castells 1997: 39, emphasis mine)

It is clear that the decisive phrase in this passage is 'by itself', since it allows the content of the statement to become obscured through an unelaborated qualification. It ought to be equally clear to any 'new' South African that this inference has the most portentous implications for the promotion of national unity in post-apartheid South Africa. If it is correct, it may well leave us stranded with a rainbow in our eyes but without the pot of gold in the form of the (non-racial!) 'nation'.

Castells' analysis of the national question in the former Soviet Union and the resurgence of ethnic conflict after the collapse is of the utmost importance to South Africans. It points to the fact that we ignore the social reality of ethnic and racial identities inherited from the past at our peril. The converse of his doubts about the nation-building capacity of the state is his insistence on the tenacity ('perdurability') of nations, as he phrases it, 'beyond, and despite, the state' (Castells 1997: 41). I want to put the matter as clearly as possible from a South African perspective: we must accept without any qualification Castells' caveat against 'fabricating' a South African nation. In particular, we have to guard against any Jacobin social engineering. Said (1995: 356) calls this 'the process of identity enforcement', a theme which many South African liberals and neo-liberals, sometimes quite disingenuously, have taken up recently (see especially Rhoodie and Liebenberg 1995). On the other hand, we face the real problem in this country that if we do not promote national unity, that is, arrive at a core of common values, practices and national projects (regardless of the class character of the political leadership for the moment[4]), we shall, as in similar cases in recent historical experience in Europe, Africa and Asia, fall apart into warring ethnic groups, each with a more or less separatist agenda. If that were to happen, similar events to the north of us would pale into historical insignificance.

... we ignore the social reality of ethnic and racial identities inherited from the past at our peril.

This is the reason why in the course of the past three years or so I have consistently warned against the ill-considered institutionalisation of the Commission for the Protection and Promotion of the Rights of Cultural, Religious and Linguistic Communities (I call it 'The Commission' for short). But before I deal with this grave question, it is necessary that we accept the proposition first popularised by Benedict Anderson (1983: 55) that administrative units 'create meaning'. This is simply another way of saying that states can – under certain conditions – create the material, that is, territorial, economic and general infrastructural, framework within which a sense of national unity (consensus, 'culture' even) can evolve. If we reject this point of view, all the talk about rainbow nations is no more than wishful thinking. That, of course, is not a good enough reason to espouse the proposition I have advanced. Voluntarism is ultimately as false as determinism. In all such cases, the key to the success of such a project is to be found in the peculiarities of the history of the social formation concerned.

In our own case, both those who were compelled at the beginning of the 1990s by geopolitical and domestic political developments to hand over the trappings of office and those who inherited these from the apartheid bureaucracy were agreed on the need to maintain the territorial integrity and the coherence of the state (see Alexander 1993, Marais 1998, Bond 2000, among others). This is the reason why we have been witness to the most astounding ideological and intellectual acrobatics – among other things, the spectacle of yesterday's dyed-in-the-wool racists becoming today's reconstructed anti-racists and of many a communist becoming a champion of privatisation and free-market economics. With the exception of rabid Volkstaters, the entire leadership of nationalist political organisations is committed to South Africa as a coherent political entity and there is total consensus in respect of 'building a nation' in a new South Africa. The whole of the period of Nelson Mandela's administration was focused on producing what he imagined to be 'reconciliation' and national consensus or national unity. Whatever one's criticisms of the modalities and contradictions of this strategy, it has to be said that a combination of economic necessity, massive propaganda and the socio-economic integration of the black and white middle-class elites, has given rise to a surprisingly united, non-racial political class in a surprisingly short space of time. While this could simply be written off as the co-optation of the black middle class and its political leadership by the white capitalist class, it would not minimise the social reality of the recasting of the capitalist state in South Africa in a superficially non-racial mould. In spite of the continuities between apartheid and post-apartheid South Africa, especially in respect of the fundamental hardware of property and economic relations as is manifest in the continuing abysmal wealth gap between most black and most white people,[5] or in the spatial segregation of the majority of the people, it is indisputable that a new image of a multicultural society is being projected.

The national question today

I have no doubt that at present, much of this is no more than cosmetic. This view is certainly substantiated when we consider the (cultural) software of identity politics. At this level of 'building the nation', things are clearly moving at a glacial tempo. The neglect in previous decades of the question of racial prejudice in its own ranks by the liberation movement is coming to haunt it at the beginning of the 21st century. Moreover, considerations of power and maintaining the stability of the country are leading the leadership of the African National Congress (ANC) to make what may become disastrous strategic moves. Of these, the most important, in my view, is the impending establishment of 'The Commission', to which I referred previously. This event is about to make the national question into the most explosive issue on the terrain of South African politics. I consider the concession that was made to General Constand Viljoen – who is one of the leaders of the Volkstaters – and his men in the new constitution (sections 185, 186 and 235) to be the perfect opening for those elements who want to undermine or water down the liberal-democratic dispensation of the New South Africa. These articles represent no less than the constitutionalisation of ethnic politics in the post-apartheid dispensation and while they do not necessarily have to signal the beginning of the end of that democracy, they can be used to attack it and to place it on the defensive.[6]

In accordance with the projections of Castells, economic, political and socio-cultural transformations in South Africa and globally have catapulted all its traditional communities into a crisis of identity. This is most noticeable among those groups who were constructed as racial minorities in ruling-class ideology, that is, the so-called Coloureds and whites. Among the latter, it is especially the Afrikaans-speaking group that has been destabilised.[7] Today, the speculations of a Lionel Forman more than 40 years ago suddenly assume a lethal relevance and one is tempted to ask, despite arguments against the 'ifs and buts of history', whether our situation might have been different if his questions had been treated more seriously when they were raised. Among other things, he posed what were then looked upon as at best unnecessary, at worst very awkward, questions, which followed directly from the theories of nationality that prevailed in the Congress Movement at the time:[8]

> If the people struggling are indeed nations, then an important part of our policy must be the demand that these nations have the right to self-determination. If they are not nations, and if they are national groups, aspiring to be nations, then in turn they have the right for the conditions to be created by which they may become nations with the right to self-determination. This means that it will become part of working-class policy to guarantee those nationalities which have not their own territory that they will be given territory which they will be able to

> administer autonomously, in which their own language will be one of the official languages and in which their national cultures may flourish ...
>
> Which of South Africa's peoples are nations? I would not like to say. Possibly there are several communities in South Africa which are full-fledged nations. But I think the majority of communities which have common language and psychology in South Africa are not full nations, but national groups. That is, I think they are aspirant nations, lacking their own territory and economic cohesion, but aspiring to achieve these ...

Forman's questions were obviously generated from his reading of Stalin's various tracts on the national question. I shall not try to discuss the debates captured in many volumes in many different languages and from many different points of view on the validity of Stalin's approach to the national question. Two relatively recent comprehensive surveys in the English language, one by a radical scholar (Munck 1986), the other by a more traditional academic (Connor 1984), have once again drawn attention to the problematic relationship in theory and in practice between Marxism and nationalism. Both arrive at the conclusion that the theoretical frameworks used by Marxists of whatever tendency were, and are, mostly inadequate to understand the phenomenon of nationalism. Munck (1986: 2) even asserts that 'essentially, Marxism has no theory of nationalism'.

For Forman to have raised the kind of questions he did at the time when the architects of apartheid were alive and busy carving up the South African body politic to fit into their Procrustean ghettos took great courage indeed. It also points to the historical specificity of South Africans' experience of identity politics and goes a long way towards explaining the apparently contrary – against-the-current – responses of most South Africans to questions of social identity. While I reject Forman's logic, I believe he was clairvoyant in trying to fix our attention on the potential for ethnic fragmentation in South Africa. I also consider it to be of the utmost importance that we do not repeat history and that we should devise and promote strategies which will reinforce the centripetal, not the centrifugal, tendencies in our social formation. It can be said without any disrespect to the memory of Lionel Forman that men such as General Viljoen would, today, agree with every word quoted here. They have arrived at a similar position to that of Forman because of their class interests and their particular racial–ethnic ideologies.

This is not the place, and it is not my brief, to give advice to the South African governing elites. However, given the analysis which Castells has provided us with, we could do worse than to revisit some of the historic debates that were conducted in the Second and Third Internationals on the national and colonial questions. Moreover, given the flux that has come into being because of the post-1968 challenge to traditional identities and concepts of identity, it may well be a useful exercise to go back to the ideas of the Austro-Marxists, people like Renner, Bauer and others, whose work tended to seek the overlap between national and sub-national identities, meshed in ways that strengthened the whole without threatening the parts.[9] In my view, we have to look for the answers in a careful balance between constitutional guarantees of individual rights and legislatively mandated, perhaps even expanding, powers of self-management accorded to voluntarily associating social groups, some of which will have a longer sense of historical (traditional) belonging than others.[10] Provided that, whatever form the cultural cantonisation of South African society eventually takes, we do nothing to encourage or entrench any racial identities based on the past or on contemporary affirmative action programmes. Judging by what Castells thinks of the prospects of a 'Rainbow Coalition' *á la* Jesse Jackson[11] and with due consideration for the historical and sociological differences between the United States and South Africa, I suspect he would be extremely sceptical about our chances of success in 'building a nation' at the southern tip of the continent.

A multilingual nation?

There is another proposition which Castells puts forward in this context, which is of great importance to the debates and projects in which we South Africans are engaged at this moment. Because of considerations of space, I shall refer to this only briefly. It is Castells' considered opinion that:

> The attributes that reinforce national identity in this historical period vary, although, in all cases, they presuppose the sharing of history over time. However, *I would make the hypothesis that language, and particularly a fully developed language, is a fundamental attribute of self-recognition, and of the establishment of an invisible national boundary less arbitrary than territoriality, and less exclusive than ethnicity ...* (Castells 1997: 52, emphasis his)

Leaving aside inevitable ambiguities deriving from the crudeness of writing as a technique (what, actually, is a 'fully developed' language? What does 'the sharing of history' actually mean?), this position is located within the classical, essentially 19th century, European Marxist polemic between those for whom nations were primarily political communities and those for whom they were cultural communities. To put the matter bluntly, if we were to accept this terminology and the conceptual universe whence it derives, we would necessarily describe South Africa as a multinational state. At issue here is the use of the term 'nation'. It is without any doubt, certainly in the English language, a most imprecise term. Without entering into tedious Marxist apologetics, I want to say that in the post-war African context, the word 'nation' is, and should continue to be, used in order to denote the population that resides within a given independent state, not because the state and the nation are coterminous but because, in the post-colonial African context, the state, generally speaking, creates the conditions in which meaning (identity, and also identities) is created. For this reason, we have expounded on numerous occasions why it is that 'community of language' is not an 'essential attribute' of the nation, why, in other words, the crucial issue is the capacity of the citizens to communicate with one another effortlessly, regardless of the language in which they do so. For this reason, too, the work of scholars such as Benedict Anderson has been of immense value to those of us who have tried to escape out of the Eurocentric conceptual cages that made it impossible for our predecessors to make any advance in these matters. In numerous essays and books,[12] my colleagues and I have explained how important it is to promote multilingual awareness and multilingual proficiency as well as lingua francas in a state as ethnically diverse as South Africa. Sub-national identities, whether the basis of affiliation is language, region, religion, gender or any other significant social marker, constitute part and parcel of the patchwork which is framed by the national identity. While the degree of, and even the potential for, the development of a sense of national unity varies from one territory to the next, the crucial task of the political leadership, and of other elements in the ruling elite, is to ensure by democratic means that no intersection of economic interests and ethnic consciousness takes place. One of the necessary ways of doing this is to reduce the Gini co-efficient in South Africa. For, unless the extreme inequality of incomes between the top 20 per cent (largely white) and the bottom 20 per cent (black) strata of the population is done away with, the danger of such intersections, through ethnically mobilised sectors of the society competing with one another for a better position at the national trough, is very great

... 'nation' is, and should continue to be, used in order to denote the population that resides within a given independent state ...

indeed. We do not have to look much further than this province (the Western Cape) itself to see how real this danger is.[13]

The national state between the local and the supranational

It is a fact that in most independent African countries, sometimes very conscious and determined attempts at implementing such strategies have failed, with the resultant ethnic conflicts and all too often genocidal wars which have come to be seen as one of the elements that stereotype 'the hopeless continent', where the prevailing mood is that of 'Afro-pessimism'. This is the point at which, I believe, Castells' insights are most useful to us. Firstly, because he points to the danger inherent in the power of language and in what Edward Said (1995: 353) calls 'the logic of identity'. Against the depredations of a homogenising culture spread through the globalised media networks, defensive nationalist reactions most often fall back on language which, '... as the direct expression of culture, becomes the trench of cultural resistance, the last bastion of self-control, the refuge of identifiable meaning' (Castells 1997: 52). Much as I would like to mine this rich vein, I can do no more in the present context than to refer to the plight (as seen by certain Afrikaners) of the Afrikaans language and the rearguard actions many of the speakers of this language are fighting against English, 'the global language' (Crystal 1997).[14] Even more to the point, however, is the fact that other linguistic communities, especially Venda- and Tsonga-speakers, who are beginning to define themselves and are defined by others as 'minorities', are similarly beginning to mobilise not so much *against* the dominance of English as *for* their place in the sun, usually defined as hours broadcast in their language by the South African Broadcasting Corporation. This is as it should be. However, it must be obvious to all who have studied these questions that statecraft should be anticipating possible conflictive situations through a process of completely transparent language planning. While some of this is happening at a surface level, it is obvious that the governing parties do not (yet) see the need to prioritise the language question by making budgetary provision for resourcing essential strategic and tactical projects. We can only hope that we shall not have to wait for a Zimbabwe-type land-invasion campaign – with all its potential for violent conflict – before priorities are reordered. There is a real danger that a language faultline will displace the racial faultline, which, however, continues to demarcate an unbridgeable gulf between those who are 'in' and those who are 'out'.

Castells' lucid analysis of how the dynamics of the network society disempowers the nation state and transforms it into an agent of global capital flows and of the global institutions that try to manage these flows provides us with a particularly helpful framework for evaluating the challenges and the achievements of the post-apartheid government. With hardly any exception, his description of the situation in which the state finds itself at the beginning of the 21st century tallies with the reality of the New South Africa. The choices made by the political class – 'black and white', as we say here – were in a sense scripted for them by global forces beyond their control, since they could not countenance one or other variant of a delinking strategy (Amin 1990) without inviting the uncertainties of a protracted and bloody civil war.[15]

The Mbeki administration, because of the choices made at the beginning of the 1990s, is doing exactly as Castells' theory predicts. It is attempting, on the one hand, through regional and subregional (Organisation of African Unity, South African Development Community) cartels, involving, among other things, the rhetoric of the African Renaissance, to gain a better place for itself in the global pecking order. On the other hand, it tries to regain and maintain its legitimacy with its own citizens by devolving power to the lower levels of government, that is, to the provinces and to local government authorities. This represents some guarantee of a liberal–democratic future, although the real source of the guarantee is to be found in the social pluralism of the country and in the unequal distribution of economic (white) and political (black) power. Even the proximate cause of the constitutional architecture of the New South Africa, that is, its proto-federal character, has more to do with the need to accept a trade-off between a centralising united democratic South Africa and a federalising consociational democratic system based on 'groups', than with any immediate sense on the part of the new regime of having to legitimise itself. Legitimacy had been conquered in the course of decades of struggle and for the present, much to the frustration of right and left alike, the accumulated interest of the liberation movement ensures that there is no viable alternative to the ANC-led government.

It is clear to me that at present, the Mbeki administration can still string the clamouring 'minorities' along. Many right-wing and not so right-wing Afrikaners have frequently expressed their frustration at what they see as government tactics to bring about the anglicisation of South Africa via the gradual but ineluctable scaling down of Afrikaans and of other South African languages. The establishment of Groep 63 (the Group of 63) recently is a clear signal from these quarters that they are not going to be outwitted by such Fabian tactics. Lest I be misinterpreted, let me state clearly that the South African government is motivated by a range of intersecting and interconnected considerations. These include (unresearched) considerations of 'the costs of multilingualism',[16] the convenience as well as the empowering effects of an English-mainly and even an English-only policy from the point of view of the middle classes, the genuine belief (but it is only a belief) that English is the language of globalisation and that it is a Canute-like strategy that would promote any alternative, the related view that English is, or can be, the national lingua franca ('the Kiswahili of southern Africa') in the short term, in spite of the fact that it is not used or heard outside of middle-class forums and on popular TV (in an Americanised version), and last, not least, fear of the unknown.[17] In the present context, it ought to be clear that the imperatives of globalisation which, among other things, in the brutal phrase used by Castells, discards 'used-up or irrelevant locales and people', whether they know it or not, are driving the rulers of South Africa in all sectors of our society in a very specific direction, that is, towards becoming a deeply divided society in which, as in all countries today, the division is determined by class. In South Africa, however, because of the legacy of 350 years of colonialism and apartheid-capitalism, this division continues to coincide to a very high degree with racial and ethnic divisions, which, under 'favourable' circumstances, can very easily be exploited by separatist elements or even by the state itself to gain economic or political advantage. This is the danger that a capitalist government in South Africa has to avert if it wants to maintain its place in the new world order. The dilemma is captured by Castells when he states that:

> [The] more states emphasise communalism, the less effective they become as co-agents of a global system of shared power. The more they triumph in the planetary scene, in close partnership with the agents of globalisation, the less they represent their national constituencies. End of millennium politics, almost everywhere in the world, is dominated by this fundamental contradiction.[18] (Castells 1997: 307–308)

Concluding remarks

This leads us directly to the question of the role and historic status of social movements. Again, I can only point to the importance and the complexity of the issue in the South African context. Here, too, we have over the past two decades at least experienced what Castells refers to as the split between the self and the net, that is, the growing alienation of groups and sectors of the population organised, or organising themselves, either defensively or proactively to come to grips (or to terms) with the usually devastating effects of the information-technology paradigm. Thus, we have, as it were, in miniature, everything from 'Islamic' and 'Christian' fundamentalism, to ethno-nationalist movements for increasing autonomy and eventually a separate state as well as Pan-Africanist ideas of a United States of Africa, the women's (and increasingly also, the men's) struggle against patriarchy, the movement for environmental justice, the banding together of the 'traditional' leadership of the country for a larger slice of the national revenue, a children's movement, an incipient co-operative movement and last, not least, the labour movement against the depredations of globalised capital.[19]

Is it possible that out of these criss-crossing networks the post-apartheid state can weave a socio-historical fabric that is tough enough to withstand the kinds of pressures that are being and will be brought to bear upon it from the workings of the global system into which it has been pulled willy-nilly? Or, will some of these movements become the stumbling blocks which trip up the state in its attempts to be an effective agent of global capital and of the global capitalist institutions? There is still much that speaks for a period of heightened class struggle in South Africa; the issue has by no means been decided. Strategic projections ranging from the adoption of more state-interventionist, neo-Keynesian economics to limited delinking *á la* Samir Amin are being debated in different public and more confidential forums. All of them are geared towards recapturing and maintaining the sovereignty of the South African state.[20] Given the choices that have been made and the fact that capital holds all the strategic positions, I doubt whether such projects have much hope of success, especially if they are conceived of as projects to be undertaken by the state itself, or in conjunction with the state. Castells (1997: 109) is undoubtedly correct when he asserts that 'the ability, or inability, of the state to cope with the conflicting logics of global capitalism, identity-based social movements, and defensive movements from workers and consumers, will largely condition the future of society in the twenty-first century'.

There is still much that speaks for a period of heightened class struggle in South Africa; the issue has by no means been decided.

The radical project, under these circumstances, has to be one that finds relevant answers to the question how social movements that are based on challenging the individualising and barbarous logic of the global economic networks can transform them into one that has as its major term the survival and continued evolution of the human species as a biological and social category of free and autonomous beings, bound together by the profoundly humanistic ethos of ubuntu in the universe. If we are not to end up in the position of Goethe's sorcerer's apprentice (not rescued by the Grand Master), we have to conceptualise information technology and the micro-electronic revolution in a non-determinist manner and be bold enough to visualise the alternatives so that these can be planned and strategised for globally.

In South Africa, we also say, as do so many people in other parts of the world: There Must Be An Alternative – 'Themba' for short. The point is that in the Nguni languages, the word 'themba' means 'hope'.

Notes

1 See works by Alexander, in particular, 1986 and 1999. The position suggested by Castells is gradually becoming the orthodox view especially in the countries of the South. See, among many others, Amin (1978); Amin (1990); Chatterjee (1993).

2 'With a certain ferocity Gellner makes a comparable point when he rules that "Nationalism is not the awakening of nations to self-consciousness: it invents nations where they do not exist ..." The drawback to this formulation, however, is that Gellner is so anxious to show that nationalism masquerades under false pretences that he assimilates "invention" to "fabrication" and "falsity", rather than to "imagining" and "creation"...'.

3 See, among many other modern references, Amin 1978; Munck 1986.

4 The struggle between different and conflicting classes continues as the leadership of each of these formations attempt to put their particular stamp on the emerging, or evolving, nation.

5 The latest socio-economic statistics relating to this gap are conveniently summarised in Wilson (2000: 18–24).

6 For a more detailed exposition of this view, see my article entitled 'Language and the national question', in G Maharaj (1999). One of the ironies of the present situation in South Africa is that those within the ruling alliance who used to oppose any concessions to 'group rights', even against the advice of their Soviet allies at the time, are today willing to flirt with this, in the South African context, extremely divisive political strategy. See Van Diepen (ed.) (1988, especially 149–50).

7 For reasons of space, I can only refer to the ongoing discussion on the changing identity, composition and future of 'the Afrikaner' in the Afrikaans media and to the wider debates that ensued after then

Deputy President Mbeki extolled his African being as an inseparable aspect of a multicultural, not to say hybrid, nation in a significant speech, made on behalf of the African National Congress, in the Constitutional Assembly on 8 May 1996.

[8] Cited in Alexander (1986: 78–79).

[9] A recent succinct analysis and evaluation of this almost forgotten episode in the history of European Social Democracy is that by Plasseraud (2000).

[10] The perennial debate in South Africa between those who believe that human rights vest in the individual and those who insist that they also vest in groups is a classic example of a Rylean 'category mistake'. This is not a theoretical question; it is a historical question, the outcome of which is always decided by means of political conflict and negotiation. The Austro-Marxists' principle of personality is an example of a relevant compromise between these two extremes which is undoubtedly capable of adaptation in circumstances where ethnic competition has been eliminated or where ethnic passions have never been mobilised for political ends.

[11] He refers to this project as '... a process of building a political identity that only if fully successful in the long term could create a collective, cultural identity that would be necessarily new for both whites and blacks, if it is to overcome racism while maintaining historical, cultural differences ... But in the ghetto trenches, and in the corporate boardrooms, historical African-American identity is being fragmented, and individualised, without yet being integrated into a multiracial, open society' (Castells 1997: 59).

[12] For a recent bibliography, see Alexander (1999); Alexander (2000); Heugh et al. (1995).

[13] Jameson (1998: 74), echoing Castells' argument, notes that if the national state is seen as a source of despotism and a broker of unequal distribution, cultural and social arguments are used to affirm federalist demands in spite of the recent failures of these 'solutions' in places as diverse as the ex-USSR, Canada and Yugoslavia. He also confirms the defensive nationalist response, identified by Castells (1997: 52), to the cultural homogenisation which is inherent in the globalised networks (see Jameson 1998: 74–75).

[14] Alexander (2000) represents a concise attempt at analysing the relationship between language, class and power in South Africa at the end of the 20th century.

[15] A sophisticated and critical description of the political economy of the transition has just been published by Patrick Bond (2000);

for an earlier but equally compelling account of the moral, political and theoretical debates and agonising that took place within the ranks of the Congress Alliance prior to and in the course of the negotiations, see Marais (1998); also Saul (2000).

[16] This 'argument' is exploded by my colleague, Kathleen Heugh (2000), in an article to be published soon in the journal, *Perspectives in Education*.

[17] This last point was persuasively argued by Lydia Ramahobo, Dean of Education, University of Botswana, at a recent symposium on Multilingualism and the Judicial System held in Bloemfontein at the University of the Orange Free State.

[18] The whole of this passage represents a brilliant generalisation, such that the preceding paragraph is well worth citing at length because it has well-nigh universal applicability and demonstrates the penetration of Castells' analysis:

> [In] the 1990s, nation-states have been transformed from sovereign subjects into strategic actors, playing their interests, and the interests they are supposed to represent, in a global system of interaction, in a condition of systemically shared sovereignty. They marshal considerable influence, but they barely hold power by themselves, in isolation from supranational macro-forces and subnational micro-processes. Furthermore, when acting strategically in the international arena, they are submitted to tremendous internal stress. On the one hand, to foster productivity and competitiveness of their economies they must ally themselves closely with global economic interests and abide by global rules favourable to capital flows, while their societies are being asked to wait patiently for the trickle-down benefits of corporate ingenuity. Also, to be a good citizen of a multilateral world order, nation-states have to co-operate with each other, accept the pecking order of geopolitics, and contribute dutifully to subdue renegade nations and agents of potential disorder, regardless of the actual feelings of their usually parochial citizens. Yet, on the other hand, nation-states survive beyond historical inertia because of the defensive communalism of nations and people in their territories, hanging onto their last refuge not to be pulled away by the whirlwind of global flows.

[19] In this paragraph, we find the beginnings of the explanation of numerous contemporary South African paradoxes ranging from the abandonment of the Reconstruction and Development Programme (RDP) in favour of Growth, Employment and Redistribution (Gear), to South Africa's policy towards the

European Union and towards southern Africa, including intervention in Congo, Zimbabwe, etc., and the tension in the relationship between central and provincial government.

[20] If Castells' analysis holds, it is ironic and problematic that at the very time when the social contract is being undermined and negatively amended in most countries of the North because of the individualising effects of information technology and the global economic networks, it is one of the main planks in the South African labour movement's platform. Perhaps this explains why the National Economic Development and Labour Council (Nedlac) is such a lame-duck institution!

References

Alexander, N (1986) 'Approaches to the national question in South Africa', *Transformation,* 1: 63–95.

Alexander, N (1993) *Some Are More Equal Than Others: Essays on the Transition in South Africa.* Cape Town: Buchu Books.

Alexander, N (1999) 'Language and the national question', in G Maharaj (ed.), *Between Unity and Diversity: Essays on Nation-Building in Post-Apartheid South Africa.* Cape Town: Idasa/David Philip Publishers.

Alexander, N (2000) 'English unassailable but unattainable: the dilemma of language policy in education in South Africa', *Praesa Occasional Papers,* No 3. Cape Town: Praesa/University of Cape Town.

Amin, S (1978) *The Arab Nation: Nationalism and Class Struggles.* London: Zed Press.

Amin, S (1990) *Delinking: Towards a Polycentric World.* London and New Jersey: Zed Books.

Anderson, B (1983) *Imagined Communities: Reflections on the Origin and Spread of Nationalism.* London: Verso.

Bond, P (2000) *Elite Transition: From Apartheid to Neoliberalism in South Africa.* London and Pietermaritzburg: Pluto Press and University of Natal Press.

Castells, M (1997) *The Information Age: Economy, Society and Culture. Volume 2: The Power of Identity.* Oxford: Blackwell.

Chatterjee, P (1993) *Nationalist Thought and the Colonial World: A Derivative Discourse.* London: Zed Books.

Commission for the Protection and Promotion of the Rights of Cultural, Religious and Linguistic Communities. Website: http://www.gov.za/reports/1998/pansalb.html

Connor, W (1984) *The National Question in Marxist-Leninist Theory and Strategy.* Princeton, NJ: Princeton University Press.

Crystal, D (1997) *English as a Global Language.* Cambridge: Cambridge University Press.

Du Preez, M (2000) 'Screwed back into my box', *The Star,* 4 May.

Gellner, E (1983) *Nations and Nationalism.* Ithaca, NY: Cornell University Press.

Heugh, K (2000) 'Beyond myths and legends: languages other than and alongside English – or why not?', *Perspectives in Education.* (Forthcoming)

Heugh, K, A Siegrühn and P Plüddemann (1995) *Multilingual Education for South Africa.* Johannesburg: Heinemann.

Hobsbawn, EJ (1990) *Nations and Nationalism since 1780.* Cambridge: Cambridge University Press.

Jameson, F (1998) 'Notes on globalisation as a philosophical issue', in F Jameson and M Miyoshi (eds), *The Cultures of Globalisation.* Durham and London: Duke University Press.

Maharaj, G (ed.) (1999) *Between Unity and Diversity: South Africa and the National Question.* Cape Town: David Philip Publishers.

Marais, H (1998) *South Africa: Limits to Change – The Political Economy of Transformation.* London and New York: Zed Books.

Munck, R (1986) *The Difficult Dialogue: Marxism and Nationalism.* London: Zed Press.

Plasseraud, Y (2000) 'Wie kulturelle Minderheiten besser zu schützen wären. Die vergessene Geschichte der personalen Autonomie', *Le monde diplomatique,* June 2000.

Rhoodie, N and I Liebenberg (1995) *Democratic Nation Building in South Africa.* Pretoria: Human Sciences Research Council.

Said, E (1995) *The Politics of Dispossession: The Struggle for Palestinian Self-Determination 1969–1994.* London: Vintage.

Saul, J (2000) 'SA's tragic leap to the right', *Mail and Guardian,* June 23–29.

Van Diepen, M (1988) *The National Question in South Africa.* London and New Jersey: Zed Books.

Wilson, F (2000) 'Globalisation: a view from the South', *Comparative Human Relations Initiative* (Southern Education Foundation, Atlanta) publication. (Forthcoming)

Neville Alexander is the Director of the Project for the Study of Alternative Education based at the University of Cape Town. He obtained his master's degree from the University of Cape Town and completed a doctorate at the University of Tubingen (Germany). He was a fellow at the Alexander Von Humboldt Foundation, Johann Wolfgang Goete Universitat and Yale University. During his ten years' imprisonment on Robben Island he was a lecturer and teacher to fellow prisoners and wrote one of the struggle classics, *One Azania, One Nation,* whilst under house arrest for five years.

crain soudien

Re-imagining, remaking or imposing identity

At the close of his introductory talk in Cape Town, Manuel Castells emphasised how much the process of constructing a European identity turned on the recognition of existing identities and on the principle of working with shared experiences. How, he asked, could a bridge be constructed between this European discussion and the South African discussion? What emerged in attempting to engage this question was a complex bricolage of cues, constructions and theorisations. Central, amidst a range of issues, was the question of the South African state and its relationship with the world and the rest of Africa. At several points of an engaging discussion, talk turned to the location of South Africa in Africa, its relationship to the process of globalisation, its potential for remaking itself and, critically, its function as a state. In this review of the discussion no attempt is made to summarise the many propositions and arguments which were proffered in the course of the morning and early afternoon. Instead, an attempt is made to recast the discussion as an engagement around what one might call statecraft and identity.

There were many points of agreement in the course of the morning and early afternoon. Building on Castells' ideas of national identities and local identities, no one contested the idea that identities were complex and were amenable to construction and reconstruction. It was accepted that one could be, simultaneously, several things. More troublesome, however, were 'how' type questions, issues of procedure and the role of agencies such as the state in working within a paradigm of multiplicity, as opposed to one of singularity and homogeneity. A fundamental sticking point, worth pausing over, was the basis on which a new South African identity or identities could be constructed and the role which the state could play in this process.

While there was some debate around the efficacy of the modern state, arising out of panelist Abebe Zegeya's analysis of the African National Congress government's weak capacity to deliver, there was agreement that the modern nation-state, as a network state, had already reconstituted itself. This reconstitution, in the context of globalisation, compelled it to present itself as an engaged presence. It had to engage with its neighbours and the wider world in which it found itself. Despite the fact that in places such as East Asia and in very different ways in the former Union of Soviet Socialist Republics the new informational economy had subverted the regulatory authority of the state, the state still commanded both influence and power in relation to a whole range of social and economic functions. It had to create the modalities for co-operating with its neighbours. It was obliged to respond to renegade behaviour within the international community of states. There was agreement that the Samir Amin (1990) route of an African uncoupling from the world was not a possibility.

Uncontentious as this characterisation of the state was, there were, however, complications with the ways in which it articulated and represented itself. At one level, these complications manifested themselves as the difficulties of representing itself internally and externally, but at another level, no less complex, involved the relationship, and the contradictions around this relationship, of its inside-face to that face which it presented to the outside world.

In the discussion in Cape Town, it was the internal articulation which took precedence. Aside from a fleeting moment of *frisson* around the need for an overarching African identity ('Why,' asked a participant, 'would anyone want to construct a European identity? The idea of constructing an African identity is strange') the nuances of this inside–outside relationship were not explored. Even less explored, interestingly, were the forays onto the global stage of South Africa in the person of President Mbeki, as the voice of a renascent Africa, as the voice of a less than supplicant Third World bringing to the international trading arena its unique commodity of humanism. Which Africa and which Third World were being invoked in these constructions were not discussed. An ascendant and exceptional South Africa, tutor to a deviant Africa led by gangsters and rogues, was, instead, circulated in the discussion.

An ascendant and exceptional South Africa, tutor to a deviant Africa led by gangsters and rogues, was ... circulated in the discussion.

In this discussion of South Africa's internal face, the path taken was that of emphasising the strategic necessity for presenting a united South Africa to the world. The challenge which crystallised in the discussion was how South Africa would construct this new unity for itself. In response to Castells' enunciation of his identity as Catalan and his assertion that Zulu identity was not an invention of apartheid, the issue arose of the valency of ethnicity. An important tension emerged here around the issue of the transportability of terms and definitions. If Spain could be constructed as a multinational state, of Catalans and Andalusians, why did this possibility not exist for South Africa where Zulus have had a self-identity for more than two hundred years? The critical issue, averred Castells, was moving South Africans towards a super-ordinate identity, what he called a project identity, where 'togetherness became a material experience'. Togetherness required, however, actors who shared this project. If the state was the only actor in the process, it imperilled itself, because failure would delegitimise it. Such a project identity would thus work only when social actors themselves became also state actors. Out of such a process would emerge a state which saw itself as a participant in the process of *inducing* new identities.

It was in this context that the difficulties within the process of constructing the state's internal face became most evident. Two categories of difficulty surfaced in the discussion. One category of discussion centred around issues of power and was manifested in concerns around class and social interests in relation to the national good. Another category of discussion revolved around issues of language and culture and fairness and justice.

In terms of the former category, interestingly, the term 'power' itself was invoked only occasionally, but it was clear that it gave body to the conceptual constructions which were outlined and deconstructed in the seminar. Power, and the issues around it, was recycled several times in a number of different forms expressing a range of interpretations. One participant asked whether interests did not constitute the core of identity work, while another enquired whether identities in Europe were not being constructed out of the collective action of groups such as the working class. Behind these interjections lurked an anxiety with the vocabulary of 'shared experience' in relation to expressions of power. While the point was not made, the inference was that 'shared experiences', as a point of entry into understanding South Africa, was somewhat less than sufficient. Castells' responses to these questions were that class projects or projects constructed around interests, were, by themselves, problematic and could not provide the wherewithal for building a national identity. The theoretical frame out of which this response emanated was essentially that of identity as being plural and complex, and of the possibility of constructing youth, gendered, class and other identities. In terms of this, young people could be involved in identity projects. Trade unions fighting in Europe could have as their objective the consolidation of a working-class identity. These identities and the processes of building them did not construct a world where people could 'live together'. This project of people living together, he argued, was possible. He urged caution against the idea of constructing identity as an oppositional project. Interests, he argued, provided the basis for recreating class divisions and fragmentation. Instead of identity being built on opposition, it had to be perceived too as a question of the possibility of people being able to live together. Alexander's response to this was that perhaps the question was not so much that of building a united nation-state coerced into a condition of national unity as that of promoting national consensus.

The second category of question which emerged related to language and culture, and the building of a single state. In response to Castells' assertion of his Catalan identity, his description of nations as entities seeking to express themselves as nations whether they have a state or not, and his essaying of the possibility of a multinational South Africa, a number of comments were made. Njabulo Ndebele, Vice-Chancellor of the University of Cape Town (UCT), commented that he was brought up speaking Zulu, conversed in Tswana and thought and wrote in English. Zimitri Erasmus, a sociologist at UCT, asked where in a multinational state those who were on what she called the 'edges' belonged, those who were both Zulu and Xhosa. Alexander reminded the meeting of the debate around nations and national groups which had taken place in the 1950s. The debate had not been taken very seriously, he argued. As a consequence, and problematically so, South Africa was currently facilitating the establishment of a Commission on the Rights of Cultural Groups. His view was that the Commission was constitutionalising ethnic politics in an ideological climate where culture had become synonymous with race. The real question on the political landscape of South Africa, he felt, was that of attenuating racial identities, not for the purpose of displacing them, but to facilitate the emergence of other identities such as linguistic, religious and regional identities.

The real question on the political landscape of South Africa, [Castells] felt, was that of attenuating racial identities, not for the purpose of displacing them, but to facilitate the emergence of other identities such as linguistic, religious and regional identities.

Much of the difficulty in engaging this discussion came from the ways in which terms were used. It was clear that the term 'nation' carried different meanings in the different contexts in which it was used. For Castells a nation was a nation if people sought to fight for it. This was clearly a notion which the post-apartheid South Africans present at the seminar found uncomfortable. Alexander explained that, unlike in Europe, language and nation were not coterminous in post-colonial Africa, and as was shown above, people such as Ndebele provided a practical example of the conundrums which must be the lot of many urban South Africans. Zegeya also commented that the consolidation of South Africa would arise only in the context of an absence of the fear of differences. For its success, democracy in South Africa did not need overarching identity categories. In listening to the South Africans, Castells accepted the possibility that perhaps a different category of language would have to be used to explain plurality and statehood. However, he repeatedly made the point that the problem could not be solved in words. It was of supreme importance that a notion of the state developed as a state which protected its people and not the nationalities within it.

Ultimately, it became clear that much more critical dialogue was needed. As Castells noted in his summing up, the discussion had not been about the building of a new society but that of constructing a new state. The question which remained was that of addressing the conditions for constructing this new state in its contradictory diversity where conflict and wealth disparities were important characteristics of the society. Urgent action, he felt, was needed around education and the redistribution of wealth. The rich had to begin to share their wealth and more determined means of connecting with global wealth had to be sought. Diversity, productivity and social justice were crucial and essential for countries to grow. If these were present, then identity could assert itself.

Diversity, productivity and social justice were crucial and essential for countries to grow.

Interestingly, the cornerstone of Castells' talk , namely the mechanisms for what he called 'growing up new identities' and creating canvases of common expression in the new European identity, was not pursued in the discussion. In this part of his talk Castells referred to ten mechanisms for growing identity. Of the ten, the first three were directly educational. He referred to the massive Erasmus project in Europe where European students were moving around within the system, the integration of programmes at some levels across countries, and the deliberate teaching and learning of other people's languages. Two major principles undergirded these mechanisms, namely the building of existing identities and the growth of new shared experiences. Why this terrain was not entered has much to do with the extent of the clearing of the ground which still needs to take place in South Africa. South Africans are not at the point where they can say with any degree of confidence that there is substantive agreement amongst themselves about questions of language, culture and race. Even though the state has proceeded to dismantle the iconography of apartheid, its ventures into re-presenting itself have been limited to renaming initiatives, re-signposting and so on, and while these have not been without their significance and have indeed been assimilated into the popular imagination, the content of that which has been renamed and re-signposted remains profoundly problematic. The excision of the old colonial signification embodied in the name 'Orange' in the new Free State, for example, is ingenious, but, ironically, is grist to the new lampooning mill. Current newspaper reports on hearings being conducted by the Commission of Human Rights describe black people walking miles and miles to tell stories of marauding white gangs terrorising rural communities. These stories may, of course, be sensationalised in the news, but they are symptomatic of the yet-to-be-filled content of places like the new Free State province. It is against this backdrop that one understands why the major educational initiatives of the state, such as the controversial Curriculum 2005,[1] cannot address issues such as identity directly. They do not yet have a consensus on which to draw. Until then, the sparring will continue about how to present South Africa to itself.

Notes

[1] Curriculum 2005. Website: http://education.pwv.gov.za/policies_reports

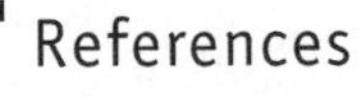

References

Amin, S (1990) *Delinking: Towards a Polycentric World.* London: Zed Books.

Crain Soudien is Professor in the School of Education, University of Cape Town and teaches in the fields of Sociology and History of Education. His research interests include race, culture and identity, school and socialisation, youth, teacher identity, school effectiveness and urban history. He has published over fifty articles and book chapters in the areas of race, culture, educational policy, educational change, public history and popular culture. He is also the co-editor of two books on District Six, Cape Town. Apart from his academic work, he is actively involved in a number of social and educational projects including the Primary Open Learning Pathways Project which is concerned with child literacy, and the District Six Museum, which he and colleagues established in 1989. He was educated at the University of Cape Town and holds a Ph.D. from the State University of New York at Buffalo.

section three

technology and development

3

There is a new economy, exploding throughout the world, unleashing productivity and creating prosperity but in a very uneven pattern.

manuel castells

Information technology and global development[1]

Introduction

The world is experiencing a major technological revolution, centred around information and communication technologies and genetic engineering. At the same time the Internet is the epitome and the most powerful medium of this revolution. Under the impulse of new technologies and flexible forms of organisation and management we are witnessing the formation of a new economy, characterised by rising productivity growth and global competition. During the late 1990s most of the world experienced reasonable rates of economic growth, in spite of the Asian crisis of 1997–1998. The prospects are for a continuation of this economic dynamism in core economies as well as in selected areas of the developing world. The United Nations (UN) Human Development Reports indicate some improvement in living conditions (education enrolment, life expectancy, infant mortality) around most of the world, when data are considered from a historical perspective. Besides, the last decade has witnessed an extension of political democracy, the beginning of globalisation of human rights and the opening up of horizontal communication channels via the Internet. This has led to people having more say today in public affairs than in any prior time in history. Furthermore, there is a major cultural revolution, as feminism has risen in the last three decades, and emancipation of women seems to be an irreversible trend.

Yet, at the same time, people around the world feel threatened by globalisation and by new technologies, and a widespread social backlash against the new techno-economic system is emerging, in different forms, from reactive movements to alternative projects enacted by proactive movements. This is not, as some would think, a matter of misunderstanding or an expression of ideological irrationality. UN Secretary General Kofi Annan's (2000) report to the Millennium Assembly provides a good empirical basis to understand many of these concerns. They arise from a multiplicity of reasons: similar fears have taken place in all rapid social transition periods and there are fears of uncontrolled use of technology (for example, in genetic engineering). These fears are founded and may be illustrated by the fact that, for example, there are also growing environmental concerns about the consequences of our development model, precisely because we know more about these consequences, thanks to advancement in science and technology.

Governments seem to be facing a major crisis of legitimacy. The UN Gallup survey of public opinion cited in the Secretary General's report indicates that two thirds of respondents of a global sample of citizens around the world do not think that their country is governed by the will of the people. Some of this distrust is linked to widespread corruption and lack of accountability. But the main reason is that governments are in fact the main globalisers. Therefore, if globalisation is perceived as a threat, governments are not credible in the eyes of many citizens, because they are responding to global interests rather than serving their local constituencies. Furthermore, people's lack of trust also arises from the perception of the gap in opportunities and from the fact that, rather than living in a world divided between rich and poor (an old feature of human societies), we are entering a new world characterised by a cleavage between those who are 'in' and those who are 'out' of the new system of wealth and power. Let us examine this process and then elaborate on the policy implications of this analysis.

The Internet, the new economy and global development

There is a new economy, expanding throughout the world, unleashing productivity and creating prosperity, but in a very uneven pattern. This economy is characterised by three inter-related features:

- Informational productivity and competitiveness are based on knowledge and information, powered by information technology. This translates essentially into the need for a technological infrastructure, and the critical role of highly educated human resources.
- Networking. The new economy ensures productivity and flexibility on the basis of information-powered networks – networks within firms and among firms, networks between regions, and decentralised networking around nodes. An important example of dynamic nodes in developing countries is Bangalore, India, a major software and electronics region, linked to the major technological centres of the world, particularly to Silicon Valley. The new global architecture is built around flows between dynamic nodes. The negative aspect of this dynamic is that the system allows for the switching on and off of regions and even countries according to their contribution to the value chain structured around these global networks.

The new economy is a global economy. It is an economy that has the capacity to work as a unit in real time on a planetary scale. This capacity is technological, based on telecommunications, fast transportation and information systems. It is institutional, based on deregulation, liberalisation and privatisation. And it is organisational, based on the networking of business firms, and on flexible forms of management and work. The key dimension of globalisation is financial globalisation – financial markets are now globally interdependent and electronically enacted in real time, bypassing government controls, and determining the fate of economies (for instance, in 2000, on average, currency markets exchanged about US$2 trillion per day). But also, the core of production of goods and services is globalised, organised around multinational corporations and their ancillary networks, accounting for about 30 per cent of global gross domestic product (GDP). International trade is also an important dimension of globalisation, but the expansion of trade is mainly a function of the internationalisation of production, as multinational corporations and their networks account for about two thirds of international trade, including about 40 per cent of trade that takes place within a given firm and its networks. Science, technology and highly skilled labour are also organised on a global scale. And migration of unskilled labour is increasing everywhere. The global economy is highly segmented: not everybody is included, but everybody is affected.

The key dimension of globalisation is financial globalisation ...

This new economy has new rules. Firstly, it is powered by the Internet – the equivalent of the electrical engine of the Industrial Age – making possible the operation of the network enterprise, the historical equivalent of the industrial factory. Information technology, including information-based transportation systems, is the basis of connectivity and knowledge-based production. Secondly, there are new rules for labour. Highly skilled labour is critical – flexible, adaptable, self-programmable, able to innovate by working in flexible enterprises. Thirdly, there are new rules for capital: financial markets are the core of the realisation of value. Growth of value of stocks substitutes for profits as the determinant of the new economy, since it is the main criterion to attract investment. Market valuation is led by information – of which profit is one of the elements, but not the only one. In the long term, profits (expressing productivity) have to be there for growth to be economically sustainable. But profits arise as a result of investment in labour and production, and this investment is attracted by stock valuation mechanisms that are driven by information turbulences in financial markets. As Paul Volcker writes: 'Flows of funds and their valuation in free financial markets are influenced as much by perceptions as

by objective reality – or, perhaps more precisely, the perce
the reality' (Volcker 2000: 78). This is not speculation, si
process generates value out of investment – in goods, in services,
increasingly in material production (software, entertainment, consulting, research, and so on) In this sense there is no financial bubble, because we have entered a period of systemic financial volatility. Rather than waiting in vain for the bubble to burst, so that we can return to a state of market equilibrium, we must learn to live in sparkling water. Growth of value of stocks is determined by expectations and trust, and their right combination: in emerging markets, there are high expectations but low trust, so capital is always ready to flow in and out – as is the case, in advanced economies, in day trading and dotcom companies. In this new, brave financial world, stocks have become currency, as companies use their stocks to acquire other stocks, and to pay their most valuable employees and consultants with their stock options. The immaterial economy has become the real economy. The performance of firms in this information-based, information-driven and information-valued economy determines the fate of people and countries.

Consequences for development

The networking logic of the new global system makes it possible to integrate everything into the network that is valuable, while switching off from the network everything that is devalued, according to the dominant criteria in the global networks of capital, information and power. As a result, the world is no longer divided between North and South but between areas and people who are switched into and off these networks. This trend raises the key issue of how to diffuse dynamism from the Southern nodes of global networks into the South at large.

Global connectivity and information technology infrastructure are necessary, albeit not sufficient, conditions for development. However, in an underdeveloped, impoverished country, why invest in expensive infrastructure if there is no use for it? This becomes a vicious circle, perpetuating underdevelopment.

Human resources are the essential infrastructure, without which technology means nothing. The new economy is a people-based economy. This means education, but not in the sense of the warehousing of children. The key issues are the training of teachers, and the reform of the school system into a new pedagogy adapted to the Information Age. The university system plays a pivotal role in the new development strategy, both in training and in research. Furthermore, beyond the school system, there is a growing need for a multi-faceted process of social learning over the lifetime.

Global financial markets ensure access to capital sources from everywhere, but also leave countries vulnerable to sudden reversals of financial flows. Trust has to be built along with expectations.

Trade alone will not work as a development tool. It is trade as expression of an international production system, so the critical matter for a country or region is its integration in this international production system. Development means, in fact, the ability to enhance the value produced in each node, increasing competitiveness on the basis of higher productivity. For instance, the percentage of international trade over GDP in sub-Saharan Africa is lower than in Organisation for Economic Co-operation and Development countries. But what Africa exports is increasingly devalued *vis-á-vis* the value of advanced services and high technology goods. The upward spiral of competitiveness works through higher productivity. The downward spiral works by cutting costs, particularly labour and environmental costs. There is a virtuous circle of expanding demand and productivity for everybody, through informational development. And there is a vicious circle of striving to be cheaper than other competitors, so most countries end up being poorer, while only the dominant economies benefit from this pattern of international competition.

The upward spiral of competitiveness works through higher productivity. The downward spiral works by cutting costs, particularly labour and environmental costs.

Productivity in the new economy requires a strong technological basis, of which the Internet is the most direct expression. So, countries do not need to produce an Internet or develop an Internet industry. But all countries, to be productive and competitive, need to produce, sell and manage with the Internet. Information technology is the electricity of the Information Age, and the Internet is the equivalent of the electrical engine, at the root of organisational forms: the factory in the industrial era, the network in the Information Age.

The social consequences of uneven informational development

The UN Human Development Reports and other UN documents in the last five years have provided evidence of increasing inequality in the midst of this extraordinary process of technological innovation and economic dynamism. Poverty is persistent in many countries and for many people: close to 50 per cent of people in the world survive on less than US$2 per day; in the United States, 20 per cent of children live in poverty; in the European Union, pockets of social exclusion persist, while there has been a substantial increase in inequality, and in child poverty in the 1980s and 1990s. In the United States, real wages declined until 1996; in the European Union, there was still double-digit unemployment on average until recently. So, at first sight, it seems as if the 'trickle-down' theory is not working. Overall, in the 1990s, even counting the tens of millions that have benefited from globalisation in China, India and Latin America, a conservative estimate would put about two thirds of people in the world who have either not improved their condition or have seen their condition deteriorate, particularly in Africa.

Correlation does not necessarily imply causality, but I contend that there is a systemic relationship between the new, knowledge-based, global network economy, and the intensification of inequality, poverty and social exclusion throughout the world. The trend is not related to technology or to globalisation *per se*, but to the institutional conditions under which globalisation proceeds and the information technology revolution expands. In summary, the mechanisms connecting the network economy to increasing inequality and social exclusion seem to be the following.

Firstly, networking and flexibility make it possible to connect the valuable and discard the devalued – for people, firms and territories.

Secondly, extreme underdevelopment of technological infrastructure in most of the world is a major obstacle for development. Diffusion of the Internet in 2000 is still at around three per cent of the world's population versus over 40 per cent in the United States and Scandinavia, and 25 per cent in the European Union. When connections are made in developing countries, they concern very restricted linkages via satellite, extending the global networks but with great differences in teledensity between metropolitan centres and the rest of the country. Internet content providers and the Internet industry are highly concentrated spatially (Zook 2001). Yet, Internet usage will grow exponentially (nine million users in 1995, 300 million now, 700 million by the end of 2001, over two billion in 2007). But this trend of the Internet induces a new round of social inequality:

- Firstcomers shape the uses and the structure of Internet (as is also happening in biotechnology).
- Educational ability and cultural capital are unequally distributed and this inequality is amplified by the Internet.
- Education, technological literacy and research and development are unevenly distributed in the world. As they become key development resources, countries lacking these resources become locked in their backward conditions.

- Financial volatility, induced by global financial integration, leads to recurrent crises with devastating effects in the more vulnerable areas.
- Governments are often bypassed by flows of capital and technology, and increasingly restrained in their policies by international financial institutions and private lenders – thus suffering a double crisis of functionality and of legitimacy.
- In the wake of crisis and poverty, the global criminal economy develops, further delegitimising governments, and creating a parallel economy that benefits from globalisation.
- As economies and societies come under stress, corruption, ethnic strifes, banditism and civil wars disintegrate states and societies.
- Massive movements of population follow, accelerating urbanisation without conditions to integrate people in cities. Millions of urban dwellers live on the edge of ecological catastrophe. Non-sustainable processes of migration and urbanisation contribute to the rise of epidemics of different sorts.
- Children are the most vulnerable members of our societies, and they are abused more than ever, because of the dynamism and global reach of the exploitative economy, the sex economy and the criminal economy – and if children are wasted, we are implanting in the minds of our future people the seeds of despair and destruction.

Thus, while we have unleashed extraordinary creativity and technological innovation, the contradictions of the development process are sharper than ever. Yet, there is no fatality in history. Human action, if we react in time and with sufficient knowledge and determination, can reverse current destructive trends – by redefining the *problematique* of development.

A new model of development: info-development

'Trickle-down' theory does not work. Even in the unlikely event that it would, over time, the time lag for diffusion of the effects of economic growth throughout the planet would be too long. Before the sharing of wealth would take place, it is likely that we would witness social and political reactions that would block development.

A world of networked 'Silicon Valleys', isolated from the rest, is not viable morally, politically, ecologically or even economically.

It is not viable economically because of the contradictions introduced in the new economy by two gaps. The first gap is that between the rate of growth of productivity and the rate of growth of demand, leading to a structural overproduction crisis, particularly in the high technology sector. The second gap is that between the rate of growth of high technology industries and advanced business services, and the rate of growth of the pool of talent needed to foster productivity. Here lies the explanation for the paradox of hundreds of thousands of high-paying jobs not being filled for lack of skilled workers, in the midst of a world struck by unemployment.

The information technology revolution changes everything. Under the current parameters of international division of labour, poor countries and regions are threatened with structural irrelevance associated with their technological obsolescence. On the other hand, if properly used, the information technology revolution could spur a model of informational development that would allow developing countries to leap-frog beyond the industrial stage in their process of development. This leap-frogging strategy is difficult, complex, and still unclear in its actual contours. But it offers the best prospect to overcome structural, global inequality. Indeed, there are already numerous projects and programmes around the world implementing development along these lines. We must build on these accomplishments, but for development to be cumulative and synergistic we need to redefine development in a global perspective, and implement a co-ordinated, global strategy. Let me review the main elements of this new approach to development.

... if properly used, the information technology revolution could spur a model of informational development that would allow developing countries to leap-frog beyond the industrial stage in their process of development.

Knowledge and information are the keys to productivity; connectivity is the key to global competitiveness. Knowledge and information can be applied to all activities, both in production and in the delivery of goods and services. Development today is, above all, development of the capacity to process knowledge-based information efficiently and apply it to production and to the enhancement of the quality of life. Under the informational paradigm, two key factors of production are necessary: information processing and communication infrastructure, and human resources able to use it. The Internet is the most direct and fundamental expression of both infrastructure and human resources. The new economy is therefore, in its essence, a mind-based economy.

The building of an Internet infrastructure requires the revamping and extension of the telecommunications system, counting on new technologies based on cellular telephony and satellite communication – the mobile Internet is the new, universal medium. Internet access community centres can be built in neighbourhoods and small towns around the world – and they are being built in some instances. Yes, people need an electrical grid together with the Internet, but in a developmental sense rather than in this 'obvious' statement of starting with the basics first (such as electricity) that in fact belies our current technical capabilities. If I may give an anecdotal example, my friend Cliff Barney is a Berkeley Net-journalist who lives, together with his wife, an artist and anthropologist, in a Mexican fishing village without electricity. And yet, he regularly publishes his *Rewired* Net-magazine, writing from his village and posting it on the Net. He uses satellite transmission, and he powers his computer with a small generator that he shares with the only cantina in the village, so that both beer and Net writing are definitely cool. In a more technological sense, in early 2000, Transmeta, an innovative Silicon Valley company, unveiled a new chip with standard processing capacity but using considerably less energy than current chips. The projections are for solar-charged computing devices, using low-energy-consuming chips, able to hook up via satellite into the network where memory and processing power are stored.

Under these conditions, the 'common sense' statement about electricity preceding the Internet is more questionable than it looks. Yet, the important point stands on the relationship between Internet-based development, and the broader range of developmental needs. The key issue is that the provision of public services and facilities such as water, electricity, sewage, transportation, health services and the like are the concomitant factors of development, not its prerequisites. The key issue is how to generate economic resources that would allow a country to provide these facilities to its people, not only by building the infrastructure, but being economically and technologically able to maintain, repair and upgrade it. So, the issue is not that people should choose between eating or using the Internet. The policy proposition is that only an Internet-based economy can generate enough value in the new, global economy to enable countries to develop fast enough to provide for themselves without having to resort to international charity on a permanent basis.

The key to using the Internet for developmental purposes is people's capacity to find the appropriate information, to analyse it, and focus it on whatever task they want or need. Which ultimately means, education for everybody. The expansion of education in quantity and quality is thus the real precondition for informational development. But how would it be possible to engage in this major educational extension with limited teaching capacity in

The most important element in improving the quality of primary education is to train the teachers.

many countries? The most important element in improving the quality of primary education is to train the teachers. Based on the innovative Brazilian experience under the Cardoso administration, distance learning, based on television and the Internet in tens of thousands of schools around the country, can help considerably. Distance learning has to be coupled with face-to-face teaching, conducted by better-trained teachers. This requires better pay and working conditions for the teachers. But the process of reforming and improving the education system from the bottom up is too slow for urgent developmental needs, in a world whose dynamic segment is speeding away from the rest of the planet. Thus, leap-frogging is necessary. And distance learning for teachers is a key element of this leap-frogging. To be sure, a new pedagogy has to be developed together with the technology. Individualised tutoring on-line is essential, and tutoring requires qualified tutors. However, the possibility exists of different layers of tutors, where the most qualified are at the top, tutoring tutors, who tutor other tutors, who ultimately tutor the teachers, who teach the students. If the whole process is made interactive, with constant feedback and rectification of the pedagogy, it could be a powerful tool of educational development. This could be possible only now because of the possibilities offered by the Internet. Furthermore, universities must develop at the same pace – including first-class universities as engines of development. In those areas of the world where research resources are scarce, regional international universities could be created, combining resources, linking them up to sponsoring universities in the main research centres around the world, with joint programmes and on-line training and research co-operation.

Adult education and on-line vocational training are critical to incorporate the whole population into the new techno-cultural system, to avoid deepening the current age divide. There is an absolute need to upgrade technological literacy in the short term. Short-cut strategies include community technology training centres; information technology extension programmes, both public and private; co-ordinating and combining existing resources; and fostering on-line development programmes.

Public services can be dramatically improved in the short term through distant delivery, particularly health services, and information on public services.

The main elements of this strategy are widely known, and many countries are convinced of the need to engage in this new model of info-development. The problem is that this strategy requires a huge, expensive transportation and telecommunications infrastructure. It also requires massive investment in human resources, in upgrading and rationalising services. The private sector is taking up some of this investment, particularly in telecommunications. But for obvious business imperatives the privately built infrastructure tends to serve advanced business centres and wealthy social groups. Ultimately business-led, informational development links up a few valuable nodes in developing countries to the developed world, but does not incorporate the majority of the population, and does not dynamise economic and human resources at large. Thus, there is a need for non-profit oriented investment in informational infrastructure. If this investment would take place, not only would it provide the basis for future development but it would have an immediate impact in stimulating the economy, in job creation, in training, in learning by doing. This is the public works programme of the Information Age. And there is a long tradition in economic policy of using public works both as an economic stimulus and as an improvement of the general conditions of production. The catch here, of course, is where the money would come from. I will examine this essential matter at the end of this piece.

... there is a long tradition in economic policy of using public works both as an economic stimulus and as an improvement of the general conditions of production.

However, I must first consider an additional obstacle to an informational development strategy. Who manages development? How useful is it to provide resources to a wasteful, inefficient and sometimes corrupt administration? How to act upon an economy and a society with a weak institutional basis, with no civil society, in the midst of violence, war, banditism and corruption? In the first place, a close-up look shows that the situation is not so bad in many countries. Societies and institutions have reacted to the devastation of the 1980s and early 1990s. Mozambique was destroyed by civil war, then suddenly surged and was making substantial progress until natural disasters set it back – all recoveries will be fragile for a long time, affected sometimes by natural disasters, sometimes wars, sometimes financial crises. This is why a sustained aid policy from the international community has to be there for the harsh moments – taking care not to make the crises worse by misled interventions. Yet, even acknowledging the difficulty of rebuilding societies and economies without solid political institutions, how to break through the vicious circle: poverty leads to clientelism and corruption, which perpetuate poverty. The answer is: in a positive feedback loop strategy. Starting from the current state of institutional disorganisation, the effort to reorganise, consolidate and rationalise the institutional framework has to be given a goal, a development plan, a perspective. This is not government planning: it should be multifaceted, with non-governmental organisations, business, government, international institutions building ad hoc networks for specific projects. The meaning of all these projects, however, cannot be simply remedial, but developmental, built on a new development strategy appropriate to the Information Age. In designing this strategy, attention has to be paid to the extraordinary diversity of situations in the so-called developing world. Brazil is not the same as Sierra Leone. The south of Brazil is not the same as the north of Brazil. South Africa is not the same as the rest of Africa. Botswana is not the same as Namibia. So, in some cases a comprehensive, multilateral aid programme throughout the country is needed. In most cases, specific projects for specific regions, or aimed at specific dimensions of the developmental infrastructure (education, technological literacy, health services) are more suitable. The key, however, is the coordination of various projects, and the process of learning from other experiences.

What could be the potential outcome of an informational development strategy? The building of one, two, many Bangalores linked to their hinterland, being intermediaries of shared info-development, rather than subordinated appendages of the First World. The most important outcome would be the diffusion of knowledge and technological capacity throughout economy and society, so that people in all societies decide what to do with them, using their entrepreneurial skills to create new markets and compete in these markets. Or else, to use their informational capacity to build alternative social models based on different sets of values. Informational capacity is not limited by any means to high technology industries and services. It could be used in sustainable agricultural development. An info-development model is based, in developing countries as everywhere, on on-line work, on-line service delivery, on-line learning, all linked to local economies and local communities. Nodes and networks which grow and incorporate people. Poverty will still be there for a long time, but there will be hope from the poor segments of the population to link up to the dynamic segments of the country and of the world. The historical horizon could then be an open, global economy, based on the enforcement of social rights, human rights and environmental rights, in a gradual homogenisation of the world's chances. With development, income growth, growth of markets and increasing expansion of the development process in formerly poor areas would provide markets and talent for the informational economy, without confining this economy to the current restrictive networks of capital and information.

An info-development model is based, in developing countries as everywhere, on on-line work, on-line service delivery, on-line learning, all linked to local economies and local communities.

However, the main problem to tackle in the implementation of global info-development is how to inject resources in the first place in areas with no hope of yielding returns in the short term. There is a need for a Big Bang, a massive, sudden investment in technology and human resources, on a scale large enough, and in various areas of the world, to prime pump the process of informational development. These resources can only come from where they are, from the rich countries, from the largest corporations, from the centres of innovation and learning, and from the international organisations funded and supported by the wealthiest countries in the world. The new *problematique* of development requires a new strategy of international aid that would be not remedial but developmental, not bilateral but multilateral, not governmental but multi-faceted on both sides; donors and recipients, governments at all levels, non-governmental organisations and business, should be involved in a joint effort. Let us examine this new landscape of international aid.

For a 'Technological Marshall Plan' in the Information Age

What follows is the expression of some very general, strategic ideas, without pretending to propose any institutional design. Any strategy for development should be participatory and shared between international institutions and governments; between governments and non-governmental organisations; between public and private sectors; between global actors and local civil societies.

The current vicious circle between the lack of conditions for informational development in many countries and regions in the world, and the dynamics of networks, including all sources of value while excluding those who have no economic or technological value, must be broken by deliberate action. Only a massive, sudden, co-ordinated injection of resources and know-how can reverse the current dynamics, which is fragmenting the planet. To give an image, I label this initiative a 'Technological Marshall Plan' in the framework of new, international Keynesianism. As the Marshall Plan did in Europe, this new plan would help the reconstruction of the world, while helping companies of the donor countries in their long-term business interests. International Keynesianism means to stimulate global demand by public works in creating a new infrastructure – this time in high technology industries. The benefits for developing countries are obvious, on condition that they develop the appropriate human resources infrastructure to adapt technologies to their own needs, and to their own economic structure, and do not just build high-tech islands in an ocean of underdevelopment. For the North, for the United States, for the European Union, for Japan, besides assuming moral responsibility and taming potential sources of geopolitical instability, there is a fundamental economic and technological interest. On the one hand, demand (particularly for high technology markets) will be expanded in various ways: (a) the immediate impact of subsidised infrastructure building; (b) the future expansion of dynamic high-tech based economies; (c) the development of new uses of advanced technology to satisfy needs that are not marketable at this point, for instance in health care on-line expert systems or distance learning education.

On the other hand, the most important bottleneck for high technology development is the lack of a large enough pool of talent. Without Indian or Chinese engineers, Silicon Valley could not operate. In Europe, leading technology companies are desperate on the matter. The development of a new technological system is so fast that it requires the mobilisation of human resources all over the planet. The argument about educating people in each country rather than resorting to disruptive migration patterns may be correct in the long run, but it takes time, and not everybody wants to work in technology. Besides, broadening the potential labour market (including on-line) increases flexibility and adaptability of labour. Is this global mobility of talent impoverishing poor countries, inducing a massive brain drain? Well, not exactly. It is first about putting minds to use, minds that otherwise would be wasted, and it is about giving these educated people the opportunity to do something with their education, where they can be useful and productive: if engineers leave India it is because they can do better somewhere else. But the most important point to be made is that the traditional 'brain drain' debate is obsolete. Today's reality is one of networks of highly skilled workers and entrepreneurs, moving back and forth between different nodes of production and innovation. Many people who come to Silicon Valley from Bangalore go back to Bangalore, and to India, set up companies, and live between California and India. The same process is happening between the United States and Taiwan, Singapore, Israel, Mexico, China and lately, Russia. The key here is to expand the networks and increase the size and quality of the nodes throughout the developing world, bringing in more talent from the whole planet to these networks, so that ultimately innovation works back and forth regardless of country boundaries. Utopian? Well, it really depends on immigration policy, and on

The development of a new technological system is so fast that it requires the mobilisation of human resources all over the planet.

company policy. Transnationalism from below is the reality for millions of immigrants that bridge economies and societies between countries – for the benefit of their families, of their companies, and of their countries.

Conclusion

This new development policy based on technological innovation and diffusion seems to be the appropriate tool for development in the Information Age. All this sounds like techno-fantasy, when the pressing problems are hunger, sanitation, epidemics, basic stuff. In fact, it is through technology-led development that we can leapfrog stages of the development process to provide efficiently for human needs, because only productivity, competitiveness, educated labour and efficient management can overcome, in a stable pattern of economic growth, the obstacles that exist today for countries to engage in a sustainable development process.

In this context, it is comforting to see – for the first time in a significant and coherent way – the new strategy for development proposed by Secretary General Kofi Annan in his recent report to the Millennium General Assembly. A Global Compact agreement, with the support of governments, corporations, non-profit foundations, non-governmental organisations, specific programmes based on the development of Internet and new technologies, transferring human resources via a Netcorps of volunteers. All these are critical initiatives that may signal a transformation of development strategies. I hope this will be seriously considered by the General Assembly, and that there will be action upon it. I also hope that other international institutions, and particularly the World Bank, can co-operate in the matter.

A global development strategy for information technology and diffusion could be devised, specified by regions, countries and issues, then transformed into projects that would receive funding, technical support and human resources from participating partners in the Global Compact agreement, such as proposed by the Secretary General. I know many corporations are ready to take up the challenge. I know taxpayers in many countries would be ready to foot the bill if they are assured that their money will actually remedy poverty and spur development, rather than financing bureaucracy and corruption. I know there are thousands of dedicated professionals ready to trade their stock options for their life options. And I know, throughout the developing world, of hundreds of projects that are using/diffusing technology in the service of human needs. These projects, often conducted in heroic conditions, have already provided the experimentation on which we can build, so we could already embark on a large-scale programme of technology-led development in many areas of the world. Many problems remain to be solved, particularly in terms of ensuring political accountability and superseding bureaucracy. Yet, if there is political will, resources and ideas are there.

This may sound utterly unrealistic. In my view, the most unrealistic view is that we can proceed with our current pattern of development, destroying our environment, and excluding the majority of humankind from the benefits of the most extraordinary technological revolution in history, without suffering a devastating backlash from society and from nature.

Problems

Notes

1 Keynote address at the Economic and Social Council of the United Nations, New York, delivered by Manuel Castells on 12 May 2000.

References

Annan, K (2000) *We the Peoples: The Role of the United Nations in the Twenty-First Century*. New York: United Nations.

Volcker, P (2000) 'The sea of global finance', in W Hutton and A Giddens (eds) *On the Edge: Living in Global Capitalism*. London: Jonathan Cape.

Zook, M (2001) 'The geography of the Internet industry.' Berkeley: University of California, Department of City & Regional Planning, Ph.D. dissertation (unpublished).

alison gillwald

Building Castells in the ether[1]

Introduction

Mastery of technology, especially strategic technology, reflects the ability of social institutions such as the state to propel a society into the new economy, into an era characterised by Manuel Castells as informational capitalism. This tenet of Castells' three volumes on the Information Age counters the widely held view that Castells' profound work on globalisation reveals the end of the state as a significant political institution in the new economy and society. For Castells the state remains a central player, though the nature of the state and its functions change in the informational era. To be effective it must function as an enabler of national technological development and innovation, for example – elements critical to survival in the networked society of this era.

This paper will also contest the use of Castells' theories in some circles to justify what Richard Heeks (1999) in another context has referred to as technological fetishism – the belief that the provision of technology in itself can solve social and economic problems from poverty to global competitiveness. The paper will examine these issues to review how South Africa is responding to what has been described as the two most dominant social trends in the world today: unprecedented urbanisation and a growing reliance on telecommunications-based relations (Graham 1999).

In doing so it will address Castells' assessment of what he describes as the Fourth World. In this context it will weigh his contention that, because of the endemic nature of the predatory state in Africa, South Africa should not try to lead the 'flying goose formation' in order to catalyse strategic growth within the region, but rather go it alone.

The state

Information and communication technology (ICT)[2] policy debates in South Africa have fallen prey particularly to the first two misconceptions about the nature of the state and the role of technology in development mentioned above. Neither of these can be drawn accurately from Castells' work. It is true that with globalisation we have witnessed the dispersing of traditional state powers: both upward into bodies of global governance such as the World Trade Organisation and the International Monetary Fund, and downward into local structures such as city governments.[3] This reconfigures the nature and role of the state from the nation-state in the industrial era to what Castells calls the networked state in the informational era. However, as Brenner contends: 'Rather than simply eroding the territorial governance of modern nation-state ... the processes of globalisation seems to be supporting the rescaling of institutional regulatory and territorial governance' (Graham 1999: 930).

The significance of the state in developing technological capacity, through what Castells describes as the 'developmental state',[4] is a constant refrain in his work. Throughout history, but particularly in the informational era, Castells sketches the state's developmental role (1996: 182). From Silicon Valley in the 1970s to Japan's Tokyo–Yokohama and more recently the Asian Tigers in the 1980s and 1990s, he emphasises the role of the state in creating the conditions for innovation and entrepreneurialism.

The nature of such state intervention is highlighted in Castells' consideration of the state's potential to accelerate, but also to retard the process of technological modernisation. The significance of this is that, from his account, it is able to change the fate of economies and societies within a few years (Castells 1996: 7).

Castells' analysis of the strategic guidance provided by the state in Japan to its ICT sector distinguishes it from the inability of the statist Soviet state to incorporate 'informationalism' – the technological ability to process symbols as a direct productive force (Castells 1998: 98). This phenomenon has been fundamental to the restructuring of the global economy, precisely through state intervention and control. He contrasts these two examples from the Chinese state whose integration into the global economy Castells ascribes to the transition from statism to state-led capitalism.

Castells' detailed accounts of why interventions by the state have had such profoundly different results in various countries provide insights into recent policies and trends within the ICT sector. They can also provide an understanding of why South Africa appears to be struggling to transform itself into an informational society, despite considerable political will to do so.

The parallels between the Soviet state as described by Castells and the apartheid state, with its inward focus and isolation, are stark. This was at a time when developmental states in other parts of the world were enabling the design of new products for diverse markets or the cloning of innovations from other parts of the world. This resulted in South Africa entering the last decade of the last millennium with an isolated ICT market, not catalysed by innovation from other markets or local research and development. Where the state intervened it was in the form of large state research institutions disengaged from entrepreneurial endeavour.

Has the African National Congress (ANC) overcome this legacy by transforming the state into what Castells calls the developmental state? It has certainly sought to. Central to President Thabo Mbeki's call for an African Renaissance since 1997 has been the acknowledgement that the nervous system of the new economy and society are modern information and communication networks.

The South African information and communication technologies sector

As Castells describes in his trilogy, technological and economic drivers towards convergence and liberalisation are indeed transforming the contemporary South African communications landscape, as they have around most of the world. The R58 billion ICT industry[5] contributes increasingly to gross domestic product (GDP) which in 1998 was R730 billion. The R6 billion broadcasting industry represents just over half a per cent of GDP. While relatively sluggish considering the number of new entrants in this market, growth of over 15 per cent (Independent Broadcasting Authority 1999) is projected for the next few years. This is way above national growth figures which over the next couple of years are anticipated to be below three per cent.

The last five years have seen massive changes to a sector once characterised by inefficient monopoly provision in the case of telecommunications and by an expensive state propaganda organ in the broadcasting sector. Despite efforts at isolation and self-sufficiency by the apartheid regime, global developments began irrevocably impacting on the information and communication sector in South Africa as in other parts of the world. These processes saw economies throughout the world become interdependent, introducing what Castells describes as 'new forms of relationship between economy, state and society in a system of variable geometry' (Castells 1996: 1).

In the late 1980s the apartheid government, acknowledging the significance of telecommunications development to economic growth and in line with global imperatives, corporatised the telecommunications public utility, Telkom. It was only after 1994 that the state, under the control of the ANC government, intervened to partially deregulate the market – this, despite earlier efforts in the dying days of the apartheid regime to privatise Telkom, as part of a broader strategy to reduce the new state's assets.

It was in fact broadcasting that provided the best example of state intervention under the apartheid regime that enabled the introduction of innovative modern subscription television technology. Like other successful interventions of this kind elsewhere in the world, it was the product of co-operation or collusion between a political and economic elite. The state monopoly was broken in the politically strained 1980s with the granting of a subscription broadcasting licence to the Afrikaans and English newspaper groups as part of a pact with the Nationalist government. The service could be narrowly provisioned to provide relief to the voting public from the realities of guerrilla warfare and other disturbing evidence of social and political dysfunction prevalent at the time, and simultaneously deal with a range of political favours. It provided – together with a web of media, education and cultural threads – the appearances of normality and even technological and economic progress to the populace, who had lived so long under a series of states of emergency that they had become the norm. It provided the state's hegemonic partners, in the form of the newspaper cartels, with a valuable source of revenue, which they claimed had declined for the print sector since the introduction of television in 1976. These constructions of normality were fractured by the burgeoning of (usually short-lived) resistance media – community free-sheets and illegal radio stations.

These were the various responses to local and global economic and technological developments that the ANC found when it came to power in 1994. They were channelled during its first term in office into what have become characterised as 'Washington consensus'-type policies and practices of privatisation, liberalisation and independent regulation. It was only then that South Africa's communication sector more formally entered the terrain of global economic competition, offering a geographically and culturally distinct site for capital accumulation.[6]

The establishment of an independent regulator for broadcasting, the Independent Broadcasting Authority, in 1994 was a result of the negotiated settlement with the focus at the time being on ensuring free and fair elections in South Africa's new democracy. However, the policies to expand services soon reflected the desire for South Africa to become a site of direct foreign and local investment in broadcasting.[7]

The monopoly of the free-to-air television market ended in 1998 with the introduction of a free-to-air competitor to the public broadcaster. E-TV is jointly owned by a local empowerment consortium dominated by trade union investment arm Hoskens and Time Warner, who have the foreign holding of 20 per cent. E-TV commands around eight per cent of audience share (South African Advertising Research Foundation 2000). The South African Broadcasting Corporation (SABC) still dominates the market with three channels and around twelve million viewers a day. The SABC also run 19 radio stations, of which two are national commercial stations. The other stations service the eleven official language groups and a number of cultural and regional interests.

The astronomical growth of the terrestrial subscription service, M-Net, over the last decade has tapered off with the launch of South Africa's technologically cutting edge direct-to-home satellite broadcasting service, DSTV, and the migration of its subscribers to satellite.[8] This highly profitable elite satellite service was in fact able to get off the ground by exploiting the early entry provided to them by the apartheid government with the issues of a terrestrial subscription service. It provided them with the financial and technological leverage to make the most of a loophole in the broadcasting legislation to create a direct-to-home satellite broadcasting business that extends across Africa, the Middle East and into Europe using cutting edge technology. While this is currently one-way digital service, it has the potential to become the dominant interactive gateway to the home – despite government policies that, had they been more effectively drafted in law and regulation, would have prevented their launch at that time.

An extensive terrestrial signal distribution network has been developed by the common carrier, Sentech, over the years and considerable satellite capacity is available.[9] Its only major competitor is the private signal distribution company, Orbicom, which is dominantly placed in the area of satellite provision with its main function being the provision of satellite facilities to an affiliated company which is the sole provider to direct-to-home satellite broadcaster, DSTV.

Developments within the telecommunications sector moved more systematically through a consultative Green and White Paper policy process before passing into law. Seeking not to be excluded from the logic of the globalising capitalist system the new state delivered a final position in line with International Telecommunications Union and Bretton Woods institutional requirements for privatisation of telecommunications companies, liberalisation of the market and the establishment of an autonomous regulator.[10] The Act established a three-tier separation of policy, regulation and operations between government, the regulator and operators respectively.

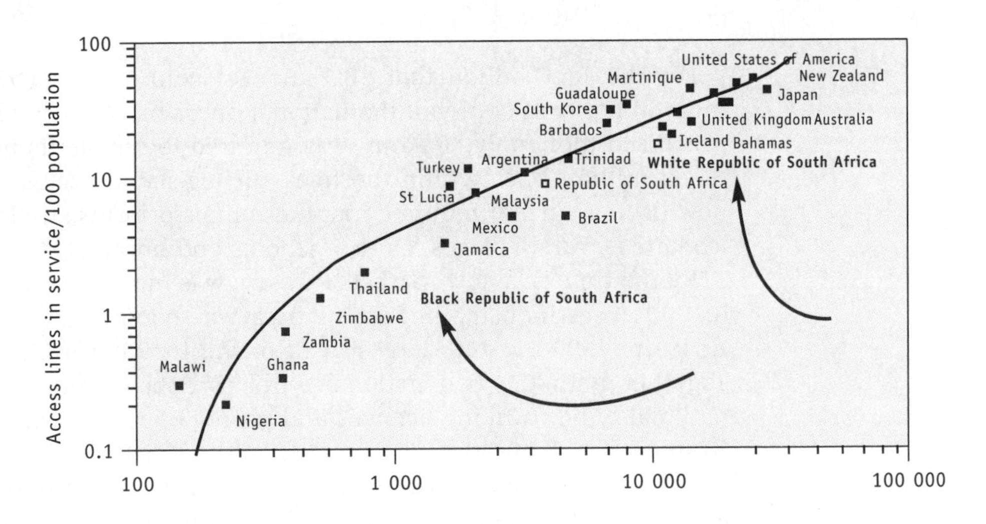

FIGURE 1: The phone gap – access lines in service per 100 population

Source: The South African Telecommunications Regulatory Authority (Satra) 1998

The policy did seek to redress the uneven development within the sector by focusing on the low teledensity (number of phones per households) and the racial disparity it reflected. The indebtedness of the telecommunications company, the poor state of the network, which was substantially analogue, and a management unprepared for impending competition were also major considerations.[11] In the mid-1990s the new government found itself with a rural infrastructure no better than in the rest of Africa where teledensity among the rural black population was one per cent, while over 50 per cent of white households enjoyed service. The overall teledensity for the country was nine per cent (International Telecommunications Union 1996). The model adopted was to acquire the necessary injection of capital, and technical and management expertise through the partial privatisation of Telkom. In order to encourage the kind of foreign investment necessary and to maximise the sale price for the national fiscus, the monopoly in voice services, local, national and international was extended for five years, with an option of a sixth if all roll-out targets were met.

This excluded the two mobile cellular operators who in the dying days of the old regime had been granted duopoly licences. The policy also anticipated the partial liberalisation of the sector in data services, value-added networks (VANs) and private telecom networks (PTNs), and ultimately resale sometime prior to the introduction of a fixed line competition (South African White Paper on Telecommunications 1996).

For the R5,6 billion that SBC and Telecom Malaysia paid for their 30 per cent equity of the national operator, the new partially privatised monopoly, Telkom, was required to double its network to six million lines within the five-year legislated exclusivity. Its new licence further required that these lines prioritise under-serviced areas, rural villages, clinics, schools and libraries.[12]

By the time this new market structure was introduced the fledgling Internet industry in South Africa was booming, with South Africa in 1996 the 14th largest user of the Internet in the world. Together with the two national wireless data communications, national radio trunking licences and paging operators which were 'grandfathered' into the new legislation, the VANS and PTN operators, Internet access and service providers are statutorily required to acquire their telecommunication facilities from the monopoly provider. This has provided the most fodder for regulatory disputes. Within months of the regulator coming into being the Internet Service Providers' Association had lodged an unfair competition complaint against Telkom, which had belatedly but aggressively entered into the Internet market.

With the granting of exclusivity in 1997 Telkom sought to eliminate any haemorrhaging of revenues. It began with the new callback operators and then moved onto the nascent but burgeoning Internet Access Providers (IAPs). By this stage these were not only corporate clients. With Telkom's launch of an Internet Access Provider (SAIX) and Internet Service Provider (ISP), Intekom, they had become competitors. Telkom now argued that the provision of Internet access was in its exclusive domain. Within months of coming into office the new regulator declared callback operators illegal in terms of the law but ruled against Telkom in favour of Internet access provisioning being in the competitive domain of value-added network services. The callback operators took the South African Telecommunications Regulatory Authority decision on review and Telkom took the Internet decision on review. Both matters have been in the courts for over three years, placing the Internet industry, dependent on Telkom for bandwidth, in a weak and vulnerable position. This, together with the high costs of local calls, has been blamed for the slowing down of the growth of the Internet industry over the last few years.

While such developments provide evidence of restraints being placed on innovation and growth of essential aspects of the info-economy, there are nevertheless 120 estimated ISPs, virtual ISPs, Access Providers and content aggregators that allow South Africa to boast a top twenty world ranking when judged by number of Internet nodes. These promising statistics for the usage of

Internet in South Africa highlight the dilemmas of uneven development with current usage and site hosting taking place among the urban elite and primarily white male elite (South African Information Technology Industry Strategy 1999).

These statistics reflect global trends towards uneven development, not just between developed and developing nations, but even between networked global cities and their surrounding hinterland. Castells describes the process inside each country, where the networking architecture reproduces itself into regional and local centres, so that the whole system becomes interconnected at a global level. Territories surrounding these nodes play an increasingly subordinate function, often becoming irrelevant or even dysfunctional (Castells 1996: 380).

Access and affordability

So, has the model of exclusivity in exchange for roll-out been an effective developmental strategy over the last three years? Telkom's target to double the network to six million subscribers, of which 1,7 million lines had to reach under-serviced areas together with high payphone targets, will undoubtedly contribute to achieving universal access. However, there would still be over three million households left unserviced at the end of the exclusivity. William Melody has also shown that while growth in main telephone lines was up to over eight per cent from 1995 to 1998, this was below the 10,4 per cent growth in the rest of Africa over the same period and the 10,8 per cent of the Upper Middle Income countries with which South Africa is classified by United Nations agencies (Melody 2000).[13]

Perhaps more important than this is the issue of affordability. The roll-out reporting to the regulator simply has to indicate how many households have been reached and there is no requirement to monitor and report on how many people stay on the network. The figures on churn – the number of subscribers who leave the network – are difficult to ascertain precisely. It has been conservatively suggested that it is around 20 per cent (Benjamin and Stavrou 2000) for all lines connected but in poor rural areas over 50 per cent, and that in some weeks more people come off the network, largely due to payment failure, than the number of new lines that are connected.

International studies suggest that basic telephony should cost a household no more than 0,7 per cent of its total income (Benton Institute 1997). The most recent figures available for South Africa suggest that the total spent by all households is 2,87 per cent of monthly income – made up of 0,65 per cent of rental and 2,22 per cent on calls (Stavrou and Mkize 1998). This is reflective of the higher communications costs associated with greater discretionary income of the historically white users whom the network was developed to serve. Because of the high infrastructure cost of a sophisticated network design to meet the high-end of business need, it is unlikely that in South Africa we will manage to realise telecommunication expenditure at less than one per cent of total household income. Realistically, telecommunications expenditure as a percentage of household income could be anticipated at between two and three per cent.

Results of studies undertaken by the South African telecom regulator show that after a lead-in time of seven months, households spend an average of between R21 and R30 per month on telecommunications (Stavrou and Mkize 1998). Given the commitment by Telkom to tariff rebalancing and an increase in local cost during the period of exclusivity of as much as 25 per cent on local calls, the study determined that the minimum a household needs to spend on telephony each month would be around R30.

Using two per cent of household income allocated to telephony and an expenditure of R30 per month as a benchmark, then 44 per cent of all households (3,8 million people) would be unable to afford to use the Telkom service. This percentage rises to 69 per cent or just over six million households whose monthly expenditure is set at R70, which would include the cost of the line rental at R50. The study concludes that on currently available data only 3,7 million households (42 per cent) can afford to install and maintain a telephone without assistance.

The 1996 Telecommunications Act allows for subsidies for needy people through the Universal Service Fund. However, with a R20 million ceiling on the fund by ministerial directive the real development potential of providing subsidised universal service is severely limited. This is one motivating factor behind the telecentre strategy that sought to provide at least access to affordable services.

Universal access, as opposed to service, has indeed increased dramatically over the last five years. Access is defined as the number of people who have access to a telephone within a 30 minute walk from their homes. This has risen dramatically to over 80 per cent for all South Africans. This has been partially due to Telkom's public payphone obligations. The greatest contribution to telephony access, however, probably has come from the introduction of prepaid cellular services, which doubled the number of subscribers on the MTN and Vodacom networks in 18 months of their introduction. This occurred despite initial scepticism of the ability of South Africans, with a declining national per capita income of R15 000 per annum (derived from the South African Reserve Bank Annual Report 1998) being able to afford such high upfront costs and tariffs. So successful has the take-up been that the number of wireless subscribers overtook fixed line subscribers in the middle of 2000 (BMI-Techknowledge 2000). In fact far more people have been serviced through a very unequal customer market than through the myriad of initiatives to extend services including the exclusivity model and not highly effective telecentre model.

Universal service and access* figures for South Africa

Percentage of households with service and access (fixed and cellular combined)		All	African	White
All	Universal service	42	18	82
	Universal access	80	74	93
Urban	Universal service	64	32	82
	Universal access	94	93	94
Non-urban	Universal service	9	5	84
	Universal access	59	56	98

* Access measured as 30 minutes' walk from a telephone

Source: Peter Benjamin on basis of South African Census October Household Survey 1999
See CommUnity at http://link.wits.ac.za/projects

Competition

Despite these various interventions by the state the ICT sector has also failed to show the dramatic growth anticipated in the mid-1990s when policy was being formulated. If some of the critical ingredients for development of the sector include political will and pent-up demand for service, why have the policies of the last few years not met expectations both locally and in terms of becoming globally competitive? Castells argues that the form of state intervention that has been successful in the era of informational capitalism links competitiveness, productivity and technology into an explicit strategy. 'The new developmental state supports technological development in their countries' industries and in their productive infrastructure as a way of fostering productivity and helping "its" firms to compete in the world market' (Castells 1996: 89). The integration of the countries into the global economy links the political interests of the state with the fate of economic competition for firms located in the country.

The strategic importance of competitiveness, stresses Castells, relates to the relative position of national economies.

The strategic importance of competitiveness, stresses Castells, relates to the relative position of national economies. This is a major legitimising force for governments in the informational era. In South Africa, the state is not intervening developmentally to protect its firms within the ICT sector in order to make it more competitive internationally. Neither the state nor industry appears to have recognised this critical relationship. Industry continues to bay for freedom from the state and regulation rather than demanding its protection and nurturing during this vulnerable stage of the sector's development. This 'protectionism' is one of the hallmarks of many of the societies that have rapidly modernised their ICT sectors.

The state on the other hand faces a severe conflict of interests in the telecom sector. It is questionable whether the state is able to play a developmental role at this stage of the sector's development when its interests as the dominant shareholder of Telkom coincide with those of the monopoly provider. Currently, it is compelled to protect the national telecommunications company as a state asset on the sound social intention of delivering universal service – but possibly at the expense of a much more significant national asset, namely the ICT industry as a major driver of national economic growth. The protection of a private monopoly with a significant foreign interest such as SBC and Telecom Malaysia have in Telkom, may have a greater negative impact on the development of local business. Under the state monopoly Telkom saw itself as a supplier of services and facilities rather than as an existing or future competitor.

Will the state in South Africa enable or retard technological and the associated economic and social development? Has there been the kind of state intervention that enables innovation, entrepreneurialism and development, which is likely to propel South Africa into the informational era? It is by all Castells' accounts the important alchemy of state intervention together with entrepreneurialism that creates an environment conducive to innovation and this seems to be one of the critical missing elements in South Africa. In the recent survey of universal access in South Africa by Peter Benjamin and Aki Stavrou, one of the major reasons identified for the failures of telecentres has been the lack of entrepreneurialism in their conception and practice (Benjamin and Stavrou 2000).

Technology

A major flaw of the intervention of the new state has been the preoccupation with technology as the end in itself rather than as the tool to reach a certain developmental, social or economic end. This view that technology is the panacea to social and economic problems is reflected in debates in South Africa on the role of ICTs in development. Castells has often been cited as seeking technological solutions to underdeveloped communities' problems. It is true that Castells does place great importance on the use of strategic technology for societies to succeed under the conditions of informational capitalism. However, it is the concept of 'informationalism' described earlier that is central to Castells' thesis:

> Information processing is focused on improving the technology of information processing as a source of productivity, in a virtuous circle of interaction between the knowledge of sources of technology and the application of technology to improve sources of technology and the application of technology to improve knowledge generation and information processing. (Castells 1996: 17)

While originating in the productive process, the technology and its associated relationships spread throughout the whole society, so influencing power relationships. It is not that technology *per se* determines historical evolution and social change, Castells argues, but the technology (or lack of it) that embodies the capacity of society to transform itself as well as the uses to which societies decide to put their technological potential (Castells 1996: 7).

This has often been confused with a kind of technological determinism, which Castells dismisses in his first volume. He argues that while knowledge and information have been central to the process of production in previous eras, it is only in the informational mode of development that the 'action of knowledge upon knowledge itself' is the main source of productivity. In this epoch, information generation, processing and transmission become the fundamental source of productivity and power (Castells 1996: 7).

How have South Africa's information and communication policies developed this fundamental source of productivity, power and transformation over the last five years? Arising from a policy that sought both to provide services to the vast majority of population denied them in the past and create a globally competitive ICT sector, Telkom was partially privatised with the specific intention of technological modernisation, and incremental liberalisation of the telecom sector was introduced. While privatisation and liberalisation may be prerequisites for economic growth under conditions of global capitalism, Castells points out that they are not automatically developmental: 'countries that are left exclusively to the impulses of market forces, in a world where established power relationships of governments and multinational corporations bend and shape market trends, become extremely vulnerable to volatile financial flows and technological dependency' (Castells 1996: 89).

It is therefore ironically the case that, because of the interdependence of markets in the global economy and the deregulation of markets that has been associated with it, the state must take up the cudgels on behalf of its economic constituencies.

> Deregulation and privatisation may be elements of the state's developmental strategy, but their impact on economic growth will depend on the actual content of these measures and on their linkage to strategies of positive intervention, such as technological and educational policies to enhance the country's endowment in informational productive factors. (Castells 1996: 90)

Policies in South Africa have not been integrated in this way. Despite various efforts and public commitment to human resource development, both with regard to producers and users, the growth of human capital has lagged behind the needs of the sector, as have research and development and innovation strategies. In addition, behind many of the policies and implementation strategies in South Africa has been the kind of 'technological fetishism' described earlier. Strategies have focused on getting technology out to areas that have been denied services and development opportunities in the past rather than contextualised information and appropriate methods to process it. Laudable as these intentions are, millions of rands have been spent fruitlessly on getting technology into telecentres, multipurpose community centres and the like, without any attempt to contextualise their usage. The effect of this is that the technology in itself is unable to meet the needs of people and there is little diffusion of the innovation or knowledge, which are critical to sustainable growth and development.

State policies and strategies need to reflect an understanding of the process of technological modernisation. A networked society is not one that just uses information technology but rather a social structure associated with what Castells calls an 'information paradigm' (1996: 60–69). This is associated with the diffusion of knowledge and innovation, not technology *per se*. The stocking of access centres with computers or the provision of Internet addresses without reference to the information or skills needs of the target audience is unlikely to contribute to the development of a successfully networked society. Rather than putting vast amounts of state resources into implementing high-end technological training and development currently being undertaken, as Peter Benjamin (2000) has argued, the focus should be on developing local content and applications. Such products are derived from the local context of a developing country and likely to be pertinent to other developing countries. With two thirds of the world's population falling into this category, there must be an export market for these kinds of content and applications.

As Nicholas Garnham has argued, understanding access in terms of traditional telecom measures, number of lines, is not sufficient.

> In evaluating levels of entitlement [of citizens from the welfare state] we need to take into account both the range of communication options made available – and these must be real options and not mere choices between products and services with minimal real differences – and the ability of people actually to make use of these options, to achieve relevant functionings. (Garnham 1999: 33)

Uneven development

While at the domestic front the South African state has struggled to nurture its fledgling information economy effectively, its significance in making South Africa a global player is acknowledged. At the moment South Africa is experiencing few of the benefits of the global economy and many of the constraints and negative consequences. In its efforts to transform the country into a model global player it has bowed to global pressures to improve market access to foreign companies and other related requirements of the Bretton Woods institutions. Among other things it has given undertakings to the World Trade Organisation that will allow entry into its markets before its own companies have had a chance to develop. It has been bound by the shift to the patents of products only, not processes, from which it could have benefited. It is faced with global changes to the accounting rate regime effectively imposed by the United States Federal Communications Commission, which will impact on it negatively and affect its ability to roll-out affordable services. At the same time it has not enjoyed high levels of foreign direct investment, high exports, employment growth and technological innovation associated with globalisation.

Foreign direct investment flows to Africa amounted to US$5,5 billion in 1996, representing 1,5 per cent of the total global investment flows. The consequence of this process of disinvestment throughout Africa, Castells argues, is that at the precise historical moment when the information technology revolution has transformed the infrastructure of production, management and communications elsewhere, there has been the delinking of African firms and labour from the workings of the new economy characterising most of the world, while linking up African elites to the global networks of wealth, power information and communication.

Brenner warns that a key result of this process of state 'rescaling' evident in the shift towards liberalised, privatised and internationalised telecommunications regimes has been to intensify capital's uneven development (Brenner cited in Graham 1999: 930). This is not only happening as it has conventionally between developed and developing countries, or between North and South. It is occurring between the 'constellation of urban networks that have developed across the globe and the isolated hinterland between these centres' (Graham 1999: 936). Based on the removal of national barriers to telecommunications competition, Stephen Graham argues that profound reorganisation of the global telecommunications industry is taking place. The most resistant nations of the world are giving way to 'the construction of multiple competing and uneven infrastructures centred on large metropolitan markets'.

Graham explores this relationship between the growth of a planetary network of global financial, corporate and media capitals, and the merging global and urban information infrastructures that interlink and underpin such centres. He argues that the increasing importance of large urban regions or 'global cities' to the economic social, political and cultural activities of the world presents a 'reconfiguration of space through telecommunications'.

Graham documents how fully liberalised regulatory environments are becoming key assets in the competitive race between corporate operations and their telecommunications hubs. 'Finance transnational and media firms demand an increasingly complex and seamless package of broadband connections and service within and between the global cities where they operate' (Graham 1999: 929).

Graham refers to a survey[14] conducted in 1998, which ranked the competitiveness of telecom provision in 25 global cities encompassing five per cent of the world's population (Graham 1999: 938). The first five cities ranked were all from the United States and had multiple competing fibre-optic infrastructures. New York led the way with nine competing fibre-optic networks. London was the most competitive city outside the United States, with six separate grids. Other European cities trailed behind due to insufficient network competition, relatively high tariffs and a lack of access to cutting edge services. The reason for global cities in the developing world being at the bottom of the table is attributed to them being located in nation-states that are generally reluctant to privatise or liberalise their telecom regimes.

> The poorer cities in our survey – defined as such in terms of GDP per capita – trail far behind, victims by and large of local reluctance to allow competition. Of these four 'poorer' cities – Mexico City, Johannesburg, Beijing and Kuala Lampur – only Mexico City makes a reasonable showing, mainly because it has been efficiently colonised by foreign-owned telecom operators taking advantage of Mexico's liberal regulatory structure. The others have a long way to go before they join the global elite. (Graham 1999: 939)

The frustrations of this for metropolitan centres in South Africa are already evident. Initiatives are already under way in Johannesburg and Cape Town to create cybercities – independently, on top of or despite the national grid – to deal more effectively with their own communications needs. Currently Johannesburg Metro can only get a two megabit facility from the national monopoly incumbent to operate its metropolitan infrastructure. Successful global information hubs elsewhere in the world are receiving at least ten megabit or even gigabit bandwidth, and among the most successful ones, multiple networks of this capacity exist.

While these competitive networks clearly contribute to the competitiveness of global cities, Graham warns that the advantages should not be overstressed. He argues that while competitive networks are probably necessary, they are not sufficient for global competitiveness. Advantages diminish over time as infrastructure and technology assets diffuse to a broader range of cities and are overtaken by possibly cheaper, more cutting edge options. He draws on the work of Castells, which highlights that the rise of informationalism is entwined with growing inequality and social exclusion throughout the world. Graham warns that for all countries, but for developing countries in particular, these cities are likely to be the main focus of highly uneven development.

In addition, as Elkins contends, the traditional modern notion that nationhood is partly defined by the ability to roll-out universally accessible infrastructural grids to bind the national space is completely destroyed by the new infrastructural logic (Elkins cited in Graham 1999: 948). Instead, the logic of the merging electronic infrastructures is to follow directly the global city networks, through direct global–local interconnection. This inevitably 'punctures and unbundles any notion of national infrastructural sovereignty' (Graham 1999: 948).

'Once relatively homogenising national infrastructures have become splintered into customised global–local grids designed to meet hegemonic interests' (Graham 1999: 948) of transnational corporations, the inclusion of the centres into the global network provides opportunities for global inclusion that largely did not exist before. But while benefits might accrue to the communication elite,

> ... peripheral regional and marginalised social groups often actually lose out and fail to reap the benefits of competition, as they are left with the rump of old Post and Telecommunications infrastructures, relatively high prices and poor levels of reliability and innovations. Highly uneven microgeographies of splintered telecommunications development thus replace the relatively integrated and homogeneous networks developed by national telephone monopolies. (Graham 1999: 936)

South Africa and 'the black holes of informational capitalism'

The question arises then of whether avoidance of such information and communication networks would allow countries to pursue a more even developmental national path? This is very unlikely. The imperatives of globalisation are likely only to result in further exclusion and marginalisation without the resources of development.

Castells considers the value of a disengagement strategy where Africa sets its own terms and attempts to meet it own needs internally. He concludes however that the 'selective articulation of elites and valuable assets, together with the social exclusion of most people and the economic devaluation of most natural resources' mean that the delinking of Africa would take a revolution. He argues further that:

> the vision of a new South African becoming the engine of development for much of the continent through its multilayered incorporation into the global economy (in an African version of the 'flying geese' pattern so much liked by Japanese strategists), seem at closer examination, utterly unrealistic. (Castells 1998: 127)

The reasons for this, Castells argues, are that the economies of South Africa and her neighbours are competitive rather than complementary and that South Africa's re-entry into the global economy will require that it devote all its resources to ensuring that it is not further marginalised. He concedes that regional co-operation programmes may help the development of a transportation and technological infrastructure in the neighbouring countries and that some spill-over from South Africa into southern Africa may alleviate extreme poverty conditions. For him these are unlikely though to transform the region or the continent.

However, it is precisely for these reasons that South Africa can afford to disengage neither from the global economy nor from the rest of Africa and particularly the region. While the exclusionary nature of informational capitalism may mean that it is not sustainable in the long run, especially as long as two thirds of the world's population remains excluded from participating in it, its collapse is not imminent. While the large majority of the world's population is marginalised from it, it impacts nevertheless on all of them directly and indirectly.

South Africa, with urbanisation levels of around 60 per cent, does not have the kind of subsistence economy found elsewhere in Africa that might permit disengagement. More importantly there are unavoidable political, economic and social realities – from Aids to common markets – that compel it to work with the southern African region and the continent more generally to build the infrastructure and ensure the connectivity essential to offering the services needed in modern economies.

... slow but steady gains have been made at the continental and regional level to enable the development of an information society in Africa.

Even since the writing of Castells' *Information Age* trilogy, slow but steady gains have been made at the continental and regional level to enable the development of an information society in Africa. Firstly, the importance of creating the infrastructure so essential to the basic and more advanced services of the information society is now more widely accepted as a given. During the late 1990s, several continental initiatives by international development organisations and local non-governmental organisations have focused national government's attention on the developmental significance of national information and communication infrastructures and the need for affordable services.[15]

Lack of connectivity directly between African countries continues to be a strategic fault line in the integrated development of the continent. Currently US$400 million is lost to the continent each year in the routing of calls to other African countries via European destinations. As Ernest Wilson has pointed out (Wilson 1996: 6) this constitutes around two thirds of total United States aid to the continent annually.

At the same time, there have been some spin-offs of global developments that have increased the possibilities of connectivity and more symmetric engagement for underdeveloped regions of the world. The multiple fibre-optic grids of the global local cities described earlier are of little use, as Graham points out, without the seamless global interconnections for corporate and financial networks to link together the corporate and financial networks for which the infrastructures have been developed. While the focus of this is on linking the geostrategic metropolitan zones of the three dominant global economic blocs, North America, Europe and East and South East Asia, Graham highlights the importance of many previously poorly connected metropolitan regions and nation-states becoming connected en route (Graham 1999: 948).

Arising from this and the potential of untapped markets, a number of proposals to connect African countries have arisen. In response to a study of telecommunications demand in Africa that indicated a growth that is set to double annually over the coming years, Africa One, a United States telecommunications company, committed itself to securing investment of US$1,6 billion to provide broadband fibre-optic cable network that would offer telecommunications connections between African countries. The system will also be connected to Global Crossing's worldwide network linking 25 countries and 200 cities around the world.

To fulfil its own telecommunication ambitions within Africa, in 1998 Telkom led an initiative to roll-out jointly the first 100 per cent undersea telecommunications cable for Africa, which was expected to cost R2,75 billion. The project aimed also to link to the Far East in support of telecommunications needs in Africa and the diversification of traffic routes between South East Asia and Europe with a 20 Gb/s to 40 Gb/s connection.[16]

It has been argued that the lack of infrastructure provides some advantages to countries without large sunken costs in 'old' technologies. New high bandwidth technologies such as fibre-optic cable and satellite can be deployed if the right investment environment is created. Several governments in Africa are beginning to realise that in the appropriate policy and regulatory environment, ICTs and services can generate large revenues – though not from traditional sources, which may in fact decline.

Wireless and mobile communications are also presenting new opportunities for easier and affordable services. Even with costs of mobile telephony as high as they currently are, wireless has overtaken fixed line voice services in Africa (*Business Day*, 2 September 2000). With the introduction of Wireless Applications Protocols (WAP) to provide basic email and Internet services and the even greater potential of next generation mobile cellular telephony to fill a much wider range of communications needs, the possibilities of bringing large numbers of Africans into the information society and new economy are enhanced. Even with the reducing costs of equipment and charges, the services will provide access to the wealthiest portion of the population. But the technology for the first time does have the potential – at a couple of hundred US dollars – to facilitate access to information and communication previously only attainable through a several thousand dollar personal computer or television decoder.

Also at the continental level, the defunct telecommunications arm of the Organisation of African Unity, the Pan-African Telecommunications Union, was allowed to disintegrate and give way to a new, more dynamic structure and leadership in the form of the African Telecommunications Union (ATU).[17] A clearly more modern agency, the vision of the ATU is to make Africa an equal and active participant in the global information society with the mission being to promote the rapid development of info-communications in Africa in order to achieve universal service and access, in addition to full inter-country connectivity.

Although the organisation is once again under-resourced and in its infancy, its leadership by former Kenyan telecom operator, Jan Mutai, holds promise and already a far more appropriate programme of action is under way. He has already worked with the different regions of the continent to co-ordinate their efforts and activities, and has been involved in the establishment of regional regulator bodies.

Almost half of Africa's countries have now introduced telecom regulators. Though their lack of capacity is usually a major restraint this is very similar to the percentage of European countries that have introduced regulators.

In the Southern African Development Community (SADC), progress has already been made with the various communication protocols agreed to by governments that have resulted in the introduction of harmonising 'model' telecommunication legislation, band planning and interconnection regimes for adoption by states within a period of time (Telecommunications Regulators Association of Southern Africa 2000). By Castells' own account regional institutional arrangements are the most effective in addressing the challenges of globalisation. Individually the countries of SADC do not provide very large or affluent markets for investment or political persuasion. Regional integration though as a free trade bloc may allow collective regional resources to be marshalled to negotiate terms of international engagement, even around issues of international radio spectrum negotiations and licensing of services.

In fact Castells' most recent papers suggest a shift to a more positive outlook for Africa under certain conditions. In a presentation to the Economic and Social Council of the United Nations in May and revised in July 2000 (reprinted in this volume as Section Three Chapter 1), Castells calls for a 'Technological Marshall Plan' to deal with the 'vicious cycle between the lack of conditions for informational development in many countries and regions in the world and the dynamics of networks, including all sources of value, while excluding those who have no economic or technological value' (Castells 2000: 17). He proposes that only massive injections of resources can turn around what has commonly become known as the digital divide. The plan aims to stimulate global demand by public works in creating a new subsidised infrastructure capable of bringing to the countries of the South developmental gains associated with high-tech based economies and developmental applications in the areas of health, education and the like. It is not just on moral or geopolitical stability grounds that the support and subsidisation of these developments should occur but because they will also provide the North with significant economic opportunities, Castells argues.

The biggest barriers to southern Africa shifting to an 'informational paradigm' as a region are not so much lack of access to financial capital and technology but rather the lack of political will and lack of specialised human capital required in this sector.

Whether South Africa can become the engine of development for much of the continent and lead the flying geese formation, or abandon this mission to save itself from being drawn in to 'the black holes of informational capitalism' (1998: 161–65) as Castells suggests, the geese will need to fly if the region is going to survive in the informational era. The biggest barriers to southern Africa shifting to an 'informational paradigm' as a region are not so much lack of access to financial capital and technology but rather the lack of political will and lack of specialised human capital required in this sector. These two elements are in the hands of regional decision-makers to transform. There is evidence that among many countries within SADC that such shifts are taking place. These are creating at least the awareness and conditions that would enable the region's participation in the type of Technological Marshall Plan that Castells proposes.

Finally, Castells sounds an important warning. Countries that fall victim to their own ideology see their technological and economic positions rapidly deteriorate relative to others. South Africa is about to embark on a second policy phase to deal with convergence and the further liberalisation of the market and listing of the monopoly incumbent. As we enter into this new phase of policy formulation and delivery in South Africa, and as we consider our relationship with our SADC partners in the context of new economy and information society, let us strip off our ideological swaddling and analyse the gains and losses made to date.

In this way (with apologies to Bertrand Russell I believe), while we build innovative Castells in the ether, we can be sure we are firmly rooted to the ground.

Notes

[1] I would like to thank Peter Benjamin for his contribution to the original presentation of this paper made at the First and Third World Perspective on Globalisation seminar, organised by CHET in June–July 2000, in Gauteng as part of the Manuel Castells Seminar Series.

[2] Heeks (1999) builds a useful model of ICTs in which he identifies a number of elements that make up the 'information system' including the technology itself, the information on which it operates, the process of purposeful activity and people to undertake those processes. Information and communication technologies have been defined by Heeks as 'electronic means of capturing, processing, storing and communication information'. However, he distinguishes these from 'intermediate' technology, still largely based on analogue information held as electro-magnetic waves such as radio, television and telephone. The convergence of traditionally distinct broadcasting and telephony infrastructures together with information technology and the streaming of digitally encoded content across all of these makes such conventional distinctions difficult. For this reason, I will use ICTs in the more encompassing sense that Castells does to refer to the converging set of technologies in microelectronics, computing, telecommunications and broadcasting.

[3] These metropolitan infrastructure-concentrated centres with high-speed capacity connections to other similar metropolitan complexes across the globe have been referred to as 'glocal' cities (see Graham op. cit. at 929–949).

[4] Castells describes a state as developmental when it establishes as its principle of legitimacy its ability to promote and sustain development, understanding by development the combination of steady high rates of economic growth and structural change in the economic system, both domestically and in its relationship to the international economy.

[5] Of this the telecommunications industry accounts for 39 per cent, the information technology industry 42 per cent and the equipment supply side 19 per cent (derived from BMI-Techknowledge 1999 and 2000 South African Reserve Bank data).

[6] See Horowitz (1997) for a detailed account of the political and economic history leading to this point.

[7] Despite a statutory mandate protecting the viability of the public broadcaster during the transformation from state broadcaster to public broadcaster, the regulator in four years privatised six of the public broadcaster's commercial regional radio stations, which are independently owned, and licensed 80 community radio stations. In addition six greenfield metropolitan radio stations were licensed in Cape Town, Durban and Johannesburg.

[8] Despite the high cost of receiving equipment, DSTV has over a quarter of a million subscribers and operates throughout Africa. As the broadcasting legislation of 1994 was outstripped by developments within the sector, it failed to provide specifically for satellite broadcasting and the satellite operator currently operates without a broadcasting licence. With the new broadcasting legislation of 1999, the IBA is required to regulate these areas and examine ways of encouraging competition.

[9] The state-owned distributor is currently preparing for partial privatisation through the introduction of a strategic equity partner.

[10] The resulting legislation removed the regulatory functions performed by Telkom and the Government and vested them in a telecommunications regulator, the South African Telecommunications Regulatory Authority (Satra).

[11] See Horowitz op. cit. for details on these factors.

[12] The incumbent cellular operators are also required through a similar 'pay or play' principle to meet specified community service obligations and contribute to national industrial strategic objectives. However, the poorly formulated obligations were linked to very low subscriber projections, which were outstripped in the first years of operation, requiring contributions from the operators, which in no way reflected their super profits. The new legislation recognised the conservatism of the original market projections and required the new regulator to investigate the introduction of further competition in the mobile cellular market within two years of coming into office. This process was set in motion in order to meet this statutory deadline but has been fraught with controversy and charges of corruption and political interference. The matter currently (January 2000) stands before the high court on review and in a counter-appeal by the Minister of Communications before the high court.

[13] These trends are confirmed by recent studies undertaken by BMI-Techknowledge, which show that while Telkom has improved its main telephone roll-out to 11,5 per cent in 1999, this is still well below many other similar markets.

[14] The Yankee Group and Communications Week International conducted the study.

[15] See www.bellanet.org on the African Information Society Initiative (AISI) which is the African mandate to use information and communication technology to accelerate economic and social development in Africa. Adopted by the Economic Commission for Africa (ECA) Conference of Ministers of Development and Planning in 1996 by resolution 812 (XXXI) as the African Information Society Initiative: an action framework to build Africa's information and communication framework, ECA was mandated to work with partners to implement the Initiative throughout Africa. The African Development Forum 1999 held in Addis Ababa under the auspices of the AISI set out a concrete series of programmes to build a network of telecentres, bring computers to school, and draw on the African diaspora for intellectual and financial capacity.

[16] http://www.computingsa.co.za. The two projects, SAFE and SAT-3, began separately. Key players in the SAFE project include Telkom SA, Telecom Malaysia, Mauritius Telecom, Cable & Wireless and France Telecom. Leading the SAT-3 project are Angola Telecom, OPT Benin, Cote d'Ivoire Telecom, Ghana Telecom, Sonitel (Niger), Telkom SA and Togo Telecom.

[17] ATU was established by the 4th Extra Ordinary Session of the Conference of Plenipotentiaries of the Pan-African Telecommunications Union (PATU) on 7 December 1999 as the successor to the Pan-African Telecommunications Union, which was established by the 12th Assembly of Heads of State and Government of the Organisation of African Unity (OAU) at Addis Ababa on 7 December, 1977 as the Specialised Agency of the OAU in the field of telecommunications.

References

African Information Society Initiative. Website: www.bellanet.org

African Development Forum. Website: www.bellanet.org

African Telecommunications Union. Website: www.atu-uat.org

Benjamin, P (2000) 'Community use of information and communication technologies.' Doctoral research-in-progress, unpublished.

Benjamin, P and A Stavrou (2000) Telecentre 2000 Project. Website: www.sn.apc.org/community

Benton Institute United States. Website: http://www.benton _www.benton.org

BMI-Techknowledge (1999) *Communication Technologies Handbook 1999.* Johannesburg: BMI-Tech.

BMI-Techknowledge (2000) Industry Briefing (seminar), Johannesburg.

Castells, M (1996) *The Information Age: Economy, Society and Culture. Volume 1: The Rise of the Network Society*. Oxford: Blackwell.

Castells, M (1998) *The Information Age: Economy, Society and Culture. Volume 3: End of Millennium.* Oxford: Blackwell.

Castells, M (2000) 'Information technology and global development.' Keynote address at the Economic and Social Council of the United Nations, New York.

Graham, S (1999) 'Global grids of glass: on global cities, telecommunications and planetary urban networks', *Urban Studies,* 36: 5–6.

Garnham, N (1999) 'Amartya Sen's "Capabilities" approach to the evaluation of welfare at 33' in B Cammaerts and J-C Burgelman (eds) *Beyond Competition: Broadening the scope of Telecommunications Policy.* Brussels: VUB University Press.

Heeks, R (1999) Information and Communication Technologies, Poverty and Development. Website: http://www.man.ac.uk/idpm/diwpf5.htm

Horowitz, R (1997) South Africa Telecommunications: History and Prospects, Virtual Institute of Information. Website: www.vii.org

Independent Broadcasting Authority (1999) Discussion Paper on Satellite Broadcasting, Johannesburg.

International Telecommunications Union (1996) *Africa's Telecom Indicators.* Geneva: ITU.

International Telecommunications Union (1999) *World Development Report.* Geneva: International Telecommunications Union.

Melody, B (2000) 'Creating opportunities: lessons from global experience.' ICT 2000 Conference: Innovation, Delivery and Development, LINK Centre, Wits University, Johannesburg.

South African Advertising Research Foundation (2000) First Quarter, Johannesburg.

South African Reserve Bank (1999) *Annual Report.* Johannesburg.

South African White Paper on Telecommunications (1996) Government Gazette No 16995 of 13 March 1996, Pretoria, South Africa.

Stavrou, A (assisted by Khumbalani Mkize) (1998) *A Telecommunications Universal Service Policy Framework for Defining Categories of Needy People.* Johannesburg: Satra.

Telecommunications Act 103 of 1996, Pretoria, South Africa.

Telecommunications Regulators Association of Southern Africa. Website: http://www.trasa.org

Wilson, E (1996) 'The information revolution comes to Africa', *CSIS Africa Notes*. University of Maryland, June, No 185. Website: http://www.bsos.umd.edu/cidcm/papers/-W

Alison Gillwald is the director of the Learning Information Networking and Knowledge (Link) Centre at the Graduate School of Public and Development Management at the University of the Witwatersrand, Johannesburg, South Africa. Prior to that she was a presidential appointee to the founding Council of the South African Telecommunications Regulatory Authority (Satra). She was previously responsible for establishing the Policy Department at the Independent Broadcasting Authority and was an advisor to the Independent Media Commission in 1994 for the first democratic elections held in the country. With a Masters thesis on democratic media policy she has worked as a lecturer in journalism and politics for many years and as a journalist on many of the major South African newspapers.

manuel castells

Think local, act global

This paper will address the effect and impact of globalisation on policies and strategies for local development. Firstly, national economies have been largely replaced by globalisation which has become the new framework for management, production and consumption. However, the fact that there are no national economies does not mean that nation-states no longer exist. This is an inescapable reality, but not a fixed one. Rather, it is a moving institution, with the ability to transform according to interests, values, projects and strategies that are rooted in societies and political processes.

To think in terms of global as against local is limiting. Instead, the reality is the interaction between global and local. Neither technocracy nor financial markets dominate in the world without contest, nor is the world being sub-divided into localities where the last stand of political autonomy is mounted. Whilst nation-states and national governments have been the main political instruments of social and political control of macroeconomic forces and technological forces, this is in fact changing. It is national governments which have become the globalisers. Their main function today is to diffuse and create the conditions for globalisation in their economies.

National economies usually create the conditions to homogenise national production, management, distribution and skilled labour. They homogenise the conditions of operation for capital technology, production and management throughout the world, and the institutions in society that are affected by these processes tend to be local and regional. National governments establish the basic infrastructure for the country to prevent it from marginalisation from the global economy, and local and regional governments relate to this with strategies in terms of the interests of their constituencies. They do so as they have little power in terms of macro forces. National governments too have little power because they have no power over national currencies and no power over technological flows. There are, naturally, gradations of power. National governments have some capacity, however; local and regional governments have less capacity, and it is within this interaction that they try to shape conditions of integration in localities and regions to develop an economy. Regionally specific contexts are what regions deal with. National governments should be aware of the world in order to position their constituencies, that is the people, in this global network of production and wealth. Regional and local governments are increasingly organising productivity, competition, redistribution and the quality of life for people living their local lives. In other words, people are not global, people are local. Their economic system is global and the articulation between the local lives of people and the global economic system comes through regional and local development strategies.

The financial markets, the production system and international trade as an expression of this production system are all part of globalisation. Financial markets are the core of this globalisation in a capitalist economy since capital is global. If there is no investment there is no economy. Profits determine the surplus, which determines the state of the economy. However, what drives investment nowadays is not profit, but the growth of value of stocks, which is only partially induced by profits. In the United States the majority of people hold onto their shares on average for only one year, that is a hundred per cent annual rotation in shares. Then if one loses money it is a matter of bad timing and not of making a bad choice. This is not speculation, it is the change in the economic laws of the financial markets, which are driven by information turbulences of which profit is a part, but only a part. From a regional development perspective this is extremely important: the valuation of financial markets for a given region and for companies that have a strong interest in the region, largely determines the value of regional economies. In fact, this applies to national economies too. For example, a considerable part of the Asian crisis, particularly the Korean collapse, was the result of the downgrading of the Korean economy by Moody's, a valuation company. If a country goes from AA to A in the ratings, the country will decline because all companies will get no more than A in what is known as the Sovereign Ceiling Doctrine. Therefore, if South Africa is downgraded, then everything in the financial markets in South Africa will be downgraded.

... what drives investment nowadays is not profit, but the growth of value of stocks, which is only partially induced by profits.

Production systems are fully internationalised. Multinational corporations and their ancillary networks only employ about 150 million workers out of a global labour force of three billion. Yet, these 150 million workers produce 30 per cent of the global gross domestic product (GDP) and account for two thirds of international trade, which conditions what happens in the economies of all countries. This creates two types of economies: on the one hand, the global economy anchored in this internationalised system of production and management and the subsidiary, ancillary networks and suppliers; and on the other, the informal economy and the survival economy. (There is no such thing as just a national economy. What are called national economies today are government-assisted economies waiting to be phased out, like the Indian sick enterprises – the official term for politically important troubled enterprises rescued by the government – or the Chinese public sector.) The internationalisation of the production system is created in this way. If two thirds of international trade is around the production systems of multinationals and their networks, and over half of this is intra-firm trade, then what we call international trade is in fact the internationalisation of the production system. International trade *per se* is not what ensures the well-being of regions and nations. This is blatantly obvious in Africa where sub-Saharan Africa has a higher proportion of external sector than the Organisation for Economic Development and Co-operation (OECD) countries, in terms of its share of GDP. It has about 30 per cent external sector (imports and exports) of the GDP where the OECD countries have about 23 per cent. But sub-Saharan Africa trades coffee, cotton, sugar, whereas the advanced economies trade high technology products, advanced business services and entertainment. Trade therefore depends on what you produce – you do not trade what you do not produce. Simply put, the unequal exchange theory still stands, but under new conditions – the exchange takes place in internationalised production networks.

Labour is internationalised through the higher skilled segment of valued labour. By skilled labour I mean labour which has some highly specialised capacity to generate and regenerate information and knowledge in what it does. This ranges from advanced civil engineers, financial analysts, managers, football players, professional killers, and anyone who has a special skill which cannot be found elsewhere. Science and technology are internationalised around networks of collaboration through companies and through universities and research institutions. Labour is the integral component of this interaction. Countries that therefore block the circulation of labour are countries which stagnate their chances in the global economy. The number one concern in advanced companies in Europe and the United States is the search for talent. The United States has a very strong policy on supporting the import of foreign talent in the high technology industries. A recent study at Berkeley, by Anna L Saxenian (1999), showed that of all new companies created in Silicon Valley in the 1990s, 30 per cent are headed by either an Indian or Chinese person and would probably increase by 10 per cent if other foreign nationalities could be included. These recruits are not part of the traditional brain drain as they create global networks of production. For example, the Indian from Bangalore who comes to the United States creates a company soon after receiving a green card, and then creates a company in India, and then goes back and forth. Countries need to be part of this competitive bandwagon. Circulation of skilled labour is central to the entire world and without the right people one cannot be part of this network.

... globalisation also has an institutional framework which is represented by international institutions which manage and support criteria for homogenisation and mobility of capital and goods and services.

In addition to the need for skilled labour, globalisation also has an institutional framework which is represented by international institutions which manage and support criteria for homogenisation and mobility of capital and goods and services. The institutional framework in the global economy is mainly constituted by the International Monetary Fund, the World Bank and the World Trade Organisation, which are the key players in enforcing this new global economy. These institutions are there to ensure the homogenisation of the economic dimension of the global economy but they are not institutions to enforce social conditions for political control over the global economy. This is crucial in understanding what these institutional 'roles' are. The protest in Seattle in 2000 was saying that people need to be represented at these meetings and not have everything be decided at a few technocratic meetings by experts. The slogan 'No to globalisation without representation' stated this eloquently.

Under these conditions the first element needed for successful regional development strategy in the global economy is connectivity. Connectivity to networks forms the infrastructure of the economy in the same way that national markets were built along the railways and telegraph systems in the 19th century. Connectivity begins with transportation and communication. Transportation systems are the key to a region being in the global economy. They are information technology based. Computers assist pilots in take off and landing. As you know with Durban being a port economy the computerisation of trans-shipping trade is absolutely fundamental. The Internet is the basis of the new economy. It is the heart of the new technological system. Soon there will only be two kinds of companies, that is companies based on the Internet and dead companies, or firms surviving in their informal networks.

The mobile Internet is critical in diffusing Internet-based capacity to manage the economy. It is estimated that by the year 2004, 350 million users will have access to mobile Internet based on cell telephony. A number of key companies are developing programmes to access the network on very cheap devices. Policies will have to be developed to expand the bandwidth of telecommunications. A policy of accessible tariffs will have to be introduced by government to break down monopolies.

So connectivity is the basis. But connectivity is only as good as the people being connected. Therefore, the second key element for regional development is a good human resources policy. By this I mean not the corporate notion of human resources or education in the traditional sense, but rather the notion of learning, and learning in a social context. However, this does start with education in terms of the education system. Here local and regional policies are extremely important. Even in countries like France and South Africa, which have strong national systems of university education, the connection to the specificity of schools and universities in the local and regional context is always there, regardless of how much the system depends on the national government. The education system requires working at the three levels simultaneously. It requires installing learning capacity, rather than simply information. Universities must be institutions of research and development as well as teaching.

Distance learning can be very beneficial. It has extraordinary possibilities. In a society like South Africa this is difficult as there is a high level of illiteracy, but if we don't begin now a large proportion of the population over the age of 40 will be sentenced to functional illiteracy. The Internet offers a great deal for distance learners. All that is needed initially is to show potential learners the possibilites opened up by using the Internet. It creates the psychological ability to break the barrier of relating to the Internet. So adult education and distance learning is a major instrument which will certainly have to be based on the Internet because most of the failures of distance learning twenty years ago were as a result of the primitive technologies employed at that time.

Once you have connectivity and a good human resources policy, the third requirement in a regional development strategy is to support entrepreneurs. The informal economy is full of entrepreneurs who are able to create value out of nothing with extraordinary skill and ability. However, these are all low-value activities. The challenge is to mobilise these efforts into higher value-added activities which have to be found in the market, and not to rely on government to create these opportunities. This will result in a huge number of small and medium businesses which are a major source of jobs in all economies, particularly in developing economies. The days of waiting for the large automobile factory are gone. A public works programme may be there but only in a few years' time because the fiscal resources are not available. People creating jobs by themselves and for themselves is what needs to be supported or else mass unemployment will prevail. However, conditions need to prevail for entrepreneurs to succeed or they will simply remain in the informal economy. They need venture capital to finance innovation and they need to be kept informed about financial markets, technology and information for managing their business. The Hong Kong government under British colonial rule established the Hong Kong Productivity Centre and the Hong Kong Competitive Centre which distributed free information to small businesses, viable markets, technology, management and training. Until 1990, when the Hong Kong economy was transformed into a services economy, 85 per cent of exports were produced by local companies with less than 50 employees. This was the result of an active industrial policy that made it possible for small companies to prosper.

For regions to prosper it is imperative for power to be decentralised to local and regional governments in order for regions to have the legal power as well as the fiscal and personnel resources to achieve these aims.

For regions to prosper it is imperative for power to be decentralised to local and regional governments in order for regions to have the legal power as well as the fiscal and personnel resources to achieve these aims. This is what transformation is about. In Latin America, in the 1990s, one of the most important experiences of transformation was the gradual decentralisation of power to regional and local authorities, particularly in Mexico, in Brazil, in Bolivia, in Argentina. However, decentralisation by itself is not enough: regional public administration must be flexible and competent. In the 19th century the French model of development had many problems. It shifted from a corrupt bureaucracy to an efficient bureaucracy in the 20th century through the development of a school of administration. Paying administrators a good salary helps keep corruption at bay as in the case of Singapore which also invested in key schools to develop public managers. Other countries have emphasised the regional level as in the case of Brazil, which has regional and local administration training schools.

Corruption cannot be ignored. I cannot think of a more important political topic today. Dysfunctional corruption wrecks governments and therefore societies, and most of the corruption we see today is dysfunctional. Permanent investigation is a way of controlling government and this also permeates into the image of a region. Some international companies allow between 20 and 30 per cent of their budget for bribes, which automatically becomes part of their production costs. Eliminate this from the budget and your company becomes more competitive. A policy of transparency is fundamental. Governments should have transparent management systems as well as being open to scrutiny by the media. This is where the old formula of democracy comes in. If a government is democratic it will be subjected to regular checks at every level, particularly at the local and regional level. Democracy must be seen as an instrument of development.

Quality of life is also a development policy in the sense that it retains and attracts human resources. This encompasses many elements including economic growth, which creates employment and distributes income which in turn reduces crime. Urban safety, social services, urban planning and design are other elements which contribute towards quality of life.

Identity linked to a given place, a given region, a given locality, provides an extraordinary source of legitimacy and tends to provide meaning for the people to be there.

Identity is not a necessary condition, but it is a very important one. Identity linked to a given place, a given region, a given locality, provides an extraordinary source of legitimacy and tends to provide meaning for the people to be there. Identity enables people to accept sacrifices and still bet on the future.

An important aspect to be aware of in regional participation in global markets is the fact that everyone competes with the same information. So we have to be very careful that what Durban is doing does not undermine Johannesburg. In other words, how the strategy of mobilising your regional unit in terms of competition in the global economy can proceed without it being at the expense of undermining other regions. Here a lesson can be learnt from business, which is extremely successful in developing a culture of competition and co-operation, and establishing strategic alliances.

So, we need to establish a kind of a trade union of local and regional governments to negotiate and establish productive partnerships but on the basis of equality, with private businesses and with national governments and international institutions. The European local and regional governments have established vast networks of co-operation which can be used as examples. The Committee of Regions and Cities in Europe, which has the status of advisory body to the European Commission, is based on the local and regional governments. There is also a federation of municipalities in Europe which exchange information and share strategies. And there are a number of informal networks of regional and local governments, with considerable benefits for their participants.

At the international level, one of the most interesting examples I know is a network called the Educating City Network which is a network of local governments throughout the world with centres mainly in Europe and Latin America. It looks at ways of exchanging experiences and joint programmes in terms of how municipal governments could improve the quality of the education in their city. One example of a programme that has been exported by the city of Barcelona to other members, is the

Internet literacy campaign which is a municipal initiative where schoolchildren take their grandparents to the school to teach them about the Internet. In exchange, the grandparents tell them about Barcelona 50 years ago. So they exchange history with Internet literacy. Barcelona is now packaging this and translating it into all kinds of other contexts as a diffusion of technology through municipal-based education.

This leads me to the notion of the Barcelona model. Although there are some problems, I'd like to emphasise the positive elements of the experience, not in detail, but simply to illustrate the analysis that I presented.

First of all, the city of Barcelona is now considered one of the success stories in municipal and metropolitan development in Europe and in fact, throughout the world. Urban journals have coined the phrase 'the Barcelona Model' as a result of the way in which, in the 1980s and 1990s, Barcelona was ranked the number one city in terms of quality of life in Europe. At the same time it developed a very strong economy, good business environment and was ranked number two in Europe after London. Now, what were the factors behind this so-called successful Barcelona Model?

An important element was the development of regionally based human resources in Catalonia, in the framework of the overall improvement of the Spanish educational system. Universities improved considerably, and as in the United States, universities became the responsibility of regional governments.

Secondly, urban design and urban policy have made an important impact on people's quality of life. Monuments are used effectively in working-class neighbourhoods as an expression of local meaning. A policy to create open, public space has also helped in the strengthening of urban life. Opening up public space creates interaction. Fusion of street life is important. Grassroots associations hold festivities and celebrations. In Barcelona there are about 300 grassroots association who have a festivity a week. If people are celebrating, other problems are submerged.

Thirdly, strong support from business has assisted in Barcelona's success both at a local, regional and national level. The development of Internet, and of Internet firms, has also helped Barcelona to modernise, and to link up with the global economy.

The institutions of local governance have linked a decentralised local government with an active civil society. Civic associations exist in many neighbourhoods, and are connected to municipal government through a system of citizen participation. There are also numerous functional connections, and institutional co-ordination between the Barcelona government and the working-class municipalities of the metropolitan area thereby creating a de facto metropolitan government, which reduces the risks of segregation.

This unique city has a strong identity, as well as beauty. The identity of Catalonia grew up from centuries-old resistance to the centralising, autocratic tendencies of Madrid during the Spanish Empire, and beyond. Building on this history, pride was instilled in the Catalans. One of the most successful campaigns was a municipal campaign called 'Barcelona, Make Yourself Beautiful'. Not more efficient, but beautiful. So it was psychological, and this has a very positive feeling that involves people in the preservation of their environment. But it certainly would not have worked without the necessary political conditions. The citizen movement in Barcelona was extremely important in the late 1960s and 1970s. The neighbourhood movement was able to organise and change conditions in the city even in the face of the Franco dictatorship. And I emphasise this because I think you have some similar circumstances in South Africa in terms of the heritage of very strong, urban-based grassroots movements that have already taught people that they can change things if they organise themselves and they put pressure on authorities.

The fourth factor was effective management. During the 1970s some of the best professionals in architecture, engineering, planning and economics in Barcelona merged for political reasons with the grassroots movement. So they learned the real problems of the city and at the same time they were highly trained professionals, particularly the architects and engineers who were among the best in Europe. When the socialist/communist coalition came to power Barcelona had the chance of electing a very charismatic mayor, Pasqual Maragall, a very good urban economist who also happened to be the grandson of the Catalan national poet. He represented the socialist party, grassroots movement, urban economic management and the identity of Catalonia at the same time. So, in other words, when you have a Mandela you can change things in any country. When cities have good leaders and good mayors, they can do it.

... when you have a Mandela you can change things in any country.

Let me conclude. This global system that we are in is not a big balloon of electronic flows. It is in fact an urban world, over 50 per cent urban today, and about two thirds urban in 25 years from now. It's an urban world, articulated around nodes which are metropolitan regions, major metropolitan regions. This urban world, articulated in metropolitan regions, works around a global economy which is driven by knowledge and technology as key elements in generating high value added. The great challenge here is not simply how to grow and develop but how to link up an informational strategy of productivity and competitiveness to the development of quality of life for people at large. It just happens to be that in this kind of economy, to have people who are productive, and therefore healthy, and therefore stable, to start with, is the main resource for productivity and competitiveness.

So there is a potential positive feedback loop between productivity, which is the basis of competitiveness, and quality of life. When countries and regions fall in the downward spiral of competitiveness, which is being cheaper than the others, they become tendentially poor and poorer together. On the other hand, countries and regions can also engage in a different strategy, in a different kind of competitiveness, aiming at being more productive than the others. So that in fact there is a high road of competition through increased productivity, which is really investment in human resources and in quality of life at large.

The other key linkage that is essential in our society is the linkage between political representation and meaning, and meaning which is based on identity. It just happens to be that local and regional experiences, local and regional contexts are those that favour better the connection between identity and political representation. So that there's not simply an abstract citizenship but citizenship of a place and a society we know, we're clear about, and we find meaning.

... we do not live and we will not live in one homogeneous global society but in a network of local societies, co-operating and competing at the same time in a global system of networks of wealth and information.

From this local/regional connection between productivity and quality of life and identity and democracy, there are all kinds of linkages possible to connect to the nation-state, to the global economy and to the emerging networks of civil society through non-governmental organisations throughout the world. So in overall terms, we can say on the basis of observation, that we do not live and we will not live in one homogeneous global society but in a network of local societies, co-operating and competing at the same time in a global system of networks of wealth and information. In that sense, the control of the global starts with the local. Reversing an unfortunate slogan which I think is misleading, I would say that the critical matter today for both democracy and development is to think local and act global. Think local, as people need to be rooted in their identity, in their interests, and in their institutions of political representation. But act global, via the Internet, connectivity, media politics and international competitiveness, as the powers that be inhabit the global space of flows.

References

Saxenian, AL (1999) *Silicon Valley's New Immigrant Entrepreneurs.* San Francisco: Public Policy Institute of California.

section four

higher education and the network society

4

> ... the construction of a more stable, more promising international order in the aftermath of the Cold War requires the multilateral tackling of the developmental process on a planetary basis.

manuel castells

Universities as dynamic systems of contradictory functions[1]

Universities are institutions that in all societies, throughout history, have performed basic functions that are implicit in the role that is assigned to them by society through political power or economic influence. These functions, and their combination, result from the specific history of education, science, culture and ideology in each country. However, we can distinguish four major functions at the theoretical level whose specific weight in each historical epoch defines the predominate role of a given university system and the specific task of each university within the overall university system.

Firstly, universities have historically played a major role as ideological apparatuses, rooted in the European tradition of Church-based universities, either in the statist version of the French, Italian or Spanish universities (closely linked to the religious orders, to the Roman Catholic Church and to the national or local states) or in the more liberal tradition of theological schools of Anglo-Saxon variety, ancestors of the liberal arts colleges. The formation and diffusion of ideology has been, and still is, a fundamental role of universities, in spite of the ideology of their ideology-free role.

However, we must consider this role in the plurality of ideological manifestations. Ideological apparatuses are not purely reproductive machines, as seen in the functionalist theory exemplified by Pierre Bourdieu (1970). They are submitted, as Alain Touraine has shown (1972), to the conflicts and contradictions of society, and therefore they will tend to express - and even amplify - the ideological struggles present in all societies. Thus, both conservative and radical ideologies find their expression in the universities, although the more the ideological hegemony of dominant elites is established in society at large, the more conservative ideologies tend to be predominant in the university, with the expression of radicalism being confined to a minority of the student body as well as to some 'official radicals' among the faculty members, tolerated on behalf of the necessary flexibility of the system. On the other hand, the more the socio-political rule of society relies on coercion rather than on consensus, the more universities become the amplifiers of the challenge to domination in society at large, as it is often the case, for instance, in Latin America (Nassif et al. 1984). In such cases, universities are still predominately ideological apparatuses, although they work for social change rather than for social conservatism.

... universities have always been mechanisms of selection of dominant elites.

Secondly, universities have always been mechanisms of selection of dominant elites. Included in such mechanisms, beyond selection in the strict sense, are the socialisation process of these elites, the formation of the networks for their cohesion, and the establishment of codes of distinction between these elites and the rest of the society. The classic liberal arts college in the Anglo-Saxon tradition, including the Oxbridge version of theological schools, or the state-based European universities, played a fundamental role in the formation of the new elites of the proto-industrial and industrial societies, as family heritage was eroded in its legitimacy as the sole source of social power. Without substitution for the ideological role of universities (and actually frequently overlapping with it) elite selection and the formation of social networks became the backbone of the leading institutions of the university system, actually constructing the internal hierarchy of such systems on the basis of a scale of proximity to the values and standards generated in such institutions. The English system, built around the undisputed dominance of Oxford and Cambridge, is probably the quintessence of this elitist role of university, an extremely important function in any society. But the role played by Ivy League universities in the United States, by the University of Louvain, based on the influence of the Catholic Church in Belgium, or by the University of Moscow in the Soviet Union, is in fact very similar, and reproduces the process of elite selection and formation, while adapting it to the historical and cultural characteristics of each society.

The elite selection function should not be associated necessarily with private universities oriented toward the aristocratic or bourgeois elites. For instance, in France, where the service of the state was traditionally the most noble function, carrying with it the highest power and prestige, the elite university is fully institutionalised in the system of the *Grandes Ecoles,* loosely connected to the university system, but largely independent from it. As is well known, the *Grandes Ecoles* prepare exclusively for civil service, with the graduates committing themselves to at least ten years of service to the state. At the top of the technical *Grandes Ecoles,* the *Ecole Polytechnique* is technically linked to the French Army, and although the great majority of its graduates have probably never touched a gun, they keep climbing in the hierarchy of army officers, since their 'active duty' generally takes place in the technocracy of the French state.

As a sign of the dominance of the state over private firms in France, the elite of industrialists (but also of leading managers) is often recruited among former graduates of the *Grandes Ecoles*, after they have accomplished their 'tour of duty' in government. Thus, elite-oriented universities are linked to the specific history and composition of elite formation in each country.

The science-oriented university came, in fact, very late in history, in spite of the practice of science in universities in all times, including the achievement of fundamental scientific discoveries in universities that were by and large ideological apparatuses. In fact, the first universities focusing on science and research as a fundamental task were the leading German universities in the second half of the 19th century, although there were a few early transfers of the science university model to the United States, particularly the Johns Hopkins University, built around the Medical School.

... the third and most obvious function of the university ... is the generation of new knowledge ...

What seems today to be the third and most obvious function of the university, that is the generation of new knowledge is, in fact, the exception throughout the world. In many countries it had not yet been fully recognised as a fundamental task by the political institutions and private firms until the coming of the current technological revolution, when the examples of the decisive influence of American science-oriented universities in the new processes of economic growth (the 'Silicon Valley syndrome') won the reputation of being 'useful and productive' for the universities of the Information Age. However, this shift in the conception of the university's role should not overlook the fact that in most of Europe, research has been institutionally separated from higher education and confined into scheduled 'National Scientific Research Centres' of the French, Spanish or Italian type, while the German model (still operating on the principle of separation between teaching and research) has been somewhat more flexible in the interaction between the two functions. Many European governments have assumed the functions of scientific research in specialised institutions – not trusting the universities, which are considered too vulnerable to student pressures. In other areas of the world, particularly Japan, private firms have also distrusted universities as research-oriented organisations, and many have their own inhouse research laboratories supported by government funds, directly linked to these firms' needs and orientations.

The popularity of the research-oriented university came from the success of such models in the American university system. Both private universities, modelled after pioneering engineering schools such as the Massachusetts Institute of Technology (MIT),

Stanford or Cal Tech, and public universities endowed by Land Grants policies, particularly in the Midwest and California, played a fundamental role in generating new knowledge and in using it to usher in a new era of industrialisation on the basis of new technologies (Veysey 1965). But, while this model is now vastly imitated throughout the world, it is very specific to America (although, as I said, it originated in the German university experience), and remains the statistical exception among universities, even in the United States where only about 200 of the 35 000 universities and colleges can be considered as knowledge producers at various levels.

The science university in the United States received a major impulse from the military needs of government, during both World War II and the Cold War, since new technologies became critical to assess the American military hegemony in the second half of the 20th century. However, the interesting fact is that the science university model became fully developed in America only as an expansion of the role of another model of university, centred on a different function: the professional university.

The professional university is the university focused on a fourth function, perhaps the largest and most important nowadays: the training of the bureaucracy.

The professional university is the university focused on a fourth function, perhaps the largest and most important nowadays: the training of the bureaucracy. This has always been a basic function of the university, since its days as a Church school when it specialised in the formation of the Church bureaucrats. And it was certainly the focus of the Napoleonic model of university that inspired most European universities. Or of the traditional Chinese university system, structured around the preparation of the Imperial system of examinations as a form of access to the state bureaucracy, and a model that certainly inspired the Japanese and Korean systems. The training of the bureaucracy, be it the Imperial service or the plethora of lawyers that populated the Italian or Spanish administrations, was (and is) a fundamental function of the university in most countries.

Thus, much of the university system is rooted in a statist tradition. However, when the process of industrialisation required the training of a mass of engineers, accountants, economists, social workers and other professions, and when the expansion of the health and education systems demanded millions of teaching staff and medical personnel, universities were called upon to provide both general and specialised training for this massive, skilled labour force. At the same time, they had to equip themselves to accomplish this function, thus becoming large consumers of their own production. The professional university, focusing on the training of the labour forces, was particularly successful in those countries where it was close enough to the industrial world to be useful for the economy, but not so close that it would lose its specific role *vis-á-vis* the short-term interests of particular segments of the industry. Thus, the Land Grant universities in the United States created by state governments to fulfil the development tasks of the regional economy were the exemplary experience that opened the path for future professional universities. The agricultural schools of California and Wisconsin or the engineering schools of Michigan and Illinois, generated a culture of close interaction between the university and the business world, providing the ground for the expansion of the role of these universities in the whole realm of science, technology and the humanities, but always closely linked to their original developmental tasks. The American university experience is better represented by the professional model epitomised by MIT or Wisconsin than by elite universities such as Yale or Stanford, regional varieties or reproduction of social elites. The science-oriented university came later, and developed both on the basis of the elite university and of the professional university, until forming a more complex structure in which several functions interact with each other.

However, for the purpose of the analysis presented here, the important fact is that it was the professional university that gave birth to the science university as the needs of the economy made research increasingly important as a strategic tool to enhance productivity and competitiveness.

The ability of universities to generate research while disseminating it into the industrial world was critical for the university to keep its training function together with its scientific function (Wolfe 1972). On the other hand, those universities, as in the socialist countries, that became completely submitted to the needs of the labour market in the context of a planned economy were, in fact, unable to perform their training function, even less their research function (Peper 1984). This was because in a world where technology is rapidly changing, the critical training for engineers and technicians is the one that enables them to constantly adapt to new technologies. Engineering training that was obsolete as soon as the young engineer would quit the school, actually making him or her entirely dependent on his or her training on the job – that is exactly the contrary function that the university is supposed to perform, although practical experience is always critical in adapting and applying general knowledge.

These four functions (generation and transmission of ideology, selection and formation of the dominant elites, production and application of knowledge, training the skilled labour force) represent the main tasks performed by universities, with different emphases on one or another according to countries, historical periods and specific institutions. But universities as organisations are also submitted to the pressures of society, beyond the explicit roles they have been asked to assume, and the overall process results in a complex and contradictory reality. In many societies, and certainly in the West, the demand for higher education has reached the status of a social need, regardless of the actual functional requirements of the economy or of the institutions. This social need, as expression of the aspiration of all societies to upgrade their education, has led to the so-called 'massification of the university system', as the institutions respond to excess demand by downgrading some elements of the system and transforming them into reservoirs of idle labour, a particularly useful function if we consider that this idle labour is in fact formed by potentially restive youth. Thus, an implicit function of modern university systems is that of surplus labour absorption, particularly for those lower-middle class sectors who think their children are entitled to social mobility through the university system. But the more a university system is able to separate this 'warehouse function' from the rest, the more it is both successful and unjust. The more a university system is politically or socially forced to make coexist the implicitly excluded segments with its productive functions, the less effective it is, actually disintegrating into various organisational systems that try to recreate social segregation outside the formal institutional system.

... the demand for higher education has reached the status of a social need, regardless of the actual functional requirements of the economy or of the institutions.

Indeed, the critical element in the structure and dynamics of the university systems is their ability to combine and make compatible seemingly contradictory functions which have all constituted the system historically and are all probably being required at any given moment by the social interests underlying higher education policies. This is probably the most complex analytical element to convey to policy-makers: namely, that because universities are social systems and historically produced institutions, all their functions take place simultaneously within the same structure, although with different emphases. It is not possible to have a pure, or quasi-pure, model of university.

Indeed, once the developmental potential of universities has been generally acknowledged, many countries try to build 'technology institutes', 'research universities' and 'university-industry partnerships'. Thus, after centuries of using universities mainly as ideological apparatuses and/or elite selecting devices, there is a rush of policy-makers and private firms toward the university as a productive force in the informational economy. But universities will always be, at the same time, conflictual organisations, open to the debates of society, and thus to the generation and confrontation of ideologies. The technocratic version of a 'clean', 'purely scientific' or 'purely professional' university is just an historical vision sentenced to be constantly betrayed by historical reality, as the experience of the rather good quality Korean universities, never tamed by the government in spite of its political control, clearly shows. The real issue is not so much to shift universities from the public arena to secluded laboratories or to capitalist board meetings, as to create institutions solid enough and dynamic enough to stand the tensions that will necessarily trigger the simultaneous performance of somewhat contradictory functions. The ability to manage such contradictions, while emphasising the role of universities in the generation of knowledge and the training of labour in the context of the new requirements of the development process, will condition to a large extent the capacity of new countries and regions to become part of the dynamic system of the new world economy.

Universities in the Third World: from dependency to development

To assess the role and tasks of Third World universities in the development process we must first consider their specificity against the background of the analytical framework presented in this paper. It is certainly simplistic to consider altogether the diversity of institutions and cultures that are included in the ambiguous term of the 'Third World university'. Yet, with the important exceptions of China and Thailand, the specificity of the university system in the Third World is that it is historically rooted in its colonial past. Such specificity maximises the role of universities as ideological apparatuses in their origins, as well as their reaction against cultural colonialism, but emphasises their ideological dimension in the first stage of their post-independence period.

Indeed, in the case of the British colonies, the report of the Asquith Commission (1945) set up the conditions for the organisation of universities in these colonies around the model of the British civic university. In the case of the French colonies in Africa, a meeting in 1944, held in Brazzaville by the French provisional government, saw the universities as an extension of the French university system, and organised them as preparing the best students to follow their training in the metropolis (Sherman 1990). An even more clear expression of direct cultural imposition is the case of Zaire, where the Louvanium University Centre in Congo was an extension of the Catholic University of Louvain.

Even modern universities today, such as the University of Hong Kong, appear to the visiting faculty members, including this author, as pure British exports, keeping all the imperial flavour of Kipling's writings. As for Latin America, the much earlier independence date makes the origins of universities appear less directly relevant to their current role. However, the statist-religious character of the colonial foundations of the university system still permeates the structure and ideology of contemporary colleges, emphasising ideology and social status over the economic and labour functions of most Latin American universities (Solari 1988).

The recruitment of social elites ... became the fundamental function of universities in the Third World.

The recruitment of social elites, first for the colonial administration, later on for the new political elites created with independence, became the fundamental function of universities in the Third World. Because the political regimes were unstable for a long time, universities – in Latin America for two centuries and in Asia and Africa in the second half of the 19th century – became the social matrix of conflicting political elites, conservative, reformist or revolutionary, all competing to lead and shape the nationalist ideology of cultural self-determination and political autonomy. Thus, in many countries, for a long time, the political function of the university (what is called the 'militant university' in Latin America) – merging the ideological function and the formation of new social elites – has been predominant, to the detriment of the educational and economic tasks that the university could have performed. As several university leaders have proclaimed, the 'political preconditions' had first to be set up for universities to be able to proceed with the accomplishment of their specific role. The intellectual and personal drama of some of the best college professors in the Third World is that in order to pursue their academic endeavour, it had to be closely linked to the university system in the dominant countries, thus denying to some extent their cultural identity and taking the risk of being rejected by their own societies and considered alien to their problems and struggles. The contradictions between academic freedom and political militantism, as well as between the drive for modernisation and the preservation of cultural identity, have been a fundamental cause for the loss of the best academic talent in most Third World countries.

Nevertheless, when countries had to face the development tasks in a modern, increasingly integrated world economy in the last 30 years, the need to train skilled labour gave a new impetus to universities as educational institutions. Furthermore, the extension of the traditionally important middle class in Latin America, and the formation of a new professional class in Asia and Africa, both giving priority to the education of their children at the highest possible level, led to a massive expansion of university enrolment. In fact, the new nationalist governments used the creation of universities and the increase in the number of students as a substantial measure of their development efforts. The number of university students has dramatically increased in recent years in most countries.

However, much of this increase has taken place in traditional areas of education (law, humanities and social sciences) since the first task of the university system continued to be to recruit and train the administrative and managerial classes on which the political system continued to rely. Along with it, in the most socially oriented regimes, this took place in the expansion of careers destined for social services, particularly education and health. Indeed, educational workers (mainly school teachers) have become one of the most important occupational groups in the lower-middle-classes of developing countries.

There have also been substantial attempts in a number of countries to increase the level of training in the scientific and technical professions, particularly in engineering and in agriculture-related degrees. Yet, such efforts have faced three major obstacles:

- the lack of trained faculty in sufficient numbers who are able to instruct the students in the most recent technology
- the lack of an adequate level of funding to train students in experimental sciences and professional schools, leading to a teaching programme dominated by verbal communication and excessive numbers of students in the classroom, undermining the quality of the technical training
- the well-known vicious circle: there are few highly skilled jobs for engineers and scientists in developing countries, because few firms can operate in these countries at a high technological level, because of the lack of skilled manpower.

The net result is that much of the increase in university recruitment goes to careers without direct impact on the development process because they are less expensive, and the failures in the training are less visible. In addition, the quality of technical training is generally very low, not enabling countries to take their place in the world at large.

There is of course the possibility of breaking the vicious circle by a deliberate policy of investment in technical higher education. In fact, countries that have engaged in such policy have received substantial pay-offs. This is the case of South Korea, of China, Taiwan, and to a lesser extent, of Singapore and of Malaysia. The policy involves the recruitment of foreign faculty and/or the recruitment of highly trained nationals attracted to their home country from their positions in more advanced university systems. There is a definite trend in the last decade towards the creation of new 'technology institutes' in a number of countries, to emphasise the need to train skilled engineers, scientists and technicians. However, only some of these institutes live up to the expectations generated by their flashy names and their brand new buildings: those investing enough resources in good faculty and modern equipment to update the quality of their training. Thus, only relatively rich countries are able to provide the necessary resources to upgrade their labour force, creating a new gap within the Third World.

While the training function of Third World universities is slowly making progress, at least in some areas, the science function is increasingly lagging in relationship to the acceleration of scientific research in the advanced countries, particularly in research and development in the critical areas of new technologies. This is both for structural reasons and for institutional causes linked to the specificity of Third World universities.

Structural reasons have to do with the cumulative character of the process of uneven scientific development. Centres of excellence that take the lead attract the best researchers who obtain the best equipment and material conditions, being able to attract the best students who end up forming a closely connected network. Thus, most of the best Third World scientists migrating to the United States or Europe (or staying in these countries after their doctorates) do so because it is the only way for them to continue to do research in the cutting edge of their speciality. In fact, salary and working conditions appear to be secondary factors in relation to the basic condition: to belong to an advanced scientific milieu. This is partly linked to the amount of resources devoted to research and development by advanced countries. But there are also important institutional conditions, linked to the specificity of Third World universities, that make difficult their performance as centres of generation of knowledge. The need to preserve cultural identity, and the tensions created by the extreme politicisation of universities in overcrowded conditions, make it extremely difficult to manage the co-existence of the ideological and political functions with the scientific activity of the university. The necessary distance and independence of academic research *vis-á-vis* the immediate pressures of political conflicts become literally impossible when students, and some faculty, are engaged in changing the world or in affirming themselves as their main goal. In addition, the existence of large segments of the university population that are simply treated as surplus labour makes it rather difficult to maintain the respect for scientific activity (whose pay-offs are necessarily in the long term) on the part of students and faculty who are relatively marginal to the society or from university administrators whose main concern is to keep order and maintain the system operating in formal terms, regardless of its actual output in the generation and transmission of knowledge.

The inability to manage contradictory functions within the same system has led a number of countries to concentrate their efforts in a few technical universities (many of them of new creation), while leaving much of the existing university system to its own decomposition. This can be a short-term solution for the training of some technical personnel in certain specialities, but it will hardly respond to the needs of the scientific university. One of the key elements in the development of the universities as centres of discovery and innovation is precisely the cross-fertilisation between different disciplines (including the humanities), together with their detachment *vis-á-vis* the immediate needs of the economy. Without the self-determination of the scientific community in the pursuit of the goals of scientific research, there will be no discovery. There is certainly a major need for the linkage between science, technology and industrial applications. But it is only possible to apply the science that exists. And there will only be scientific discovery, and connection with the world centres of scientific discovery, if universities are complete systems, bringing together technical training, scientific research and humanistic education, since the human spirit cannot be piecemealed to obtain only the precise technical skills required for enhancing the quality of regional crops. Thus, the refuge of the productive functions of the university system in a few, secluded technical schools can only be a temporary measure to rebuild a complete higher education system on the basis of additional resources, better management and adequate connections with the world's scientific centres, in respect of the identity of each culture.

... there will only be scientific discovery, and connection with the world centres of scientific discovery, if universities are complete systems, bringing together technical training, scientific research and humanistic education ...

Universities in the Third World are making dramatic progress in quantitative terms but are still unable by and large to perform their developmental function. Even university systems with great scientific excellence, such as the Indian or Chinese university systems, are falling behind those systems that have been able to manage the interaction between science, technology, economy and society. The ideological and political origins of most Third

World universities cannot be ignored but should not be permitted to suffocate the necessary evolution of the university toward its central role in modernisation and development. If Third World countries are also to enter the Information Age and reject an increasingly marginal role in the world system, development policies must include the impulse and transformation of higher education systems as a key element of the new historical project.

Higher education as development policy: the new frontier of international aid

If the substantial enhancement of university systems is critical for the development process in the new world economy, and if most countries are unable to mobilise the necessary resources at that end, it follows that the new frontier of international aid passes through the territory of higher education. However, the effectiveness of such aid will be conditioned by the ability to design policies that take into account the specificity of universities as institutions, and are able at the same time to link the science and training functions closely with the needs and goals of the economy and society.

It would seem that in most countries, university systems overwhelmed by numbers and handicapped by lack of resources and excessive ideologisation cannot be restructured in their totality in the short term. Thus, this imposes the notion of selective aid, either concentrating resources in the best of the existing academic centres and/or creating new universities supported by national governments, private firms and international institutions. Yet, in both cases it is crucial that universities are conceived as complete academic centres of learning and research, with all levels of training (undergraduate and graduate, including doctorate) and with as many areas of study as possible, certainly mixing science, technology, humanities, social sciences and professional schools. The cross-fertilisation between different areas of specialisation, with flexible programmes that emphasise the capacity of students to think, find the necessary information, and be able to reprogramme themselves in the future seems to be the most effective pedagogic formula according to most experts of education who are open to the new characteristics of technology and management in the advanced economy. At the same time, the co-existence of different levels of training (graduate and undergraduate) makes possible the interaction between advanced students dedicating themselves to research and teaching, and professionally-oriented students, future skilled workers, who will receive some of their training from innovation-oriented teachers, able to open up their horizons beyond the current state of specialised knowledge.

The new Third World universities must also emphasise research, both basic and applied, since this will become the necessary ground for the upgrading of the country's productive system. Research must be connected both to the world's scientific networks and to the specific needs and productive structure of the country. This probably requires the existence of specialised organisations that must be part of the university system, organising both connections toward the world and toward the economic structure of the country (information centres, international exchange programmes, bureaus of technology transfer, bureaus of industrial or agricultural extension, university–enterprise networks, etc.). Institutional reforms of universities, or creation of new universities, should be undertaken under co-operative agreements between international institutions (such as the United Nations or the World Bank) and national governments of the host country, with the support and participation of private firms interested in the upgrading of the technological basis of countries or world regions. They should simultaneously foster institutional innovation (the setting up of new institutions or the reform of the existing ones to make them able to manage the contradictory requirements of various university functions), and provide the necessary resources for the upgrading of the system. Foremost among the needed resources is the human capital represented by faculty and researchers of top quality, fully integrated in the world's scientific and technological networks. While in the long term the new Third World universities should be able to compete for resources in the open world market, as well as generating their own high-quality academic personnel, in the coming years the sudden improvement in the quality of the universities will probably have to come from a combination of several policies:

- The training or retraining of young faculty and doctoral students in centres of excellence of advanced countries, after taking the necessary measures to provide them with the scientific and professional conditions to receive them in their home countries after their training period.

- The recruitment of nationals of Third World countries established in the universities of advanced societies, offering them equal or better conditions of work than the ones they enjoy in the universities where they are employed. Aid programmes should target specific individuals and provide the necessary support for endowed chairs and research centres in areas of priority.

- The temporary use of visiting foreign faculty in strategic fields of research under strictly planned conditions, conducive to the formation of a research group in the Third World university, and to the continuation of the linkage between the newly established group and the visiting faculty once they return to the centre of excellence from where they were recruited. In other words, the critical matter here is to use visiting faculty as priming devices for the setting up of linkages between less developed and more developed university centres.
- The use of talent existing in the private firms and public sector of Third World countries, as adjunct professors able to provide their experience and knowledge to a university world that had been generally ignored because of the low social and economic status of the university system.
- The establishment of joint research centres and training programmes between technologically advanced private firms (either national or multinational) and national universities supported by international organisations. These mutually beneficial agreements, of which there are already numerous examples, should be integrated in a broader programme of institution building, instead of being kept, as is generally the case, under the close control of the participant corporation.

Once the two basic elements of a good university are established, that is a proper institutional setting and high quality faculty, material resources in terms of equipment and physical plant can be provided without being wasted. Only after such infrastructure exists, can recruitment of students begin and the necessary funds for fellowships and tuition be facilitated.

It is obvious that such programmes of multilateral investment in higher education are expensive and will only yield substantial results in the medium term, at the earliest in a ten-year period. It is also true that such is the case for most development programmes investing in infrastructure. The key issue is to understand that the most important infrastructure in the economy of our age is the human brain and the collective capacity of a given society to link up all its brains with the brains of the world.

Still, it is an expensive programme that, given the permanent limit of scarce resources, will have to concentrate in some centres of higher education that operate, at the same time, as models for other systems, and as the providers of informational inputs for entire regions of the world. Some countries are large enough to receive aid directly to their existing national institutions, from which large numbers of people will benefit and major natural and industrial resources will be generated (China, India, Indonesia, Nigeria, Brazil, and Mexico).

In other instances, it will probably be advisable to build regional international universities (such as the University of Central America, the South East Asian Institute of Technology, the West African International University) that will concentrate financial, technological and human resources in a few centres of excellence, able to generate world-class research and training in a few years. However, the experience of several international university centres (in some of which this author has been a faculty member) shows the absolute need to anchor international universities in the national universities of the region, instead of bypassing them. It is the essential condition to be truly useful to the economies and institutions of each country, instead of creating a pool of graduates that generally dissolve themselves in the international networks or become marginal in their own countries upon their return. A possible solution to the problems I have mentioned could be the absorption of high-quality faculty members back into the national universities of their own countries, after they have spent a limited time (five years for instance) in joint centres, or regional universities, formed by association between the universities of the countries in the region. Thus, the joint centre could become an element of integration and cross-fertilisation between the various national universities, selecting the best students, and being formed by faculty of the national universities on a rotating basis.

In any case, specific organisational forms can be found if the basic principle is assumed: it is necessary to concentrate international and national resources in a few centres (either in large countries or in regional groupings of countries) that will operate in direct connection with the development needs of their societies and economies. International aid (both public and private) should be channelled through these institutions, with strict control over the proper use of the funds in respect of national sovereignty and cultural identity of the countries involved.

While it is relatively easy to agree on the importance of improving higher education for the development of the Third World, the question arises of who could be interested in supporting such a major undertaking and why countries or firms would be ready to assume the substantial economic cost and political effort required for such a new form of development policy.

Conclusion: universities at the crossroads of a new international order

At the turn of the millennium, humankind could envisage a bright future after the end of the Cold War and the demise of the Communist threat, counting on the development process that is well engaged in most of Asia, and expecting the current technological revolution to yield its promises, as yet unfulfilled, of a dramatic enhancement in economic productivity. We seem indeed to be on the edge of not the end, but of the beginning of history, if by history we understand the opportunity for the human species to fully develop its biological and cultural capacities.

Yet, at the same time there are substantial pitfalls in our social organisation, if we consider the extent of economic inequality and political oppression at the world level and the lack of harmony between economic growth and ecological conservation. Since most of these evils take root in the context of poverty and underdevelopment prevailing in large areas of what is still called the Third World, it would seem that the construction of a more stable, more promising international order in the aftermath of the Cold War requires the multilateral tackling of the development process on a planetary basis. Advanced countries, and their private firms, cannot thrive in a shrunken planet, concentrating their technology and their resources on a diminishing segment of humankind. And this is for several fundamental reasons:

- Morally, our model of society will be judged by our children by its capacity to look beyond the immediate self-interest of each one of its individual members.
- Functionally, the growing deterioration of natural resources and collective public health, directly linked to poverty and mass desperation, will affect the whole of humankind: the Peruvian cholera epidemic is only the beginning of what could be a return to the medieval plagues, if living conditions are not improved in the sprawling shanties of the Third World.
- Politically, widespread misery and functional marginality for countries and regions in the midst of a world marked by economic affluence and technological miracles, transmitted by the electronic media, will feed ideological fundamentalism, fanaticism and terrorism, as forms of negation by the excluded against the exclusionary practices of the dominant countries.
- Economically, the potential gap between the fast rate of technological innovation and the slower growth of markets can only be

solved in the long term by including new markets in the world economy – new people with new needs to be satisfied. Both the former Second World and the Third World have to be brought into a unified, dynamic world economy, in which today's aid is in fact the investment for tomorrow, in a process similar to the mutual benefits brought to the United States and Western European economies by the Marshall Plan after World War II. A much broader Marshall Plan, multilaterally financed and controlled on a planetary scale, is necessary to integrate the whole of humankind in the development process, thus ensuring material progress and social stability for decades to come. The development of the Third World is in the economic self-interest of the Organisation for Economic Co-operation and Development countries and their corporations.

Now, if we take seriously the analyses pointing toward the formation of a new economy, in which the ability to generate and process information is a key to productivity, it will not be possible to integrate Third World countries in a dynamic world economy without creating the necessary infrastructure in higher education. Because research and education policies take time to bear their splendid fruits, such policies must be placed at the forefront of international aid at the present time, when the seeds of a new world order are being sown.

Notes

[1] This paper is a section of a larger report called 'The university system: engine of development in the new world economy', presented at the World Bank Seminar on Higher Education and Development in Kuala Lumpur, 1991.

References

Bourdieu, P (1970) *La Reproduction*. Paris: Minuit.

Nassif, R, G Rama and JC Tedesco (1984) *El sistema educativo en America Latina*. Buenos Aires: Unesco-CEPAL, Kapeluz.

Peper, S (1984) *China's Universities: Post-Mao Enrolment Policies and Their Impact on the Structure of Secondary Education*. Ann Arbor: Centre for Chinese Studies, University of Michigan.

Sherman, MAB (1990) 'The university in modern Africa', *Journal of Higher Education*. 61(4): July–August.

Solari, A (1988) 'Sentido y function de la Universidad', *Revista de la CEPAL*. 35: August.

Touraine, A (1972) *Universite et Societe aux Etats-Unis*. Paris: Seuil.

Veysey, LR (1965) *The Emergence of the American University*. Chicago: University of Chicago Press.

Wolfe, DL (1972) *The Home of Science: The Role of the University*. Chicago: Carnegie Commission on Higher Education; New York: McGraw Hill.

martin hall

Education and the margins of the network society

Introduction

This paper reads between the lines of Manuel Castells' recent writing about the 'network society'. In his trilogy, *The Information Age,* as well as in a series of reports and papers, Castells touches on the implications of the network society for higher education and for Africa. I start by outlining Castells' concept of the nature of work in the new global economy, and in particular his distinction between 'individualised work' and 'generic labour'. This highlights the structural basis for social exclusion in the network society – a risk for geographical areas such as Africa, but also for the ghettos of the new metropoles. From this I move on to education and, specifically, the current claims for the potential of distance learning on the World Wide Web. Although Castells does not consider this field specifically in his work that is reviewed here, his models for the workings of networks allow us to understand some of the trends, and to infer their implications.

The global economy

World economies have existed since the 16th century. A global economy, in contrast, is 'an economy with the capacity to work as a unit in real time on a planetary scale' (Castells 1996: 92). In this 'space of flows', capital is managed in real time by globally integrated financial markets, and production and distribution are managed in a 'global web'. Today's global economy comprises the three major regions of North America, the European Union and the Asian Pacific region: 'around this triangle of wealth, power and technology, the rest of the world becomes organised in a hierarchical and asymmetrically interdependent web, as different countries and regions compete to attract capital, human skills and technology to their shores' (Castells 1996: 101). Because the creation of this global economy has involved a structural transformation in the relations of production and power, Castells sees this as a new social form, 'informational capitalism' (Castells 1998: 340).

How did this new world order come about? Castells traces its genesis to the 1970s, and to technological innovation and productivity growth driven by competitiveness and demand for profitability. Firms were driven by fears of declining profitability to adopt new strategies in order to establish new markets which would absorb a growing productive capacity in goods and services. This in turn promoted enhanced communications capabilities and information technologies: 'what has changed is not the kind of activities humankind is engaged in, but its technological ability to use as a direct productive force what distinguishes our species as a biological oddity: its superior capacity to process symbols' (Castells 1996: 92).

This transformation has profound implications for the nature of work. Because capital accumulation resides in the flow of investments, rather than in the production of goods and services, it creates a demand for mobile, 'individualised labour', which Castells terms 'self-programmable'. Members of this new elite are able to constantly retrain themselves – to 'learn how to learn' – and to take up key roles in the network economy. This successor to Organisational Man is celebrated by Charles Leadbeater in his 'blueprint for the 21st century':

> Most of us make our money from thin air: we produce nothing that can be weighed, touched or easily measured. Our output is not stockpiled at harbours, stored in warehouses or shipped in railway cars. Most of us earn our living providing service, judgement, information and analysis, whether in a telephone call centre, a lawyer's office, a government department or a scientific laboratory. We are all in the thin-air business. (Leadbeater 2000: ix)

Leadbeater's new world contrasts with the lot of those excluded from the information elite – those whom Castells terms 'generic labour'. In the network society, generic labour is exchangeable and disposable, and is assigned given tasks that do not lead to development and consequent empowerment. The critical factor in determining who has the opportunity to join the information elite and who is restricted to the pool of generic labour is, of course, education. And this in turn renders access to education as the key social issue of the network society – the large number of workers who have become unattached to traditional, social structures of work, but are not reattached to the information economy.

> In a society where education, information and knowledge are the critical sources of wealth and influence, class formation takes place in the classroom. Who gets into the education system determines who gets what in capital, communication and political influence. (Carnoy and Castells 1999)

One proxy for this new social division is the 'digital divide' – the distinction between those with access to new technologies, and those without such access. By the end of 1999, one in three Britons was on-line. But gaps in access based on wealth were increasing, with 59 per cent of the most affluent socio-economic classes on-line, and only 14 per cent of unskilled people using on-line resources (Travis 1999). The same pattern was evident in the United States, where the government has identified the 'digital divide' as a leading economic and civil rights issue. A study based on December 1998 census bureau data, found that:

- households with incomes of US$75 000 or over were more than 20 times as likely to have access to the Internet than those at the lowest income levels
- whites were more likely to have access to the Internet from home than blacks or Hispanics from home and work combined
- black and Hispanic households were two fifths as likely to have home access to the Internet as white households.

This divide had increased by more than six per cent since 1994 (National Centre for Educational Statistics 1999; National Telecommunications and Information Administration 1999).

The digital divide in Africa is well established, and the spread of the Internet can be seen as both mimicking earlier patterns of colonialism and following the contours of discrimination (Hall 1999; in press). Information technology is widely seen as the key to bridging South Africa's 'skills divide'; however, little of the country's developing information technology industry is in black hands (Templeton 2000). A recent article entitled 'Geeks in the bushveld' (*The Economist* 2000) suggests that, rather than heralding an 'African Renaissance', information technology may be widening social divisions through the extensive automation of service industries. For example Nedcor, a major financial services conglomerate, has reduced its operating costs by 25 per cent over the last three years through automated operating and customer services, thus absorbing the consequences of 'white flight' without the necessity for training skilled black professionals.

Castells' argument is that the 'digital divide' is a structural feature of the network society, rather than merely an unfortunate side effect that can be ameliorated by enlightened social policies. He sees networks as gatekeepers to 'network enterprise': 'inside the networks, new possibilities are relentlessly created. Outside the networks, survival is increasingly difficult. Under the conditions of fast technological change, networks, not firms, have become the actual operating unit' (Castells 1996: 171).

Why does this happen? Castells argues that competitiveness in the global economy depends on technological capacity (understood as the articulation of science, technology and industry); access to large, integrated and affluent markets; an appreciable differential between production costs at the production site and prices at the market; and a political capacity to steer growth strategies. Because these are all features of developed economies, the network society is reinforcing historical patterns of domination. Castells believes that this leaves Africa in a particularly vulnerable position. Writing some time before the collapse of the Asian economies, Castells argued that:

> Overall, the systematic logic of the new global economy does not have much of a role for the majority of the African population in the newest international division of labour. Most primary commodities are useless or low priced, markets are too narrow, investment too risky, labour not skilled enough, communication and telecommunication infrastructure clearly inadequate, politics too unpredictable, and government bureaucracies inefficiently corrupt (since no official international criticism has been heard about other bureaucracies equally corrupt but still efficient, for example, in South Korea until the presidency of Kim Young Sam). Under such conditions, the only real concern of the 'North' (particularly of Western Europe) was the fear of being invaded by millions of uprooted peasants and workers unable to survive in their own countries. This is why international aid was channelled to African countries in the hope of still taking advantage of some valuable natural resources and with the purpose of preventing massive famines that could trigger large-scale migrations. Yet what can be said of the experience of the transition of Africa into the new global economy is that structural irrelevance (from a systems point of view) is a more threatening condition than dependency. (Castells 1996: 135)

Can systematic social exclusion in the network society be overcome? Networks are automatons that have their own 'social morphology' that induce inequalities of consumption and therefore exacerbate the distinction between 'individualised labour' and 'generic labour' (Castells 2000); the marketing and distribution of distance education through the Internet is a good example of this 'social morphology' that will be discussed later in this paper.

This leads Castells to conclude that 'there is little chance of social change *within* a given network or network of networks' (Castells 2000: emphasis added). There are, he argues, two alternatives to the burgeoning growth of dominant networks. The first of these is the creation of 'cultural communes' that deny the logic of the network society, close in on themselves and cut themselves off from the world. The second comprises alternative projects that build different sorts of networks – 'new history making' (Castells 2000).

Higher education

First, though, it is necessary to look more closely at some of the dominant trends in education in the network society. In his 1999 report to Unesco, Castells argues that the network is the 'real operating unit' of the global economy. This is because the 'real time' of the global economy results in the simultaneous concentration of decision-making and the decentralisation of execution. This solves a major limitation of industrial capitalism – the contradiction between growth and size, on the one hand, and flexibility on the other. The possibilities of 'real time' reward flexible, individualised labour and render anachronistic the socialisation of work that was characteristic of industrial economies. It is this that leads Castells to conclude – building on his work with Carnoy – that the 'social sustainability of work flexibility' is the 'real issue for the 21st century' (Castells 1999; see also Carnoy and Castells 1999).

... schools and universities play a major role in the 'socialisation of work'.

This model can be transferred directly to higher education. Although the source of an unresolved tension in traditions of liberal education, it has long been recognised that schools and universities play a major role in the 'socialisation of work'. Indeed, Bourdieu would argue that the production of socialised labour has been the only real function of university systems (see Bourdieu 1996; Egan 1997; Ryan 1998). Today, however, the flexible and individualised knowledge economy of the Internet is seen as the key to the future of all higher education (Daniel 1996). In one of many recent policy studies of this kind, the British Committee of Vice-Chancellors and Principals has concluded that 'borderless education' will be characterised by a customer-focused approach to education and training, by the dissolution of boundaries between public and private institutions, and by the increased use of branding to ensure successful competition in the global marketplace (Tysome 2000).

Many believe that 'commodification' of education in this way is the result of 'managerialism' in universities that has led to the inappropriate intrusion of 'the market'. One of the best known advocates of this position is David Noble, recently pictured holding a hammer that was used by Luddites to smash mill machinery two centuries ago. Noble sees a clear distinction of interest between university administrators and commercial partners, on the one hand, and students and teachers, on the other. He argues that the rush to implement information technology in higher education is driven by profit motives. This commercialisation started with the commoditisation of research in the 1970s, leading inexorably to the commoditisation of the core educational functions of the university at the end of the century. As a result, the educational process is transformed into 'commercially viable proprietary products that can be owned and bought and sold in the market' (Noble 1997). This intrusion of the market is being promoted by an alliance of vendors of network hardware, software and 'content', by corporate training advocates, university administrators, 'technozealots' and charitable foundations. It is inevitable that teachers will become labour in a production process, with their activities restructured in order to reduce their autonomy. This will result in alienation from intellectual property as universities assert rights of ownership over course notes, teaching materials and other 'content' (Noble 1997, 1998a, 1998b).[1]

Noble's argument is attractive and persuasive because it tracks the authentic experience of many in universities. It is, however, inconsistent with interpretations of the contemporary global economy by Castells and others, because it casts its critique in the political economy of industrial capitalism rather than in the 'informational capitalism' of the network society. Noble would prefer the traditional residential university with small classes, face-to-face contact with small groups of students and information technology subservient to the primary purposes of education. Although, as will be argued below, these qualities are essential to counter social exclusion, it is unlikely that it will be viable to form retrospective enclaves under the emblem of the Luddite's hammer – the customer-focused, branded products of 'borderless education' will sweep by such islands, leaving them isolated.

Castells argues, contra Noble and others, that information technology is embodied in the social relationships of the network society, and is therefore part of both production and power relations, rather than a thing apart. He encourages us to view information and communication technologies (ICTs) as the essence of the ecological relationships through which humans act on their environment, and on one another. This means that, as the network society continues to grow, the Internet will become the universal tool of interactive communication and information technologies will enhance and accelerate the production of knowledge and information (Castells 2000).

Recent trends in the adoption of the Internet for the delivery of education seem to support Castells' view, rather than Noble's contention that 'the bloom is off the rose' (Noble 1998b). Between 1995 and 1998, distance education programmes in the United States increased by 72 per cent and by 1998, 1 680 institutions were offering some 54 000 on-line courses to an enrolment of 1,6 million students. The National Centre for Educational Statistics found that an additional 20 per cent of institutions intended to offer distance education courses in the near future. It seems probable that the use of the Internet will soon be universal in United States colleges and universities (National Centre for Educational Statistics 1999). One measure of the intensity of development in this area is expenditure on advertising. For example, advertising volume in the main section of the *Chronicle of Higher Education* in April 2000 was 60 per cent on-line platforms, 20 per cent information technology systems and 10 per cent hardware. The remaining 10 per cent was divided between on-line bookstores and the more traditional advertisement of financial services for the higher education sector.

... the development of new information technologies in higher education is a source of massive investment.

It is also clear that the development of new information technologies in higher education is a source of massive investment. This was evident in one of the earliest 'e-universities'. The Harvard Business School's course platform, introduced in 1995/1996 and now providing on-line learning for 1 600 full-time Master of Business Administration students, 5 000 executive education students and 66 000 alumni, cost US$8 million to establish and requires an annual expenditure of a further US$8 million to maintain (MacColl 1999). As Dale Spender, who has developed policy in this area for Australian universities, concludes:

> there is no incremental way a traditional university with bricks and mortar and schedules and lectures can be reinvented as an e-university with the necessary information technology infrastructure, the learning packages and the skilled staff to deliver to the world's students. (Spender 2000)

The British Committee of Vice-Chancellors and Principals concluded that it can cost up to £2 million to establish a single degree programme on the Web (Tysome 2000).

The complexity and cost of establishing virtual universities is promoting large-scale partnerships of common interests, often unrestrained by geographical boundaries. Recent alliances have included Princeton, Stanford and Yale (Carr 2000), Leeds, Sheffield, Southampton, York, California at San Diego, Pennsylvania State University, University of Washington and University of Wisconsin–Madison (Goddard 2000a), and the partnership between News International (publisher of the *Times Higher Education Supplement*) and twenty-one Scottish universities to market and distribute distance learning courses (Goddard 2000b). The 'Fathom' project brings together Columbia, the London School of Economics, the British Library, the New York Public Library, the Smithsonian's National Museum of Natural History and Cambridge University Press: Columbia is reported to have committed 'tens of millions of dollars' to the enterprise (Carr and Kiernan 2000; www.fathom.com). The British government's e-university initiative is based on a commitment of £200 million for set-up costs over two years, and will comprise a consortium of universities, private sector corporates and overseas partners. It will market on-line education in China, India, Brazil, Argentina and South Africa in conjunction with the British Council (Goddard 2000a, 2000b, 2000c; Jobbins 2000).

The emerging character of virtual education, then, conforms with Castells' model of trans-national organisations in the network society, in which the opportunities of 'real time' allow massive investment and growth without compromising flexibility. The potential destination of the virtual university is mapped out in Charles Leadbeater's ever-creative imagination. He sees the new 'knowledge capitalism' as the opportunity to export the British advantage in higher education through 'great academic brands like the London School of Economics'. The British Broadcasting Corporation, he believes, could link all British universities in a vast virtual library:

> if we simply put all those books on-line we could make the United Kingdom's virtual university library available to all sorts of new universities around the world. Once we have invested the fixed cost in creating a virtual university library the marginal, additional cost of making it available to other users would be quite small.

The consequence would be to 'establish Britain's reputation as a worldwide centre for learning and education'. Because marginal costs would be negligible, set-up costs would soon be recovered, and revenues would flow back from the margins to the centre (Leadbeater 2000: 243).

Virtual classrooms?

What could such virtual classrooms be like? John Tiffin and Lalita Rajasingham (1995) have produced a detailed 'vision of what education and training could become as information technology develops'. They start by casting the conventional classroom as a set of 'critical subsystems': desks (for writing and reading as an individual activity) and a blackboard ('a subsystem for reading, writing and drawing as a communal activity'). Blackboards are technologies for short-term memory, used for the symbolic representation of knowledge and problems, while textbooks are technologies for long-term memory. From this, they move to the concept of the 'virtual learning space' – 'any kind of distributed virtual reality that can be used for learning' – enabling in turn the 'virtual school' in which there are no restrictions of size, or in the distance between learners. Critical subsystems are then recast as information systems employing new technologies and operating in 'real time', unconstrained by distance: e-mail to guarantee individual access to teachers and quick turn-around in assignments, discovery learning using the Web and full virtual reality to develop problem-solving capabilities unbounded by space. This is expressed in a design for a 'multi-level telelearning system' incorporating individual learners with personal computers, small group networks, course networks and 'virtual learning institutions' (Tiffin and Rajasingham 1995: 118). Tiffin and Rajasingham's 'virtual classroom' was designed in virtual prehistory. Nevertheless, many of the technological developments that they anticipated have come about over the intervening five years – bandwidth has increased in breadth and declined in price, real-time video and sound transmissions have become a reality, and connectivity has expanded.

There is, however, more to the virtual classroom than getting on-line, as Tiffin and Rajasingham well recognised:

> This weaving together of the weft of the learner and teacher with the warp of knowledge and problem is something that no text or handout can do. It is the essence of education, something we can recognise in the competence of good teachers, but something that defies analysis because it is dynamic and intuitive and does not work on demand, even with the most gifted teachers. (Tiffin and Rajasingham 1995: 63)

Far less work has been done in understanding these pedagogic implications of virtual education. Fabos and Young (1999), in their review of the literature, found that extensive claims for the efficacy of on-line education have not been matched by a demonstration of results. Communication exchange projects, for instance, seek to build classroom connections between schools, with learning projects based around the use of e-mail. This is said to have skills-benefits (writing and keyboard skills), social benefits (multicultural awareness) and economic benefits (preparing students for the global workforce). More complex forms of telecommunication exchange involve a number of classrooms and a moderator who co-ordinates collaboration and dialogue between classrooms following a particular curricular theme. Examples are the AT&T Learning Network, Apple's Global Education Network and Global Schoolhouse. But there is little conclusive evidence that any such uses of information technology have a substantial education benefit – the 'weaving together of the weft of the learner and teacher with the warp of knowledge and problem'.

> The overall emphasis of most exchanges simplistically remains on unification (e.g. promoting a collaborative global community and developing a 'sensitivity for humanity' and teamwork on a worldwide scale) rather than on self-reflection and critical understanding of difference. (Fabos and Young 1999: 240; see also Doheny-Farina 1996; Hawisher and Selfe 2000).

Michael Harris, a member of the founding editorial team of the journal *Internet in Higher Education,* concludes: 'I have not been able to uncover any systematic evidence of careful consideration to questions of the "effectiveness" of various pedagogical approaches. Neither faculty or students seem much interested in the questions of the "quality" of the learning experience' (Harris 1998: 248).

It seems apparent that any correction of these deficiencies will lead to a re-emphasis on the importance of interaction between groups of learners and teachers. Tiffin and Rajasingham are well aware of this, which is why they stress the importance of full virtual reality in their model of the virtual classroom. And this leads us to a contradiction at the heart of the e-university project. Effective learning in the virtual classroom – as opposed to the efficient transmission of information – will depend on small group size. However boundless education might become, no model for 'deep learning' has yet been developed that allows delivery on a mass scale without a concomitant increase in the number of teachers. As Doheny-Farina puts it, in criticising Tiffin and Rajasingham's vision of the future, 'if you provide synchronous distance education, you may indeed reach more students, but you must either hire more teachers or increase teachers' workloads and class sizes' (Doheny-Farina 1996: 110). This is David Noble's 'Achilles heel of distance education':

> In the past as well as the present, distance educators have always insisted that they offer a kind of intimate and individualised instruction not possible in the crowded, competitive environment of the campus. Theirs is an improved, enhanced education. To make their enterprise profitable, however, they have been compelled to reduce their instructional costs to a minimum, thereby undermining their pedagogical promise. (Noble 1999)

How many students can fit into a virtual classroom and still learn? A recent study by the University of Illinois suggests a maximum number of between twelve and 20, depending on the nature of the course, with rare exceptions where enrolments can reach 65 students: 'the scenario of hundreds or thousands of students enrolling in a well-developed, essentially instructor-free on-line course does not appear realistic, and efforts to do so will result in wasted time, effort and expense' (University of Illinois 1999). Studies of individual contexts support these conclusions. To cite just one example, a pilot study for the Open University's new course, 'You, Your Computer and the Net' (which had an enrolment of 12 000 students in 2000), found that it was essential for each tutor to form a community in which there was a continual flow of messages and ideas. This involved new skills, such as 'weaving' (an open-ended pulling together of ideas and teasing out new strands of discussion) and the encouragement of 'chat' so that students could 'see' one another (Cox et al. 2000). Such a community cannot be formed without a low ratio between students and tutors. Reflection on Ulster University's experience with a fully on-line M.Sc. in biomedical and medical sciences led the course convenor to conclude that 'the biggest thing you've got to plan for is human contact through phone, e-mail and videoconferencing' (Wojtas 2000).

Success in the network society depends on learning how to learn, and on continual access to new knowledge and training ...

This takes us back to Castells' key distinction between 'individualised labour' and 'generic labour'. Success in the network society depends on learning how to learn, and on continual access to new knowledge and training, providing the flexibility needed to 'live on thin air'. Education that will enable and support such 'knowledge workers' is offered through the Net, providing the flexibility that is essential to the new global economy. However – and despite claims to the contrary – it would seem that the essence of success to such borderless learning lies not in connectivity itself, but in the quality of interaction between small groups of learners and teachers. In turn, this suggests that, rather than declining in cost with the declining cost of bandwidth, the relative quality of virtual education will be indexed to the labour costs of specialised and highly skilled educators.

If this is indeed the case, then the rise of virtual education will accentuate the distinction between individualised and generic labour, rather than narrowing the 'digital divide'. In Stephen Doheny-Farina's words:

> The ideal is to put students into small classes with skilled, dedicated teachers, supported by communication technologies appropriate to the area of study (and sometimes books are the most appropriate). But the ideal has always been a luxury. The gap between the educational haves and the have-nots will widen, not decrease, with increased Net access. Ironically, when we talk nowadays about educational have-nots, we are talking about schools and students who have no access to the Net. As the Net becomes ubiquitous, the real problem will be limited access to face-to-face teaching and learning environments. (Doheny-Farina 1996: 116)

Virtual universities?

Increased access to quality higher education is now recognised as essential to the future of the developing world – a reversal of earlier assumptions that tertiary provision was insignificant in comparison with basic literacy. The World Bank's recent Task Force on Higher Education and Society sets out an agenda for the revitalisation of higher education, and sees distance education, using the new information technologies, as integral to this vision:

> The Task Force believes that distance education offers many exciting possibilities. Innovative curricula can be combined with interactive, Internet-based technology, traditional educational media such as television and print, written materials and direct contact with tutors. It needs, however, to be thoroughly integrated into the wider higher education system, subjected to appropriate accreditation and quality standards, and linked to the outside world. Research into how this can be achieved – and how distance education can fulfil its potential – needs much greater attention. (Task Force on Higher Education and Society 2000: 49–50)

Recent trends add emphasis to the need for further research and highlight the simplicity of many assumptions, such as those of the World Bank in establishing its African Virtual University as a panacea for university revival (Hall 1998). 'To introduce more computers into a bureaucratic school system, or to provide more Internet access without knowing what to search for, is tantamount to inducing cognitive chaos' (Castells 1999).

What direction should research into such 'alternative networks' take? I would suggest that the heart of the matter is not the extent of the 'information superhighway' or the cost of connectivity. Within a few years, wireless, broadband access will be a basic service, available to most people. The issue will rather be that of content. The structure and form of the network society seem to create an inexorable tendency to enhance social differentiation and to seek profits on the margins, where electronic delivery renders distribution costs minimal. When applied to the provision of education, this economic mode stretches the distinction between high quality learning – available to the information elite with low learner–teacher ratios at high costs – and standardised packages of information, delivered at low cost and with little or no interactivity.

The structure and form of the network society seem to create an inexorable tendency to enhance social differentiation and to seek profits on the margins.

This is evident in the form that the African Virtual University has taken. Although claimed as a revolution in learning, a closer look shows that courses comprise prepackaged video cassettes and occasional satellite feeds in which teachers in North America respond to questions put at the same time by classes of 40 students in several different countries, using the telephone. From late 2000, students will be required to pay fees for such courses (World Bank 1999). In educational terms, there is little in common with the Harvard Business School's on-line platform, or with courses at the Open University.

The challenge of the 'alternative network' in education, then, is that of providing access to learning that takes advantage of the new possibilities of the Internet while tackling the consequences of marginalisation and underdevelopment. And this raises in turn long-standing issues that have mostly been forgotten in the rush of enthusiasm for the virtual classroom: issues raised in John Dewey's pragmatism (1997), in David Kolb's work (1984) on experiential learning, by Ira Shor's 'critical teaching' (1992), and in Paolo Freire's models for literacy (2000). I would suggest that it is here that we will find the key to using new technologies to make 'new history'.

Considering this tradition of 'critical pedagogy' provides a sense of the shape of an alternative approach to networked education. The key factor will be the ability to turn the low marginal costs of commercially distributed education products – the packets of standardised information that critics such as Noble and Doheny-Farina see as an inevitable consequence of the Internet revolution – into useful education resources that empower individuals, rather than consigning them to the pool of 'generic labour'. This will require educational designs that enable people to learn from the experience of their everyday lives – from their local experience rather than from the attenuated environment of the 'virtual classroom'.

Discussion

In the lively discussion that followed Hall's presentation at a seminar in Cape Town, the following points were made:

Discarded labour as Africa's key problem

While Hall's paper focused on the dichotomy between individualised and generic labour, Castells reminded the seminar that the real issue for Africa was a third category: discarded labour, or people who are not recognised as labour by the network. (This is the basis of his devastating critique of systematic social exclusion in areas such as sub-Saharan Africa and the ghettos of the United States – areas which he has labelled the 'black holes of informational capitalism'.)

Castells explained that, according to his analysis, much of Africa fell into the category of discarded labour. Africa's predicament originated in colonial and post-colonial dependency, but was aggravated by 'predatory' African states. Flexible global networks are able to close down in areas perceived as problematic, and the effects of this 'cruel and brutal' marginalisation are felt by those whose lives are rooted in the area – 'capital disinvests, software engineers migrate, tourists find another fashionable spot, and global media close down in a downgraded region' (Castells 1998: 5). The overall result of this process is that Africa loses value to the global networks: 'the automaton would be better off if Africa could be totally marginalised'. In this context, Castells expressed a degree of faith in South Africa as 'Africa's hope' for global reintegration. (This seemed somewhat in conflict with his book, where he points out that South Africa is more likely to be in competition with its neighbours than in synergy.)

The real digital divide starts when you are connected

Extending Hall's discussion Castells problematised the technological determinism which underlies many notions of 'the digital divide'. According to such accounts, access to the Internet is all that counts in counteracting social marginalisation. Castells predicted that high levels of access would shortly be achieved, except for those who were 'switched off everything else, and therefore off the Internet'. South Africa might take slightly longer than necessary to reach this goal, and thus lose the advantage of being an early adopter, if it could not get rid of its telephone monopoly (Telkom). Nonetheless, access to the network is not an end in itself and, as Castells pointed out, 'the real digital divide starts when you are connected'. With access to the Internet, you still need the capacity to know what information you want, where to find it and then what to do with it – and education bridges this gap between information and knowledge. Consequently, 'learning how to learn' should be viewed as the critical skill and overall learning goal of the educational system. In support of this point, Castells cited Martin Carnoy's view that the key skills for success were mathematics, language and Internet literacy. Castells added that, since another goal of education was personality-building, an associated challenge for educators lay in building the flexible and adaptive personalities that could survive the fast-changing network society, but who nonetheless 'knew who they were' and had strong values.

Alternative networks require even more education

Responding to Hall's exploration of the possibilities for alternative networks, Castells agreed that it was possible to use alternative networks to change the structural logic of society – 'the fact that something is structural doesn't mean that it can't be changed'. Nonetheless, he pointed out that participating in such an alternative system required even more education than participating in the dominant network: 'if you want to change the system, you have the double task of understanding the system and figuring out how to change it'.

Education will never be the same

In relation to distance education, Castells again critiqued the technological determinist 'false promise' of on-line education: 'Log in, have education, become Bill Gates.' Traditional vocational education also came under fire. Castells recognised that the fundamental changes brought about by the possiblities of on-line education had changed the higher education playing-field forever. Nonetheless he cited the commercialised low-level degrees peddled by on-line institutions such as the University of Phoenix (the largest on-line university programme in the United States) as an example of overly focused and practical vocational training, which, ironically, has little value to business. Given the new demands of global capital, claimed Castells, such 'traditional vocational training is obsolete'.

Referring to Hall's discussion of David Noble, Castells identified the hidden elitism in this particular leftist critique of mass distance education – 'the world is not made of Cambridges and Oxfords'. In addition, education has been fundamentally changed by the arrival of the Internet – 'education will never be the same again'. Particularly for the developing world, giving up the technological possibilities of the Internet 'is plain stupid'. His reference to Oxford was particularly scathing. Oxford's claims of high-quality education are based on the system of personal tutoring, although it is self-admittedly not one of the world's leading research institutions. Castells' question, 'Without research, what do you tutor?' could certainly be applied to the current proposals to stratify South African higher education into separate research-oriented and vocational training institutions.

In contrast, Castells cited two positive examples of the use of ICTs in educational interventions. In both cases, innovative uses of tutoring and technology were deployed in combination. Brazilian scholarisation programmes *Proformação* and *TVEscola*, used video, Internet and layers of tutors for in-service teacher training in 100 000 schools. Castells' second example, The Open University of Catalonia's on-line doctoral programme focusing on life in the information society, utilises a worldwide network of personal tutors for its on-line students.

Freire is not enough

Castells' final comment on Hall's use of critical pedagogy was to express a sense that the Freirian approach had particular limitations in today's educational context, since Freire's basic premise of articulating 'what people know but can't formulate' was developed for a world where the amount of information available was not expanding at today's rate, and was not so crucial for economic survival. Consequently, for Castells, expressing what people already know remains secondary to developing people's capacity to 're-learn'.

South African telecommunications policy

In reply to Castells' recommendations that the Telkom monopoly be ended, Thami Nxasana, an executive of Telkom, explained the

1996 legislation that established the current telecommunications framework, and set Telkom's targets for universal service. In an illustration of the reach of 'borderless' education, Nxasana explained that Telkom had signed a telecommunications training agreement with the University of Malaysia. This clearly illustrated the warning that by the time South African educational institutions woke up, they could be 'outsourced on-line'.

The unpredictable complexities of South African social networks became astonishingly clear when Nxasana strongly supported Castells' notion of Marxism as a powerful analytical tool. As telecommunications executive, Nxasana could be read as a 'node' in a multinational telecommunications 'dominant network'. At the level of Castells' usual abstractions, he should consequently act and speak only the automaton's language of profit. Instead, however, he cited his experience of alternative networks – global worker solidarity in the labour movement in the 1980s – and asked: 'Why, despite all this technology, do we still have deserts of poverty?'

Castells expressed his surprise at hearing a telecommunications executive invoking Marxism, and warned jokingly that Nxasana should not push the Marxist line too strongly with Telkom's Malaysian shareholders. He restated his thesis that, in the new economy, telecommunications formed the basis of productive forces. For Castells, flat rates for Internet access and an end to telecommunications monopoly are absolutely essential in facilitating universal access to the Internet – which should be viewed as a basic human requirement: the electronic equivalent of drinkable water and electricity.

Dave Kaplan, from the South African Department of Trade and Industry, commented that difficult political choices were being made because of the state's effectively reduced sovereignty over economic issues. By focusing on the development of South Africa's competitiveness and banking on the presence of scarce skilled labour, the state was cornered into effectively advantaging the already empowered. Nonetheless, the state (in its traditional role of mediating social conflict) would be responsible for containing the possible social upheaval and political fallout that might result from such decisions. In reply, Castells agreed that Kaplan had articulated an absolute dilemma, but that the alternative was not worth contemplating – 'while you create low-level jobs, the global economy speeds away in the other direction'. He suggested that the priority focus should be on developing the 'human capital' to make the economy competitive (this includes making venture capital available to small entrepreneurs). At the same time, the government should consider embarking on social policy measures, such as the rollout of ICTs which were labour-intensive, but would also add to wealth creation.

Notes

[1] For a South African version of this argument, see Bertelsen 1998.

References

Bertelsen, E (1998) 'The real transformation', *Social Dynamics.* 24(2): 130–158.

Bourdieu, P (1996) *The State Nobility: Elite Schools in the Field of Power.* Cambridge: Polity Press.

Carnoy, M and M Castells (1999) 'Globalisation, the knowledge society, and the network state: Poulantzas at the millennium.' International Conference on Nicos Poulantzas: Athens, Greece.

Carr, S (2000) 'Princeton, Stanford, and Yale plan alliance to offer on-line courses to alumni', *Chronicle of Higher Education.* Washington: A47.

Carr, S and V Kiernan (2000) 'For-profit Web venture seeks to replicate the university experience on-line', *Chronicle of Higher Education.* Washington: A59.

Castells, M (1996) *The Information Age: Economy, Society and Culture. Volume 1: The Rise of the network society.* Oxford: Blackwell.

Castells, M (1998) *The Information Age: Economy, Society and Culture. Volume 3: End of Millennium.* Oxford: Blackwell.

Castells, M (1999). *The Social Implications of Information and Communication Technologies.* World Social Science Report. Paris: Unesco.

Castells, M (2000) 'Materials for an exploratory theory of the Network', *British Journal of Sociology.* 51(1): 5–25.

Cox, S, W Clark, H Heath and B Plumpton (2000) 'Herd cats in Piccadilly', *Times Higher Education Supplement.* 14 April: 36.

Daniel, J (1996) *Mega-Universities and Knowledge Media: Technology Strategies for Higher Education.* London: Kogan Page.

Dewey, J (1997) *Democracy and Education: An Introduction to the Philosophy of Education.* Simon & Schuster.

Doheny-Farina, S (1996) *The Wired Neighborhood.* New Haven: Yale University Press.

Egan, K (1997) *The Educated Mind: How Cognitive Tools Shape Our Understanding.* Chicago: University of Chicago Press.

Fabos, B and M Young (1999) 'Telecommunication in the classroom: rhetoric versus reality', *Review of Educational Research.* 69(3): 217–260.

Freire, P (2000) *Pedagogy of the Oppressed.* Continuum Publishing Group.

'Geeks in the bushveld.' (2000) *Economist.* 15 April: 72.

Goddard, A (2000a) 'Study resources pooled on Net', *Times Higher Education Supplement.* 7 April: 13.

Goddard, A (2000b) 'Elite mobilise for e-bid', *Times Higher Education Supplement.* 7 April: 64.

Goddard, A (2000c) 'Britain flies the e-university flag', *Times Higher Education Supplement.* 1 February: 6.

Hall, M (1998) 'The virtual university: education for all, or a segregated highway?' *South African Journal of Science.* 94(March): 1–4.

Hall, M (1999) 'Virtual colonisation', *Journal of Material Culture.* 41(1): 41–57.

Hall, M (in press) 'Being digital in South Africa', in S Nuttall and CA Michael, *South African Cultural Studies.* Cape Town: Oxford University Press.

Harris, MH (1998) 'Is the revolution now over, or has it just begun? A year of the Internet in higher education', *Internet in Higher Education.* 1(4): 243–251.

Hawisher, G and C Selfe (2000) 'Introduction: testing the claims,' in G Hawisher and C Selfe (eds) *Global Literacies and the World Wide Web.* London: Routledge: 1–18.

Jobbins, D (2000) 'Overseas push kicks off on Net', *Times Higher Education Supplement.* 28 January: 17.

Kolb, D (1984) *Experiential Learning: Experience as the Source of Learning and Development.* Englewood Cliffs: Prentice Hall.

Leadbeater, C (2000) *Living on Thin Air: The New Economy.* London: Penguin.

MacColl, J (1999) 'Platform on a pedestal', *Times Higher Education Supplement.* 1 October: 15.

National Centre for Educational Statistics (1999) *Distance Education at Postsecondary Education Institutions: 1997–1998.* Washington: Office of Educational Research and Improvement, US Department of Education.

National Telecommunications and Information Administration (1999) *Falling Through the Net: Defining the Digital Divide.* Washington: National Telecommunications and Information Administration, US Department of Commerce.

Noble, DF (1997) 'Digital diploma mills, part I: The automation of higher education.' Website: http://communication.ucsd.edu/dl/ddm1.html

Noble, DF (1998a) 'Digital diploma mills, part II: The coming battle over on-line instruction.' Website: http://communication.ucsd.edu/dl/ddm2.html

Noble, DF (1998b) 'Digital diploma mills, part III: The bloom is off the rose.' Website: http://communication.ucsd.edu/dl/ddm3.html.

Noble, DF (1999) 'Digital diploma mills, part IV: Rehearsal for the revolution.' Website: http://communication.ucsd.edu/dl/ddm4.html

Ryan, A (1998) *Liberal Anxieties and Liberal Education.* New York: Hill and Wang.

Shor, I (1992) *Empowering Education: Critical Training for Social Change.* Chicago: University of Chicago Press.

Spender, D (2000) 'Trade in your skills', *Times Higher Education Supplement.* 7 April: 16.

Task Force on Higher Education and Society (2000) *Higher Education in Developing Countries: Peril and Promise.* Washington: World Bank.

Templeton, B (2000) 'IT key to bridging SA's great skills divide', *Sunday Independent.* Johannesburg: 3.

Tiffin, J and L Rajasingham (1995) *In Search of the Virtual Class: Education in an Information Society.* London: Routledge.

Travis, A (1999) 'One in three Britons on-line, but the Net shows big gaps,' *Guardian.* Website: http://www.newsunlimited.co.uk

Tysome, T (2000) 'Act now, these are borderless times', *Times Higher Education Supplement.* 31 March: 9.

University of Illinois (1999) *Teaching at an Internet Distance: The Pedagogy of On-line Teaching and Learning.* Chicago: University of Illinois.

Wojtas, O (2000) 'Ulster enjoys its virtual birthday', *Times Higher Education Supplement.* 2 February: 13.

World Bank (1999) *The African Virtual University.* Washington: World Bank.

Martin Hall is Dean of Higher Education Development at the University of Cape Town, where he works in the areas of curriculum development, student access, quality assurance and planning in partnership with UCT's six faculties. He is an archaeologist by origin (and is currently President of the World Archaeological Congress) and an educational developer by conversion. He is the founder of the Multimedia Education Group, which is exploring aspects of ICTs in higher education in South Africa, and is writing about the Internet in higher education in the context of developing countries.

teboho moja
and
nico cloete

Vanishing borders and new boundaries

Introduction

This paper is not a debate with Castells in the sense of a dispute. Rather, it is an attempt to reflect on some of the implications of Castells' work on globalisation for higher education. The first section attempts to show that globalisation is a very different phenomenon from internationalisation, with vastly different implications. The second section explores some of the challenges facing South African higher education from the perspective of global developments.

Globalisation is not expanded internationalisation

There is a tendency to perceive globalisation as intensified internationalisation, or to use the concepts interchangeably. Peter Scott (2000) provides a convincing argument for a clear distinction between internationalisation and globalisation in higher education. The former reflects a world order dominated by nation-states; the emphasis is on strategic relationships for aid, development and exploitation. The latter reflects global competitiveness between great market blocs and intensified collaboration and competition in the emergence of new regional blocs which are not only economic, but also cultural and educational.

Internationalisation is closely linked with and dependent on autonomous nation-states which have autonomous but interdependent higher education institutions. The autonomous state has a great degree of control over its economic priorities and development projects, and usually provides, directly or indirectly, more than 50 per cent of the budget of public higher education institutions. The state also has a fair degree of control over who can provide higher education and what counts for higher education. International exchange of students and staff, and international collaboration in the production of knowledge is central to the life-world of the modern nation-state university (Scott 2000). In this system the boundaries between the state, the market and the university are fairly clear, albeit constantly contested.

In contrast, in a globalising higher education 'system', nation-states have limited or no control over policies regulating higher education. The private sector offers free higher education programmes in countries where there is no free higher education, the shape and size of the system are determined by partnerships between business and institutions, and quality assurance is determined and monitored by third party agents.

Effects of globalisation on higher education

The possibility of instant transactions, the ability to produce and disseminate knowledge globally in real time, the need for global capitalism to have restructured institutions, and the need for states that can make this new system function, are having a profound effect on higher education.

Globalisation is associated with a restructuring of the nation-state in terms of the deregulation of financial controls, the opening of markets and notions of efficiency, and redefining the core business of the state. These notions are antithetical to the classic notion of the welfare state, on which traditional European higher education depended very heavily. The new privatised, outsourced professional state is no longer clearly above or outside the market, but is now itself a 'market-type institution' (Scott 2000). This state of affairs is not imposed upon unsuspecting governments by an invisible hand; on the contrary, globalisation depends on being enthusiastically promoted and implemented by nation-states, who then, in the words of Castells at the Gauteng seminar, 'lose control'.

The restructuring of the state is to some extent mirrored in higher education institutions. So this is a major effect of globalisation on higher education: institutions are expected to become open to competition, be more competitive, identify core business, plan according to cost centre accounting and have a flexible, retrainable and redeployable staff who are efficiently line or project managed.

Restructuring also applies to the market, which no longer consists of small, medium and multinational firms. The market now sees its operations and its clients as global, adds value to what it regards as desired and 'switches off' what is regarded as not of value. The market does not only try to satisfy needs and make a profit in the process, but it also 'manufactures' desires and needs (Scott 2000). The market is not outside of culture and politics, but is becoming more embedded in them, and thus becomes part of shaping and reshaping both culture and politics (Scott 2000). The market is thus increasingly becoming a web of complex relationships and interdependencies which is integral to the state and culture, as well as to higher education. According to Scott:

> The frontiers between State, Market and Culture have been breached. They are more and more difficult to tell apart. Also as a result, State institutions, Market institutions and Cultural institutions are more difficult to distinguish. The university, for example, is all three. And, more radically still, the very idea of stable institutions is being undermined by technological innovation and organisational volatility. (Scott 2000: 5)

The second major effect of globalisation on higher education has to do with the changing role of knowledge, information and information technology. While these are quite separate constructs, they are becoming increasingly interrelated. Carnoy (1998) asserts that 'if knowledge is fundamental to globalisation, globalisation should have a profound impact on the transmission of knowledge'.

... if knowledge is fundamental to globalisation, globalisation should have a profound impact on the transmission of knowledge.

The centrality of knowledge to globalisation has contributed to the emergence of new paradigms and new social relations for the production and dissemination of knowledge. There are new trans-institutional arrangements for the development of knowledge production sites and multiple agencies are involved in the production and dissemination of knowledge. The emergence of multiple, networked, global knowledge production partners is redefining the role of higher education institutions. The Von Humboldt model of higher education which integrates teaching and research under one roof might be reaching its end, and Peter Drucker (1999), a guru of change management, is predicting the end of the comprehensive university as we know it today.

The revolution in knowledge dissemination is as far reaching as are the new modes of knowledge production. Government, corporations, international development agencies and institutions operating individually or in partnerships are promoting and supporting globalised course delivery. A new taxonomy of institutions has emerged, ranging from virtual, for profit, spin-offs of virtual institutions, to consortia of existing institutions. There are also institutions set up that enrol predominantly foreign students. A more frivolous classification is 'brick and click universities' versus 'click universities' (Levine 2000).

There are many new initiatives. These include the British Open University which has started to operate in the United States, the expansion globally of institutions such as Monash University from Australia, the announcement by Sylvan Learning that it is planning to open for-profit universities around the globe, and the World Bank initiative to set up the African virtual university (see also discussion in Hall in Section Four

Chapter 2 of this volume). Established institutions have also formed consortia to provide higher education programmes to the non-traditional clientele. For example, consortia consisting of Princeton, Yale and Stanford propose to offer on-line courses for their alumni. Entering the competition, Oxford has just established a commercial web education centre from which it is expected that 'tutors will become as familiar with teaching the public via interactive links as traditional Oxbridge dons are with musing in their studies over vintage port' (London *Sunday Times*, 7 October 2000).

The University of Maryland University College, UMUC Online.com Inc., is creating a global marketing plan to expand the reach of the college's on-line courses. The new company will seek corporate partners to develop innovations for delivering courses on-line. 'To be competitive, [universities are] going to have to market in such a way that is quantitatively different in order to be qualitatively different' (Selingo 2000).

The 'difference' will – amongst other things – mean an increasing demand for packaged and 'branded' materials that are more similar to the mass culture media than to traditional lectures. This raises the question as to whether higher education institutions will merely be the primary producers of academic materials that are processed, packaged and disseminated by global corporations. Universities could then become 'knowledge warehouses' where knowledge produced off-site is reprocessed before it is supplied to the corporation. The corporation's task would be to make the materials more 'user friendly' before passing them to the worldwide distributor, who might sell them, like old soap operas, at a reduced rate to the Third World once the knowledge was a little out of date.

Such 'edutainment' also raises the possibility that the names of world-class professors could become far more important than the institution in which they work, as has happened in Hollywood where the dominance of the studios has given way to the star power of the actors (Levine 2000).

There is a dramatic increase in the use of on-line courses and virtual institutions. In 1999 54 per cent of United States college courses were offered on-line. In April 2000 there were estimates of 878 institutions offering virtual courses (Newman 2000). There has been an extension of existing institutions to capture new markets and to provide greater numbers of skilled workers. In the United States the Education Commission has identified 650 for-profit degree-granting institutions. The rising demand for distance learning is challenging providers to provide high levels of customer service and other services that were not anticipated, such as electronic alumni magazines (Young 1999).

In February 2000 the British government announced a distance learning project called 'e-University', which has a £300 million start-up fund. It is aimed at encouraging and enabling the United Kingdom system to compete with major virtual and corporate universities in the United States and globally, in order to expand Britain's share of the overseas higher education market. Several partnerships have been formed between established institutions and for-profit companies. The *Chronicle of Higher Education* (16 June 2000) reported that nine universities on four continents have formed a venture with NextEd Company to offer on-line courses in Asia. The market in Asia is estimated to be worth US$10 billion annually. Two new associations representing Web-based education companies have started a Washington lobby group: 'a new trade association was necessary, because none of the existing higher education associations represents the interests of distance education' (Selingo 2000).

Quality assurance of many of the on-line courses has shifted from institutions or states to transitional quality assurance and accreditation agencies. Their emphasis is on the measuring of competencies (outcomes) that are relatively easy to measure. Examining agents operate at 5 000 sites in 140 countries and administered an estimated three million assessments in 1999. In January 2000 it was estimated that 1,7 million credentials had been awarded. There is also a move towards international standards and licensing (Adelman 2000). Trans-national quality assurance accreditation in the globalised higher education arena raises questions as to whom, and on what basis, should standards be set and monitored. The new arrangements in the accreditation of higher education courses will have a profound impact on traditional peer-certified expertise.

Commenting on these changes, Scott asks:

> But what is the impact likely to be? To put it simply, will the university thrive or will it wither away in this new global environment? Will it reach new heights as the leading knowledge institution in a Knowledge Society, or will it be superseded, bypassed, by more vigorous rivals (some of which, of course, may steal our name as a convenient 'brand')? And will the university of the twenty-first century, of the next millennium, be anything like the universities that have existed up to this point in history? (Scott 2000: 1)

Some responses to the effects of globalisation on higher education

The following are somewhat overstated 'positions' implicit, or explicit, in the way that the debate on globalisation is being conducted in higher education in South Africa and elsewhere.

We must increase our market share

(Or, the new global academic entrepreneur.)

Once academics – at first reluctantly, and then with some enthusiasm – have accepted the new managerial language of strategic planning, students as clients, core business, outsourcing, cost centres and privatisation, perhaps it is not surprising that the next logical step is to globalise this mindset. When the local market is saturated, then the global market must be tapped (as any good local capitalist business expanding its horizon and its market knows). As in economic globalisation, new technology is crucial in making it possible – and the core business is both knowledge driven and about knowledge.

The new global higher education entrepreneur looking for niche markets was inherent in the academic restructuring of the 1980s in the United Kingdom and the United States. Perhaps Peter Scott's distinction between internationalisation and globalisation could be viewed differently; internationalisation in the United States and United Kingdom gave them a competitive advantage en route to globalisation. Traditional academics find the unreflective way in which First World academics, and a few aspiring Third World academics, talk about expanding markets quite 'un-academic'. Rather shocking to Third World academics is that the vast majority of First World academics do not show much, if any, awareness of the cultural bias of their wares. They also show no compunction towards their fellow Third World academic colleagues who may be losing not only their students, but also their jobs and ultimately their institutions. This raises the question as to whether these structural changes may lead to the end of collegiality and international 'solidarity' amongst academics. It will in all likelihood also perpetuate the other phenomenon associated with globalisation: increasing inequality, both between academics within institutions and between academics in different institutions and countries.

I vant to be left alone

(Attributed incorrectly to Greta Garbo.)

In a recent discussion piece on globalisation and higher education Simon Swartzman (2000) said that 'Brazil will remain, for the next several years, a large and mostly inward-looking country'. This is remarkable, but not unusual. The Brazilian President, Frederico Cardoso, is arguably one of the foremost theorists and practitioners of globalisation in Latin America, but his academic community may well lag behind him. In many developing countries the government may be pursuing a vigorous globalisation agenda while the academics steadfastly remain orientated to the local. Castells argues that you cannot be indifferent to globalisation: you are either in or you are trying to get in. If you stay out, survival is what you are heading for – if you are lucky (Castells 1998). While academics may want to operate in the familiar locale, and occasionally hanker after a bit of the good old internationalisation, it seems that globalisation will not leave them alone, either in the way in which their workplaces are reorganised or through their colleagues on another continent recruiting their students through the Internet.

Fight the new cultural imperialists

Oppose Californication! (With acknowledgement to the Red Hot Chilli Peppers.)

From the previously colonised in the Third World this fighting talk sounds like just another despairing cry en route to applying for more grants; but far more serious is when the Europeans and the Canadians start making moves to oppose the 'Californication' of the world. Three types of approaches can be identified:

Protectionism

It is estimated that 70 per cent of Internet distance education materials originate in the United States. The first, instinctive response from many public institutions has been to ask the government to intervene and to put an embargo on foreign institutions. The French Minister of Education M. Allegre called for a 'counter-attack' in the battle over the right to offer distance education across national borders. M. Allegre bases his argument not on economic disadvantage, but on the preservation of national identity, culture and language (*Chronicle of Higher Education,* 10 December 1999). The Egyptian government has declared foreign distance education a national threat.

In South Africa some universities have asked that, since the government is providing five years of protection for the national telecommunications utility, the same should be done for higher education. While the South African Minister of Education seems quite sympathetic, he is clearly out of line with government economic policy of opening up competition and lifting protectionist measures. If the World Trade Organisation approves the proposal to make education a 'service' then such protectionism could be illegal.

Be competitive

The new British government-sponsored higher education distance consortium is on the one hand justified in opposing United States dominance, but on the other hand it sounds more like a revival of a much older British tactic – join the race for colonial domination. For the Third World this type of competition is very daunting. Successful competition is the exception rather than the rule, despite a South African university recently winning a contract for distance education in the health sciences from Israel and Turkey in competition against a number of United Kingdom institutions. The competitive advantage was because of cost and relevance: at more than ten South African rands to the British pound, South Africa has a competitive advantage and as a developing country, South Africa has a health system that is more similar to those of Israel and Turkey.

Form partnerships

Partnerships come in all shapes and sizes, and with all their inherent tensions and inequalities. In pursuing partnerships, appropriate guidelines for public and private, Third and First World partnerships will have to be developed. Some of the complications of partnerships are demonstrated by the decision of the Minister of Education in South Africa earlier this year to place a moratorium on new partnerships. According to the Minister's spokesperson:

> What has tended to happen in these private–public partnerships is that a number of public universities have, in the name of efficiency, outsourced the delivery of some of their academic programmes (especially distance learning programmes) to private sector partners. This in itself may not be a problem, but in our experience, these collaborations have often resulted in a compromise of quality. In the South African context, the students who are often short-changed in such arrangements are in the main black, and poor. (Kulati 2000: 2)

Similarly, First World–Third World partnerships could easily perpetuate the inequalities associated with globalisation.

Debates have started about the possibility that in the global arena where the authority of nation-states and institutional policy-making structures is weakened it may be necessary to look at the possibility of 'global policy' or 'supra-policy'. A lesson learnt from experience in the globalising new South Africa is that formulating policy is easier than making it work.

Finally, the process of globalisation is making the boundary between the state, the market and higher education much more permeable – the thrust is both a redefinition, but essentially a weakening of boundaries, and in some cases, such as 'nationless' distance education, a total obliteration of boundaries. The new possibilities of links between information technology and knowledge production and dissemination, and new forms of economic production and competition, drive these new forms of cross-border education delivery.

Challenges facing South African higher education

Higher education systems and institutions worldwide need to reconfigure their new roles. For South Africa the predominant challenge has been taken to be to address, or redress, past inequalities within a new framework of democratic participation and to respond to the competition from commercial higher education, rather than challenges arising from globalisation. From the overview above it is quite clear that there is an additional set of challenges that higher education needs to confront: information technology, knowledge, human resources, institutional restructuring and a new relationship between government and institutions, not to mention a globally competitive market.

Information and communication technologies

Information and communication technologies (ICTs) have the potential for transforming education towards the new knowledge-creation, educational model. Central to transforming education through technology is access to technology and new enabling policies.

Overall Internet use in South Africa increased in 1998 by 86 per cent, by 53 per cent in 1999 and is predicted to increase by about

40 per cent in 2000. The slowdown is reported to be due to lack of competition for the current telecommunications operator – Telkom – and the high cost especially of international bandwidth. In 1999 a 40 per cent growth was reported in corporate users accessing Internet via high-speed digital leased lines because the business sector, unlike the education sector, could absorb these costs. The costs are high and the bandwidth ordered for Internet purposes is small by comparison. For example, it is simply not possible to make good use of JSTOR, the United States-based electronic journal storage resource because it takes too long and costs too much to download journals. During early 1999 a United States consultant wrote that South Africa is some 15 years behind other developed countries in the use of ICTs for teaching, research and management purposes in higher education (Leatt 2000).

South African higher education has operated its own network for international and domestic bandwidth called Uninet. The network was owned and managed by what is now the National Research Foundation. The costs of bandwidth were high and escalating – bandwidth costs constituted a major constraint to the development of co-operative library ventures. Due to Telkom's monopoly Uninet had to purchase its international and local bandwidth from the national telecom provider. Furthermore, Uninet had done pioneering work for higher education, but it was not quite an Internet service provider (ISP) and was now facing stiff competition from the growing ISP market. It simply did not have the resources to update its technology and to become higher education's preferred service provider.

The story of how to obtain greater bandwidth for higher education is almost like another 'struggle story'.

The story of how to obtain greater bandwidth for higher education is almost like another 'struggle story'. A task team consisting of a number of higher education luminaries had their first meeting with the Minister of Communications and senior Telkom management in 1996. In October 2000, with the assistance of a United States donor consortium, a deal was finally struck, but not yet signed, to establish the Tertiary Education Network (Tenet) that will manage higher education's future inter-networking service contracts (Leat 2000).

It is hoped that the deal which higher education is about to strike with Telkom will give South Africa an adequate and affordable international and domestic service as part of the new state-of-the-art public broadband network which Telkom is currently rolling out. Good institutions will be able to access very much more bandwidth for the same sort of money they are currently paying. The donors have offered US$2 million to further augment the buying power of universities and technikons. The net result is that higher education could take advantage of much better bandwidth. It could also start to realise many of the ideas set out in the policy documents that have emanated from higher education, such as those written by the Working Group on Library and Information Technology for the National Commission on Higher Education (1997) and the report on the feasibility of a 'national virtual library'. Furthermore, higher education would be in a position to seriously consider the strategic advantages of how to integrate technologies much more effectively into higher education systems to improve the quality and scale of higher education provision in the country. The challenge is for higher education to apply technology imaginatively and effectively, and to develop new organisational systems that can facilitate, rather than retard, ICT application (Bouchard 2000).

The 'struggle for bandwith' is a very pertinent example where policy flows from innovation, and is driven by a consortium of funders and institutions, while the government oscillates between opposition and passivity. A future policy challenge will be for government to be ready, to be responsive, to policy development that flows both from the top and from the bottom.

Another challenge for South Africa is to determine where and how ICTs are best used. It is not unlikely, after the spectacular loss of confidence in dotcom companies, that a correction in the current extravagant claims for electronic distance education will occur. The challenge for South Africa is not to jump on the wrong bandwagon at the wrong time, as is so often the case with Third World countries.

Knowledge

There are at least three salient trends in knowledge production in the higher education sector in South Africa. Firstly, as far as scientific output is concerned, the best available data suggest a decline in total published output over the past two to three years. Whereas scholars at South African universities and technikons maintained an average output of approximately 5 500 publication units per year between 1992 and 1997, results for 1998 and 1999 show an annual decline of around ten per cent. This decline is mirrored by a comparable decline in our share of world output (as measured by Institute for Scientific Information statistics). The best figures suggest that South African scientists produced approximately 0,51 per cent of world science in 1998, compared to 0,7 per cent in 1994 (Mouton and Boshoff 2000).

Secondly, there is growing evidence that research being done at South African universities and technikons is increasingly directed at strategic (socio-economic and industry) goals. Although no data is available, there are indications that more contract research is being conducted, which could account for some of the overall reduction in publication output. Data from the National Research and Technology Audit (Mouton and Boshoff 2000) showed a marked decline in the proportion of basic research being done within the higher education sector.

Thirdly, there are clear shifts in the kind of knowledge produced as far as scientific fields are concerned. Data from the SA Knowledgebase show a shift over the past ten years towards more health research and applied natural sciences research with a concomitant decline in basic natural sciences research. A similar shift away from general humanities research towards more applied social sciences research is evident (Mouton and Boshoff 2000).

South African academic science faces a double challenge: to increase strategic or 'problem-solving in context' research, and to be able to maintain and ... strengthen its core knowledge-base in basic science.

Although various forces are at work within the higher education sector which are driving these changes, the overall picture that emerges is of a body of science that is struggling to maintain its current levels of capacity and that is increasingly driven by strategic and national goals and concerns. South African academic science faces a double challenge: to increase strategic or 'problem-solving in context' research, and to be able to maintain and – if possible – strengthen its core knowledge-base in basic science. This is essential, not only because it ultimately feeds into strategic and problem-oriented research, but also because it forms the basis for high-quality postgraduate training

In response to a question about issues regarding higher education and knowledge in South Africa, Manuel Castells wrote the following: 'The global economy is knowledge-based. If you do not perform in this new system, you fall into low-value added production and you never, never develop, regardless of how much you trade' (cited in Cloete 2000: 12). A point to note is that sub-Saharan Africa, excluding South Africa, has a higher proportion of its gross domestic product in international trade than average Organisation for Economic Co-operation and Development (OECD) countries; but it is mainly in devalued primary commodities.

Castells further asserts that the knowledge economy is based on the combination of technological infrastructure, connectivity and human resources. Without human resources, nothing works. Human resources require not just technical skills amongst a minority, but a broad level of education in the population at large. In addition to generating knowledge and processing information, universities need to produce researchers and innovators. The challenge for the system – in the process of transformation – is to focus on enhancing the capacity of some institutions to become research-orientated institutions. In addition, innovation will have to be specific in its connection to the knowledge economy. The implication is that institutions have to develop a cadre of academics to serve these institutions and also develop innovators to link institutions with the business sector. Such partnerships can contribute to accessing funding for research and for faculty in applied research programmes. It is important to bear in mind that key research developments happen in international networks, often working on-line. To enter these international co-operative networks there is need for a certain level of excellence to be achieved. Once this connection is made, then the system becomes self-expanding. The issue is how to prime such a system.

It is important to bear in mind that key research developments happen in international networks, often working on-line.

Given the scarcity of resources, the problem is how to concentrate resources in some institutions and in some areas, because an equal spread leads to minimal gain (see also Castells in Section Four Chapter 1 of this volume). Thus, the choice of investing in a few areas and in a few departments or institutes must be confronted. One implication is that rather than concentrating on a few universities, funding could be given to a network of very good groups in various universities for a limited period of time (five to ten years, depending on fields), which are then evaluated in terms of their performance. As part of the building of these networks, mechanisms of diffusion of their discoveries and graduates to the overall university system should be established. In other words, resources would be concentrated on innovative and excellent networks of a few groups, while, at the same time, ensuring that this is not the construction of a non-accountable elite. In general, it is not a good policy to work on selected areas, such as information technology. Yet it looks like some key areas, which are at the cutting edge, could be critical for a while. A large investment in these areas could ensure the dramatic technological upgrading of South Africa in a short time, say ten years.

The inter- and intra-institutional differentiation in South Africa will increasingly be based on knowledge capacity, which means a combination of the academic backbone of the institution and how it is organised and connected or networked. In South Africa the term 'disadvantage' is often directly linked to a shortage of financial resources, while the real difference often lies in academic capacity, of which the so-called 'academic culture' is just a symptom of differences in knowledge capacity. Policy demands for mission re-engineering, life-long education, engaging in problem-solving research and so on, all presume a certain academic capacity for modifying, or retooling, existing skills. A problem we have to confront is that Castells' 'self-programmable labour' is not in abundance, and is over-concentrated in certain institutions. In a certain sense South Africa has a largely 'generic' academic labour market – people who are left out of the information networks and who do not have the knowledge skills to rethink their occupational tasks and apply their skills in different contexts and to different problems.

The 'knowledge portfolios' (see Carnoy in Section One Chapter 2 of this volume) of academic workers are going to allow some to become increasingly market-linked and competitive, pulling them further away from the national public institutions and more into the global knowledge-production, problem-solving consultancy world. At the other end of the spectrum of generic labour, are academics who will become more local, 'switched off' out of knowledge networks, with rising frustration and resentment. For them private higher education and global edutainment enterprises will be an increasing threat. These different knowledge portfolios are going increasingly to drive differentiation between institutions, but also within institutions, leading to new meanings to concepts such as advantage and disadvantage.

Recent South African government-related policy developments (Council on Higher Education Report 2000; National Commission on Higher Education 1996; Department of Education 1997) have not addressed these issues. There is still a preoccupation with the lingering effects of apartheid on individual and institutional equity. Yet it seems quite urgent that knowledge generation and information processing require focused policy interventions. These will need different types of interventions, not to mention investigating the possibility of some institutions becoming national or focus institutions with a predominant technology mission.

Human resources

Higher education has two important functions in the knowledge economy. The one function is to produce medium-skill level professional graduates for the professions and the service sector; the other is to produce highly skilled knowledge producers for high-level innovation. As the conceptual share of the value added in economic processes continues to grow, the ability to think abstractly will be increasingly important across all professions (Greenspan 1999). Skills must be adaptable or flexible and updated through life-long learning ('self-programmable' workers). Gibbons in his World Bank paper (1998) summarises some of these skills as computer literacy, knowledge reconfiguration skills, information management, problem-solving in the context of application, team building, networking, negotiations/mediation competencies and social sensitivity. In terms of the latter, in modern democracies graduates will have to be able to deal with and manipulate different cultural symbols, operate in diverse social settings and develop complex notions of identity and citizenship. These skills and higher level understandings should not be taught in the abstract, but could be integrated into disciplinary knowledge – be it mathematics or fine art.

The South African labour market has in recent years undergone a major demand shift caused by changes in production methods and other structural adjustments. Following international trends, South Africa has undergone a massive shift in the relationship between capital and labour in production. The increasing capital intensity and the dramatic shift to micro-electronics in all sectors has resulted in a demand – which is growing by the year – for skilled professionals, technicians and managers who will develop, implement, operate and maintain the new technologies. Concurrently, this capital–technological change is displacing and replacing the unskilled and low skilled labourers, farm workers, production workers and basic service workers (Bhorat and Hodge 1999).

The South African economy is moving away from primary and manufacturing production towards a greater emphasis on output in the services sector.

The South African economy is moving away from primary and manufacturing production towards a greater emphasis on output in the services sector. The consequence of this has been a growth of at least five per cent per annum in skilled professional and managerial occupations over the past two decades. This has resulted in these categories increasing their share of total employment in South Africa from 4,7 per cent in 1970 to 15,2 per cent in 1997. It is estimated that their share will be 22 per cent by 2002. The only other occupational category to achieve remotely similar growth is the service-orientated sales and clerical group (Bhorat and Hodge 1999).

In a 1999 survey of 273 of South Africa's major employers, 76 per cent reported that they were experiencing a shortage of professional workers. This survey predicted that in the period 1998 to 2003 the job opportunities at this professional level would grow by between 16 per cent and 18 per cent, and that those for unskilled workers would decrease by around 35 per cent (Cloete and Bunting 2000). Aids will also have a negative effect on employment. According to a World Bank-sponsored investigation (Arndt and Lewis 2000) there are major differentials in skill-based infection rates, and given the current endowments in the economy (an abundance of unskilled labour and a shortage of skilled labour), the Aids epidemic will impact negatively on labour and capital. The combination of these factors poses a huge challenge to higher education to produce more graduates in a wide range of areas.

According to an international summary of the research evidence by Sadlak (1998) of Unesco, there is a clear correlation between the level of participation in higher education and economic development. For example, the participation rate in higher education in the United States is over 70 per cent. In the OECD it is 51 per cent, compared to 21 per cent for middle-income countries and six per cent for low-income countries. On a worldwide basis participation rates increased from around twelve per cent in 1980 to 16 per cent in 1995. While it could be argued that a high participation rate is a result of development, not a cause, Sadlak states that 'any society that does not give at least twelve per cent of the age group access to higher education does not have a chance to survive in the type of future that lies ahead'. In South Africa the participation rate, at least in public institutions, has slipped from around 17 per cent in 1993 to 15 per cent in 1999. A worrying aspect is that the estimated participation rate for African students is only twelve per cent. Unless substantially increased participation rate targets are achieved as one of the primary goals of higher education for the next 10 to 15 years, South Africa will face a productivity catastrophe due to inadequate high-level human resources (Cloete and Bunting 2000).

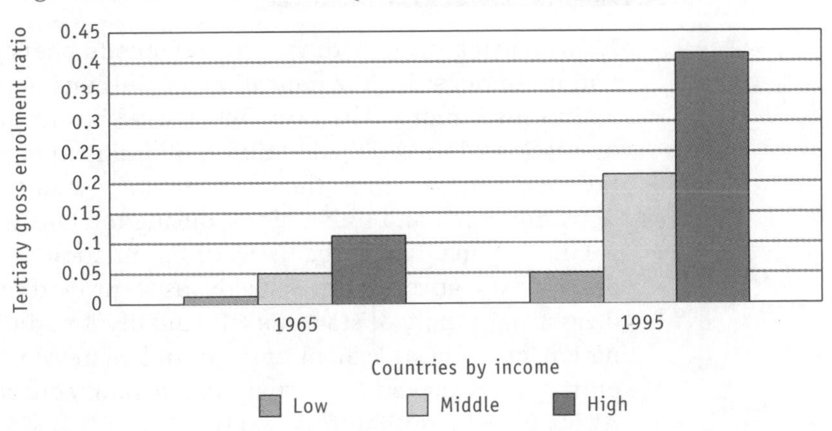

FIGURE 1: Relationship between participation rate and national income

Source: Task Force on Higher Education and Society 2000

Higher education seems to be facing two major challenges in this area. Firstly, it needs to increase its contribution to social and economic development by increasing the numbers of graduates with improved levels of cognitive skills throughout the system. Secondly, it needs to convince national government that high-level skills, the economy and Internet connectivity are connected and important. The system simply has to produce

The ultimate challenge for higher education is to influence and change the 'preglobalisation' thinking of the Departments of Finance and Labour and their policies which do not regard higher education as central to the country's development strategy.

more 'self-programmable' labour. In the next section the issues will be raised as to whether all institutions can produce 'self-programmable' labour.

The productivity section in the government's Growth, Employment and Redistribution policy does not refer to the knowledge economy, information society, Internet connectivity and its link to human resources. In contrast the whole notion of improving productivity is orientated towards a training scheme under the control of the Department of Labour and financed through a mandatory payroll skills levy. The underpinning of the report is on technical and vocational training and skills. A related problem is that after six years the Departments of Education and Labour have not yet produced an overall human resource development policy. The ultimate challenge for higher education is to influence and change the 'preglobalisation' thinking of the Departments of Finance and Labour and their policies which do not regard higher education as central to the country's development strategy.

Institutional restructuring

Restructuring deals with two simultaneous phenomena: differentiation amongst higher education institutions and reorganisation within institutions. The post-1994 period has resulted in the most dramatic and unanticipated differentiation amongst higher education institutions since the government established the racially 'separate homeland universities' during the late 1950s.

On the one hand, the new differentiation is attributed to a decrease in government subsidy as a proportion of income, a decreasing supply of students who qualify for admission (a combination of a failing school system and increasing costs) and the entry of private and international higher education into South Africa (Cloete and Bunting 2000).

On the other hand, from the argument developed in this paper, at the heart of this fragmenting system lies an interaction between knowledge capacity, connectivity, institutional resources and management capacity. These factors, within a context of a policy implementation vacuum, resulted first in intense competition amongst public institutions and second, but simultaneously, in competition between the public and the new private/international sectors.

From a system differentiated by race and ethnicity, a new institutional landscape shaped by market and globalisation effects is emerging. On the one end of the spectrum there are a number of emerging 'entrepreneurial' institutions that have been very successful in adopting market strategies to increase their student numbers. They have formed numerous partnerships, increased their contracts with industry and implemented cost-centre based accounting and planning throughout the institution (Cloete and Bunting 2000). The highest proportion of 'self-programmable' labour is concentrated in these institutions, and they are increasingly able to attract (or 'loot') people with these skills from other institutions.

On the other end of the spectrum there are a number of institutions, about 25 per cent of the system, that are experiencing serious financial problems, mainly due to a drop in student numbers, chronic management problems and a lack of capacity to respond to new opportunities. These institutions, instead of differentiating, are becoming more homogeneous in their marginalisation. These institutions, almost all black, have been characterised as 'unstable' or 'crisis-ridden', and in a number of cases the government has had to appoint external administrators and assessors for crisis management (Cloete and Bunting 2000). It is in these institutions that there is a high percentage of 'generic academic labour'.

Private higher education has proliferated in South Africa since the new Constitution declared private education a right. In 1999 the Department of Education issued an instruction requiring institutions to register; 300 applied and 65 received provisional registration. Presumably the rest do not satisfy quality criteria or are offering qualifications in post-school rather than higher education. According to an official from the Department of Education, the private institution landscape is 'a kaleidoscope ranging from almost full-time contact provision to very distant; some with courses mostly in higher education and others with courses mostly in further education'.

Estimations about the actual number of higher education students in this private sector range from about 15 000 to 115 000. If the unknown number of international Internet degree offerings were to be added, then it becomes clear that South African students have never had such a wide choice, or such a confusing proliferation, of course offerings. The landscape is not like a higher education supermarket, but more like one of the new South African huge shopping malls: a mixture of niche market boutiques (Armani-style), large supermarkets, small home-industry shops and a number of mobile pavement vendors. Competition is thus not only between public and private higher education – school-leavers have an array of post-school courses with all kinds of claims to international recognition and job opportunities never before offered in South Africa.

... South African students have never had such a wide choice, or such a confusing proliferation, of course offerings.

The differentiation and competition is not only amongst institutions, but also within institutions. The salary gap between the management with market-related packages and the professoriate seems to have widened significantly over the past few years – from a ratio of about 2:1 during the early 1990s to a ratio of 4:1 in the late 1990s (Naidu 2000). At the bottom end, the salaries and numbers of service workers seem to have declined in relative terms, particularly if outsourcing is taken into consideration. Some of the institutions have also introduced the notion of 'super-professors' who are offered substantially larger packages than their colleagues. Added to this is the increase in proportion of contract staff and temporary employees who are often exploited. The allocation of resources within the institution is differentiated into core and non-core activities, and some institutions are setting cost centres similar to those in corporations as a strategy to increase efficiency. The marketisation of higher education has penetrated the employment conditions and campus relationships, resulting in a profound change since the 1980s 'unity in opposition' to apartheid between workers, students and progressive academics. The individualisation of the academic workforce is at its highest in institutions which are the most involved in globalising. At the other end of the spectrum, unity in opposition has also dissolved, into fractious fights over decreasing resources (Nhlapo 2000).

The individualisation of the academic workforce is at its highest in institutions which are the most involved in globalising.

The development of such divergence and inequalities in the system poses a number of challenges. Firstly, will government put together a rescue plan for the faltering public institutions, and will the justification be redress, or the need to increase participation rates, or because it is very important to defend and build institutions in Africa? Secondly, entrepreneurialism has certainly led to increases in efficiency and provided access to previously excluded students. However, it is not an unqualified 'good' – in the previous section we referred to the Minister of Education putting an embargo on partnerships that do not ensure adequate quality. The jury is still out as to whether entrepreneurialism will undermine scholarship or not. Thirdly, should public institutions become like private institutions in order to compete, or should they have clearly differentiated missions? Fourthly, such vast institutional differentiation is going to require major policy differentiation, implying that new government policy will have to deal differentially with clusters of institutions. Finally, can a sense of 'campus community' be regained, or is it a notion that has no currency in a globalising (and individualising) higher education system?

Contradictory and/or complementary challenges

Higher education seems to be confronted with what could be perceived to be three sets of competing or contradictory demands.

- Firstly, the 'scholarisation' of the general population has to be improved, demanding a sustained focus on teacher education and school improvement.
- Secondly, at the lower end of the high skills band much larger numbers of students must be better educated in terms of the use of technology, problem-solving and social skills. This layer forms the backbone of the new technology and social service occupations associated with globalisation; be it as data processors or tour guides.
- Thirdly, at the high end of the high skills band more knowledge-producing and managing skills are required for global competitiveness.

To address challenges at all three levels the use of ICTs must be vastly expanded. Many institutions must be reorganised to promote, rather than obstruct, ICT expansion and innovation. To repeat: according to Castells, the central ingredients of the knowledge economy are knowledge, technological infrastructure (connectivity), human resources and institutions.

A differentiated system with differentiated policies is required to respond to these sets of demands. This may need a serious rethink, if not an abandonment, of a central policy principle of the 1997 White Paper on higher education, namely to develop a 'single co-ordinated system'. The policy was aimed at addressing differentiation based on two types of missions and historical racial differentiation. A new differentiation policy will formalise and assist institutional restructuring by providing a framework, guidelines and regulations. Differentiated institutions will be better positioned to address issues that cut across institutional types and racial differentiation to address new challenges as outlined in this paper, especially the three focus areas above.

A new system will have to be quite different from the more common undifferentiated, essentially elite Third World, and particularly African, higher education systems described by Castells in the first chapter of this section. A recent report by an advisory body to the Minister of Education tried to grapple with this problem by proposing a plan to create a three-tier system consisting of 'bedrock' institutions, mid-level (mainly master's degree-granting institutions) and comprehensive research and postgraduate institutions (Council on Higher Education 2000).

This bold proposal has met with little enthusiasm and considerable opposition from university leadership (Kotecha 2000). Firstly, the rigid differentiation ('hard boundaries') between institutional types means that institutions will be locked into a hierarchy which in South Africa will have considerable equity overtones – the historically black institutions will almost without exception be in the bedrock category. Secondly, the proposals do not provide a development rationale for the differentiated functions which can motivate institutions to develop new missions to address new challenges raised throughout this paper. Thirdly, the report hardly makes any reference to the provision of the technological and institutional capacity required to make a new system work. The result has been that many of the debates, and opposition, have been driven by arguments over institutional boundaries and by self-interest.

If the basis of the Council on Higher Education (CHE) proposal is to address the functional labour market and knowledge differentiation as outlined above, through sets of institutions that themselves have different knowledge and institutional capacities, then the differentiation (or more correctly, stratification) is theoretically correct. But it is politically flawed within the South Africa racialised context and contrary to global trends which are towards softer and more permeable boundaries.

While the focus of the CHE report is institutional differentiation, the real issue is policy differentiation. Policy differentiation is a major challenge for the government, because clusters or groups of institutions are going to require different policy and resource responses. Policy differentiation means that certain targeted policies are developed for specific periods, say five years, in order to achieve targeted effects. Targeted policies for specific periods of time are more likely to receive external financial support.

The globalising, highly differentiating, institutional cluster needs to be influenced through a high degree of incentives. If government provides these institutions mainly with block grants, they will increasingly respond to local and international market incentives that will make them drift further out of the nation-state, exactly at the moment that the nation state needs them.

On the other end of the institutional landscape, targeted institution building and knowledge capacity development support is required to enable some of the barely functioning institutions firstly to function, and secondly, to fulfil their important task in the first two bands of skill provision listed above. A five-year institution infrastructure-building project for a limited number of institutions, based on well-defined criteria, will be essential to ensure that some staff from these institutions are at least minimally able to participate in cutting-edge nodes. One of the better administered institutions in the country, the University of Cape Town, recently received such a type of grant from an international foundation to business re-engineer all their administrative procedures and technologies.

Another challenge for policy differentiation is the need that Castells raises for 'focus' or specialised institutions, and incentives, with strict accountability criteria, for cross-institutional networks in specific areas of competence and relevance. To develop some institutions, particularly one or two historically black technikons or universities, into successful technological institutions will require more than stimulating cross-institutional nodes of excellence that are part of global networks. The advantage of this is that in addition to being responsive to development needs, the upgrading of a few historically disadvantaged institutions will be a new mode of redress and will buy enormous legitimacy, which as Castells shows, is a central problem for globalising states. Also, if this does not happen, then as Castells tells us, inequality and polarisation will increase, meaning the top and the bottom will continue to separate at an accelerated pace.

Providing incentives for nodes of excellence has a double positive: it connects South African academics into the global networks and it crosses institutional boundaries.

Providing incentives for nodes of excellence has a double positive: it connects South African academics into the global networks and it crosses institutional boundaries. Policy and financial support for groupings, or consortia, can also be generalised to distance education. The proposal by the CHE (2000) for the consolidation of distance education into a single behemoth is exactly contrary to the trend towards multiple institutions in partnerships with information technology companies delivering different modes of distance education efficiently. If it is assumed that higher education cannot command a greater share of the budget, then the trade-off for greater amounts of incentive funding will require political will to close institutions which are not sustainable, and/or the strategic incorporation of some disadvantaged institutions into advantaged institutions in order to ensure a greater sharing of capacities.

Policy differentiation does not only deal with the approach of the Department of Education, but also how policies by other departments such as Trade and Industry and the national research foundations are co-ordinated around focus areas. The same applies to the numerous fragmented, mainly small, international aid agency grants which often require enormous administrative effort for modest amounts. Until government provides clear focus areas, these agencies will continue to hand out grants on the basis of their own agendas. A survey by Moja (2000) on aid in higher education in Africa in the last decade shows remarkably little demonstrable impact through multiple, one-off, small grants.

Policy differentiation also requires flows from different directions, such as the bandwith example cited earlier, and from a number of agencies such as parastatals, non-governmental organisations and consortia. The aim is to develop a web of policy actors and agencies flexibly operating in a dynamic higher education environment. This flexible, multiple-actor, targeted policy for fixed periods is exactly the opposite to a national formula-driven system trying to fix institutions into hierarchical types, resulting in the main preoccupation becoming opposition to the boundaries, rather than responding to the challenges.

An excellent example of a differentiated policy intervention in the Castellian sense, which consisted of special funding for teacher education and for high skills innovation and partnerships, is the very successful state-led reforms of the early 1990s in Finland. Amongst other things, these pulled Finland out of a severe economic crisis and contributed directly to Nokiafication (Hölttä and Malkki 2000). For South Africa, implementing the 'obvious' is much more complicated. Since 1997, when the government White Paper proclaimed the need for flexible programmes, rather than institutional differentiation, a policy implementation vacuum has developed (Cloete and Bunting 2000).

... globalisation tends to weaken the state at the very moment more state steering is required to achieve reforms and increase competitiveness.

An easy explanation for the lack of implementation is that the new post-1994 national bureaucracy and the weaker institutions do not have the planning and financial capacity for a modern steering system. More complex is that globalisation tends to weaken the state at the very moment more state steering is required to achieve reforms and increase competitiveness. The contradiction is that on the one hand, the nation-state is expected to create the conditions for economic and social development, predominantly through investing more in education and particularly in knowledge, which is the most prized commodity in the global economy. On the other hand, globalisation introduces pressures to reduce the role and contribution of central government to education, with less steering from the top (Carnoy 1999).

A complicating factor is that globalisation increases the pay-off to high-level skills relative to lower level skills, thus reducing the complementarity between equity- and competitiveness-driven reforms (Carnoy 1999). Taking increasing inequality together with the fact that the national government's capacity to steer from the top is weakened, the South African resistance to new hard boundaries between institutions is not difficult to understand.

Another apparent contradiction of globalisation is that while it 'weakens' the state, it also expects, and demands, efficient state apparatuses with well-developed civil societies that provide growing markets, stable political conditions and steady public investment in human capital (Carnoy 1999). It seems that a distinction has to be made between a state that is weakened in terms of regulating its macroeconomic policy, in setting its priorities and the level of its currency, versus an efficient state that can operate according to modern management principles. It is this reorganising of the operations of the state bureaucracy that is a huge challenge: how to become more modern, with information technology-based management systems, within a context of decreasing resources for the state – in other words, how to become a 'networked state' (see Carnoy in Section One Chapter 2 of this volume) that can steer strategically. If this does not happen, then the gap between the networked institutions and the others will grow, and the system will become differentiated along status, rather than functional, lines or boundaries.

While globalisation demands a greater role for the market, internationally the jury is out on what exactly is a good balance between private and public provision in higher education. In most countries the public/private balance developed much more as a result of a lack of provision by public institutions than due to government policy. In certain countries, such as Chile and Portugal, the private sector was stimulated as part of government policy in order to improve participation. Currently South Africa seems to be following another model, more like Kenya and Brazil, where the expansion of private higher education is due to a failure of delivery by the public system, and then all the government can do is try and impose weak and inconsistent controls. A priority for South Africa is to gain greater clarity on a constructive role for private higher education, while controlling the 'fly-by-nights'.

In conclusion, at the same time that international boundaries are both breaking down and being redrawn, with serious consequences for higher education in the Third World, within South Africa major contestations are raging about the boundaries between institutions within the public system, and between public and private higher education. At this 'scrambled' moment of disappearing, emerging and possibly hardening boundaries, it is difficult to tell which changes are contradictory and which could become complementary.

References

Adelman, C (2000) 'A parallel universe – certification in the Information Age', *Change*, May/June.

Arndt, C and J Lewis (2000) *The Macro Implications of HIV/Aids in South Africa*. Trade and Industrial Policy Secretariat, Annual Forum.

Bhorat, H and J Hodge (1999) 'Decomposing shifts in labour demands in South Africa', *South African Journal of Economics*, 67: 3.

Bouchard, N (2000) *Distance Education at Traditionally Contact Higher Education Institutions*. Report for the Council on Higher Education. (email: info@saide.org.za)

Carnoy, M (1998) *Globalisation, Higher Education, High Level Training and National Development*. Report on a Joint CHET and HSRC Seminar. Website: http://www.chet.org.za.debates.html

Carnoy, M (1999) *Globalisation and Educational Reform: What Planners Need to Know*. Paris: Unesco, IIEP.

Castells, M (1998) *The Information Age: Economy, Society and Culture. Volume 3: End of Millennium*. Oxford: Blackwell.

Cloete, N and I Bunting (2000) *Higher Education Transformation: Assessing Performance in South Africa*. Pretoria: Centre for Higher Education Transformation.

Cloete, N (2000) 'Increased government support for higher education: report for the Council on Higher Education.' Website: http://www.chet.org.za/publdebates.html

Council on Higher Education (2000) *Towards a New Higher Education Landscape: Size and Shape Report*. Pretoria: Council on Higher Education.

Department of Education (1997) *White Paper 3: A Programme for the Transformation of Higher Education*. Pretoria: Department of Education.

Drucker, P (1999) in Werner Z Hirsch and Luc E Weber (eds) *Challenges Facing Higher Education at the Millennium*. Paris: IAU Press.

Gibbons, M (1998) *Higher Education Relevance in the 21st Century*. Washington: World Bank.

Greenspan, A (1999) *The Interaction of Education and Economic Change*. Washington: American Council on Education.

Hölttä, S and P Malkki (2000) *Response of Finnish Higher Education Institutions to the National Information Society Programme*. Helsinki: Helsinki University of Technology and International Relations.

Kotecha, P (2000) South African Vice-Chancellors Association's Response to the Council on Higher Education Report: *Towards a New Higher Education Landscape: Meeting the Equity, Quality and Social Development Imperatives of South Africa in the 21st Century*. Pretoria.

Kulati, T (2000) 'Globalisation and internationalisation: some South African experiences.' Website: http://www.chet.org.za/debates/sanlameer_index.html

Leatt, J (2000) Personal communication. Cape Town: Adamastor Trust.

Levine, A (2000) *Chronicle of Higher Education,* 27 October. Website: http://chronicle.com

Moja, T (2000) 'A review of the Ford Foundation's impact on higher education in Africa.' Paper commissioned by the Ford Foundation, New York.

Mouton, J and N Boshoff (2000) 'Science in transition.' Unpublished report. Stellenbosch: University of Stellenbosch.

Naidu, E (2000) 'Varsity heads raking in the cash', *The Star,* 12 August.

National Commission on Higher Education (1996) *A Framework for Transformation.* Pretoria. Website: http://www.hsrc.ac.za/nche.html

Newman, F (2000) *Policy for Higher Education in a Changing World.* Brown University: The Futures Project.

Nhlapo, T (2000) Investigation into the affairs of the University of the North by the independent assessor appointed by the Minister of Education in terms of chapter 6 of the Higher Education Act, No 101 of 1997. Pretoria: Department of Education.

Sadlak, J (1998) 'Globalisation and concurrent challenges for higher education', in P Scott (ed.) *The Globalisation of Higher Education.* The Society for Research in Higher Education and Open University Press.

Scott, P (2000) 'Globalisation and the university: challenges for the twenty-first century.' Website: http://www.chet.org.za/debates/scott.html

Selingo, J (2000) *Chronicle of Higher Education,* 26 October. Website: http://chronicle.com

Swartzman, S (2000) 'Globalisation and higher education in Brazil.' Website: http://www.chet.org.za/debates/SanLameer/Schwartzman.html

Task Force on Higher Education and Society (2000) *Higher Education in Developing Countries: Peril and Promise.* Washington: World Bank.

Young, J (1999) 'Rising demand for distance learning will challenge providers, experts say.' A report from the conference 'Asynchronous Learning Networks', *Chronicle of Higher Education,* 11 October.

Teboho Moja is Professor of Education at New York University. She is a member of the Board of the International Institute of Education Planning in Paris. She was special advisor to South Africa's previous Minister of Education and was the CEO of the National Commission on Higher Education (NCHE) which provided the policy framework for the government's White Paper on higher education.

Nico Cloete is the Director of the Centre for Higher Education Transformation. He was previously Research Director for the NCHE and co-ordinator of the Post Secondary Education Report of the National Education Policy Investigation and the Policy Forum of the Union of Democratic University Staff Associations. He has worked at a number of South African universities, including the University of the North, University of Transkei and University of the Witwatersrand. He has published widely in the fields of psychology, sociology and education.

johan muller

Concluding comments: Connectivity, capacity and knowledge

The chapters printed in this volume stand on their own recognizances. They make their points robustly, they defend them passionately. What follows is not a commentary on them in the sense of a measured evaluation. Rather, it is a set of observations, drawing together some loose threads, and an attempt to make just a bit more sense of a man and an *œuvre* that, for a brief intense period in 2000, touched a considerable number of people and contextualised their thoughts in a common framework of debate around the central issue in social and economic life today.

Through Third World eyes

The engagements with Manuel Castells and Martin Carnoy, and the resulting chapters in this volume, are products of a particular discursive geography. First of all, each seminar took place in a different metropolitan centre, and was provided with a relatively discrete topic for discussion – economic globalisation for the first, identity for the second, and regional development for the third. Though the fit was imperfect, this meant that the discussants at the first seminar read mainly Volume 1, at the second Volume 2, and at the third Volume 3 of the Castells trilogy (leading at least one discussant to complain that he had been given the wrong book to read!). This carving up of the informationalist thesis – the 'one thread' linking up all the rest – led at times to a rather single-minded approach by the participants. Secondly, and perhaps more crucially, each seminar had a discrete set of participants: only a small core group from the secretariat travelled with the visitors. Taken together with the first point, this meant that, a few of the academic participants perhaps excepted, most participants would have had a limited acquaintanceship with the works of Castells and Carnoy, and were exposed to one facet of the golden braid only: very few, perhaps none, had read the entire trilogy and were thus *au fait* with the whole picture. Commentary therefore came from a relatively narrow and, it has to be said, sometimes self-interested base. To be fair, this was also partly due to the ambitions of the seminar organisers who wished to include as full a mix of socially relevant 'intellectuals' as possible – national politicians, technical advisors, trade unionists and business persons, amongst others – many of whom were hearing the names and ideas of Castells and Carnoy for the first time. The discussions were distinctly shaped by this configuration.

If this accounted for a certain lack of continuity in the discussions, several factors marked the participants as speaking from a broadly common perspective. The most distinctive factor was undoubtedly a political and politicist slant. Castells is well aware that a relatively high level of politicisation of discourse, of intellectual culture, and therefore also of the universities, is to be expected in newly democratic countries like South Africa, placing a heavy burden on the 'ideological' function (of universities, see Section Four Chapter 1 in this volume). This is only to be expected. But at least in the case of the universities, and by implication elsewhere too, he warns, this should not be allowed to 'smother' the efficient operation of the increasingly important 'scientific' function which exists in a contradictory relation to it, a contradiction that every society must carefully manage. In other words, as Castells put it at the outset of the Gauteng seminar, the analytical must be distinguished from the ideological and given its proper weight. On the evidence of these seminars, that point currently falls on deaf ears.

... the analytical must be distinguished from the ideological and given its proper weight.

A high level of politicisation and a relative neglect of analytical niceties in the discursive repertoires of the South Africans was evident throughout the seminar series. Participants constantly wanted to know 'what could be done' about globalisation. In the way the questions were put, it was clear the discussants were more interested in discussing plans of action (ubiquitously called 'policy') than they were in understanding the analytical diagnosis of the phenomenon at hand. Indeed, often in the same gesture, the discussants could be heard to scoff at, play down or even dismiss the existence of globalisation: globalisation was not nearly as serious a phenomenon as global elites were making it out to be – but what were we going to do about it anyway? This is only contradictory until one considers both views as part of the same framework of politicisation, in which globalisation, politicised, is seen as something of a political trick perpetrated by the agents of global capital on poor unsuspecting nations. The question 'What is to be done?' then really means, 'How are we going to combat this new trick of the ruling classes called globalisation?' From an ideological rather than an analytical perspective, this is an entirely legitimate question, but a question to which Castells, naturally enough, has no analytical answer, or rather he has a stock, calculatedly shocking, answer:

> What is to be done? Each time an intellectual has tried to answer this question, and seriously implement the answer, catastrophe has ensued. This was particularly the case with a certain Ulianov in 1902. Thus, while not pretending to qualify for this comparison, I shall abstain from suggesting any cure for the ills of our world. (Castells 1998: 378)

He does though have an analytical position on it, which is that people (and by extension countries) will always formulate innovative ways to deal with the abrasions of the new structural contradictions spanning their lives, ways rooted in their particular histories of culture, struggle and solidarity, and therefore by definition not amenable to advice: 'if there is one statement that may qualify as a social law, it is that, in any society, at any time, where there is domination, there is resistance to domination – we just have to find it' (Castells 1998: 477). Patel's discussion in this volume (Section One Chapter 7) provides a fascinating discussion of the innovative responses of the international labour movement to an analytical understanding of the problem of globalisation for international labour.

Other participants found the point difficult to grasp: if Castells and Carnoy couldn't give a political answer to what was so manifestly a political problem, then what good were they? Yet this is really to miss the distinctiveness of Castells' contribution, which is to provide a coherent framework of analysis to the emergent development regime of informationalism. Castells has been heard to lament the fact that even in scholarly contexts he has found discussants reluctant to engage with the analytical logic of his explanatory framework, preferring to deal with their more proximate anxieties about globalisation. The problem seemed particularly acute in these seminars. Kraak's anxiety (in Section One Chapter 8 of this volume), for example, is such that he has Castells 'changing his mind' about offering advice. Unfortunately for Kraak, this 'advice' refers to Castells' 'Technological Marshall Plan', an idea present in his writings from the early 1990s and presented to the United Nations just prior to his visit to South Africa (see Castells in Section Three Chapter 1 of this volume). What Kraak misses is that Castells, here as elsewhere, consistently restricts himself to outlining the conditions, as his comparative analysis suggests them, necessary for propitious development under informationalism. Even here, Castells doesn't tell individual countries what to do ('there is no universal solution', [Castells 1998: 482]). He merely suggests that the United Nations assists with putting in place the necessary technological essentials. All the national hard work has still to be done. The Technological Marshall Plan, then, is not the policy solution to the globalisation conundrum that many take it to be, nor is re-arranging the Bretton Woods architecture for that matter. These are disposing conditions, not causal factors, for developmental success.

Directly related to the discursive politicisation was a persistent anxiety regarding the future of the state. For social actors like the unions, and government intellectuals like Netshitenzhe (see Section One Chapter 6 of this volume), it was understandable that the social-democratic strong developmental state model was still the favoured one, and that any suggestion about the 'diminution' of the role of the state would be unpalatable. But many of the academics at the seminars seemed to kick against the evidence that the role of states as national political-economic actors simply had to change (see Kraak, Section One Chapter 8 of this volume). Indeed, if anything united the South Africans against the globalisation narrative, it was the forecasted contraction of the nation-state. (This did not necessarily include the other Third Worlders: Visvanathan was determinedly localist, opposing both the state and science as centralising and totalising agents; and Soludo looked not to the state alone but to restructured multilateral agencies for Africa's succour.) It is noticeable then that many of the responses in this volume accord the state a central role: Gelb in macroeconomic policy; Moja and Cloete in higher education policy; and Alexander in national identity. But these could be seen to differ markedly, from those that persisted in thinking of the state as something of a unified actor (in the old nation-state mode), and those who, like Gelb, understood the state's new productive resource to lie with what he called 'infrastructural' power (or institutional capacity) rather than with 'coercive' or sovereign power. This does not mean that the state no longer has to lead. It means that it will have to lead in a different way. Despite Gelb's show of disagreement, this is, in different words, the argument of Castells and Carnoy, although the state's leadership for Castells has not only to do with 'static' macroeconomic and monetary policy, but also with the more 'dynamic' role of generating conditions for productivity, competitiveness and redistribution (see Volume 1 of his trilogy).

There is a form of response to the Castellian narrative that comes from Third World cosmopolitan intellectuals that requires comment. This kind of discourse assumes that it is sufficient simply to challenge or refute. To denounce.[1] The Castellian analysis of the prospects of Africa and other unplugged parts of the Third World derives from analytical postulates and a plethora of admittedly dismal statistics. But to such commentators, it appears nothing more than a capricious judgement on the moral purpose of these nations, an insult that demands repudiation. These rebuttals have to them a polemical edge, as if to say, 'How dare Castells arrive at such a conclusion? Who is he to write off Africa, or the Third World?'

Castells is identified with his conclusions, as if saying that Africa was unplugged reflected his wish, not his analysis or results.

There is here usually no logical argument or empirical counter-demonstration of Castells' analysis. Rebuttal laced with moral outrage is deemed sufficient to the purpose. Further, Castells is identified with his conclusions, as if saying that Africa was unplugged reflected his wish, not his analysis or results. On the one hand this is a peculiar view of what hard sociological work is all about. On the other, it seems to mimic on the discursive plane the primary gesture of resistance identity; or in Castells' pithy aphorism, 'the exclusion of the excluders by the excluded' (1998: 374). Now, to say this about such a commentary is to invite an enraged response, and Visvanathan at the seminar made the riposte, 'I don't just want to be an excluded voice (that is, a resistance identity),' and 'If yours [Castells'] is a science, so is mine ...' But what are the propositions of such a science? The analytical arguments? The empirical demonstration? They are not forthcoming. Castells responds to such charges with some restraint: 'I'm not someone trying to propose anything. I don't have a position ... My aim,' he says, 'is to present empirical research and academic research as rigorously as possible ... to present as good knowledge as possible.' The trilogy, in other words, identifies a research programme, formulates a set of analytical propositions and sets out empirically to illustrate or refine them. For the denouncers, this counts for little.

On the other hand, Visvanathan's chapter displays a virtue that is absent from the South African responses. He tries at least to tackle what he takes to be Castells' 'grand narrative', the central structure of his sociological account. Given the scope of Castells' analysis, this is no mean feat. As the Introduction remarked, at the heart of Castells' account is a thesis about the conditions for successful development under informationalism. These conditions are simultaneously economic, political and cultural. With the first seminar devoted to the economy, the second to identity, the third to technology and development, it is perhaps unfair to judge that South Africans did not grasp the golden thread of Castells' work. But it must be admitted that in both public and academic debate, South Africans struggle to come to terms with changes to the overall logic of development. Opposition to the Growth, Employment and Redistribution (Gear) programme is perhaps the most prominent feature of public debate, but Gear is primarily concerned with what Castells calls the 'statics' of macroeconomic policy. Consequently, Gelb's chapter on the economy sticks to macroeconomics, and the chapters on technology and development hardly engage with Castells' development thesis. To do this requires an integrated discussion of issues of technology, knowledge, learning and identity, together with those of politics and economy. It is not surprising, then, that there was no serious South African challenge to Castells' overall thesis. That is also beyond the scope of this chapter. The rest of this concluding overview will at least attempt to clarify some key aspects of the discussion which, in my view, became entangled in misunderstandings that were not fully resolved in the seminars.

What is knowledge/ information?

Central to the 'informational society' proposition must lie a notion of information or knowledge. But which notion? In the conversational to-and-fro, it was sometimes hard to tell. Broadly speaking, one can say that there are two fundamentally different approaches to the sociological analysis of knowledge. The first derives from political economy and treats knowledge as a form of property or capital. The second derives from political theory and treats knowledge as intimately linked to power or sovereignty. In the first case, knowledge is seen as a productive asset; in the second, knowledge is linked to interest and domination. On the one hand then, knowledge as cultural capital; on the other, power/knowledge.

It should be clear by now that Castells writes in a political economy tradition, and his notion of 'knowledge' is a cultural capital one.[2] If one considers Bourdieu's (1986) three kinds of cultural capital, then Castells' is one of incorporated cultural capital, an embodied asset usually but not always acquired via formal education. The second tradition is likely to regard acquired formal education as a 'credential', as institutionalised cultural capital, which, in Randall Collins' (1979) account, is used as an instrument of closure and monopoly. We have thus two quite different senses here of formal education, the first productive, the second exploitative. Castells and Carnoy treat knowledge, as I have said, as a directly productive force, and also as an indubitably positive asset.

This doesn't mean that it can't be used for nefarious purposes, but in this it is no different from any other kind of asset. As Pels says, 'Credentials are not simply understood as artificial goods or relatively arbitrary entry tickets to large organisations, but also as social consecrations of real properties which do have independent social effects' (Pels 1998: 210).

This approach to knowledge is borrowed from Daniel Bell (1976), who has been criticised for being functionalist and technical (see Visvanathan in Section One Chapter 3 of this volume, for example), which is to say, in such an approach, skill is 'black-boxed' so that questions of power and monopolistic closure cannot easily arise (see Stehr 1994; Pels 1998). In some versions of conflict theory, on the other hand, skill is taken to be a power instrument only, wielded always for the sake of sectional interest, by closure, monopoly or domination. Here skill and knowledge serve merely as proxies for power. But neither of these adequately reflects Castells' position. As we might expect from his culturalist affinities, not to mention his Poulantzian (1980) sympathies, Castells has no trouble in accommodating a view of knowledge as both status–cultural as well as technical–functional. There is no reason why we cannot treat skills as both economically productive and potentially exclusionary:

Castells has no trouble in accommodating a view of knowledge as both status–cultural as well as technical–functional.

> The heart of the matter is not so much the predominance of the power-interested or 'exploitative' side over the functional or 'productive' side, but the duality of functional necessity and dispositional interests, i.e., the intrinsic entanglement or inseparability of 'good' and 'bad' dimensions. (Pels 1998: 220)

In other words, although coming from a political economy background with an inclination to treat knowledge as a technical asset, Castells' analysis is not incompatible with power/knowledge approaches – except with those radical constructivist and postmodern views of knowledge as exclusively sectarian and monopolistic, about which, as Castells says in Section Four Chapter 1 above, the less said the better.

Given South Africa's apartheid past, it should not be surprising that power/knowledge is more common in local social analysis than notions of knowledge as cultural capital. It was noticeable how frequently misunderstandings arose in the discussions with Castells as his interlocutors persistently tried to read Castells' idea of knowledge through a power/knowledge lens. The pervasive suspicions of knowledge and expertise in popular and political talk in South Africa, it has to be admitted, sometimes verge on anti-intellectualism. It should hardly need saying that this is not the way to grasp the importance of knowledge-based information under informationalism, nor to appreciate the increasingly important role of education in providing knowledge-based skills. As knowledge becomes the primary productive asset, the old dichotomies of the division of labour collapse, and all workers now spread out along a gradient of knowledge possession. Knowledge becomes the key marker of class, and it is a marker that can change as educative opportunities present themselves. This means that the state has an unprecedented opportunity to improve the lot of the disadvantaged by making quality education progressively more available. And it must do so, as Carnoy says, by reducing the selectivity of formal education. Quality schooling becomes, more than ever before, a matter of social justice. Commenting at the end of the Gauteng seminar, Carnoy said:

> [Castells' analysis] should be taken extremely seriously by policy-makers, extremely seriously; [they should] not put [their] heads in the sand and say, 'No, we're a specific case, we don't belong to this, we're in a different situation.' No. I think the message is, everybody is in a different position but in the same situation.

Yet politicians are slow to grasp the fundamental lesson here. On hearing that South African Grade Eight pupils had once again come last in the recently published TIMSS survey results (Howie 2001), Minister of Education Asmal's only reported comment was that 'it [is] problematic to compare across education systems' (*Business Day*, 7 December 2000). Such defensiveness is, at the very least, dispiriting.

Societal learning

> Why is it so hard to change the world? The answer would be: because societies don't like to learn. They would rather stick to what they know and to the rules that stabilise what they know.
> (Eder 1999: 209)

Both Castells and Carnoy have repeatedly said that the only way to properly exploit the new mode of development of network society is to prioritise the two developmental fundamentals, namely human resources and communications technology. In this connection, the term 'learning to learn' repeatedly crops up. The tiresome invocations of management gurus aside for the moment, what does 'learning to learn' really mean, and what is its connection to communications technology?

In an illuminating paper on how societies learn, Klaus Eder (1999) distinguishes between two kinds of learning. 'Substantive' learning is learning of established knowledge, or learning how to invent new knowledge within the parameters of socially accepted rules and well-accepted institutional arrangements. 'Rule learning' is learning to participate in changing the rules and institutional arrangements by which knowledge is produced, organised, stored, communicated – in a word, changing the arrangements by which knowledge is (re)stabilised. The distinction is akin to Kuhn's (1970) between normal and abnormal science – in Eder's terms, Kuhn is describing the oscillation between two different forms of learning within a particular scientific 'community of discourse' (where normal = substantive and abnormal = rule-based). This societal level Eder calls 'interpersonal' because it occurs within a community of peers rather than strangers. He distinguishes also two other levels where rule learning can replace substantive learning, namely the 'organisational' (where the organisation – the firm, for example – learns that 'exploration is better than exploitation' (Eder 1999: 206); and the 'institutional', where for example the most encompassing institutional order, the public sphere, can re-institutionalise the experience of a society (the Truth Commission, for example, helped to familiarise South Africans with human rights culture).

All societies are capable of both kinds of learning. But clearly some societies lean more to substantive learning, others toward rule learning, which is what Castells and Carnoy mean by 'learning to learn'. What predisposes a society to one or the other? For Eder, growing social uncertainty provides the irritant that spurs a society to the collective evolutionary realisation that 'choices within rules are no longer sufficient. New rules have to be chosen' (1999: 208). For Castells, the new communications technologies enormously expand the possibilities for enhancing the 'rules for inventive work' (Eder 1999: 206), and so act more as an incentive than the potentially punitive threat of uncertainty. The possibilities are there and must needs be grasped. But in both cases, there is still something missing: what predisposes a society to see uncertainty as risk, new technology as productive opportunity? When, how and why does a society knowingly grasp the nettle of 'learning to learn', and therefore institutionalise it in the learning routines of society at large? The answer is that for a society to be a learning society, it must first be an educated society.

Europe remains the paradigm case of a society that both perceives increasing uncertainty as burgeoning risk, and the new technologies as exploitable opportunities. Africa, equally clearly, doesn't. South Africa seems to be spending a long time teetering on the fence. When economists quote seemingly insulting statistics – for example, that in 1965 the American state of Illinois had a gross domestic product greater than that of the whole African continent (Judt 2000: 67) – they mean in part to express the consequence of failing to exploit these opportunities. Nor is this failure only a failure of state or governmental will; it is a dual *failure of capacity*: neither the communications technology is there to exploit, nor is the capacity in the labour force, because of poor formal educational opportunities, there to exploit it, were it in fact available to be exploited. Learning to learn is thus fatally stymied because of the generally low level of education of the populace as well as of the technical base of the country.

So to return to the site of a potential misunderstanding between economists and educationists, it should be plainly said that when economists refer to 'learning to learn' they are in the first place referring to institutional practices of knowledge stabilisation, not to individual skills that individuals may or may not possess, although this is by no means unrelated. Learning to learn is not in the first place a prescription for curriculum experimentation (as the South African authorities with their Curriculum 2005 arguably thought it was). Nor is it some kind of achievable skill platform from which individuals can launch endless forays into 'lifelong learning'. *Learning to learn is an institutional capacity and inclination to respond to both inducements and threats by improving the social base for knowledge growth and its stabilisation.* Communications technology has drastically enhanced the speed and efficiency of this capacity. And as communications technology keeps improving, as it most assuredly will in informational society, it means the capacity to keep on improving it accordingly; learning to learn must become a recursively embedded feature of social arrangements. Of course, the necessary condition to turn 'learning to learn' to productive account lies indeed in raising the aggregate level of skills in a society, by formal as well as other means. And here there are no mysteries, no progressive tricks, no cognitive short cuts. There may well be technological short cuts; in fact, Castells' wager is that there must be, because normal business-as-usual improvements in the substantive learning apparatus will simply take too long without making use of the accelerated conduits of the network society. What works for commerce will work for education. For this reason his proposal to shortcut the longer term process of upgrading the teacher knowledge base by using communications technology is not so much a pedagogical nicety as a desperate measure, a logical and necessary string to a nation's leap-frogging bow. Cultural or fundamentalist railing against globalisation and its technological paraphernalia, no matter how nicely it might play to the people at

... as communications technology keeps improving ... it means the capacity to keep on improving it accordingly; learning to learn must become a recursively embedded feature of social arrangements.

home, is at the end of the day merely an argument for retaining the customary rule-based arrangements, for delaying, sidetracking and otherwise blocking societal 'learning to learn'. This is concretely what Castells means by the attenuation of the structural contradiction between the net and the self under informationalism: it may well rest upon a particular technological dispensation that has evolved elsewhere, but its reduction is the result of policy and capacity in each local case.

Having said all that, there remains a residual danger in this kind of account, and that is to underestimate the complexities involved in *technologising education*, for relying on technology to institutionalise 'learning to learn'. Some of the tensions or ambiguities in the new global education circuits are nicely brought out in the chapters in this volume by Hall and by Moja and Cloete: Does it work? Will it really be less expensive? Whose interests does it serve? and so on. The human capital writers have no such qualms, and Castells and Carnoy are no exception, a qualmlessness that in the end comes down to a view of education as skill inculcation (albeit humanistically leavened, see Castells in Section Four Chapter 1 of this volume), and pedagogy its relay. Technology merely compresses time and space; it doesn't necessarily add or subtract anything pedagogically. In one sense this is quite true. In another, it overlooks the moral–social dimension of education. From Durkheim (1915), through Althusser (1971) to Bernstein (1971), the critical pedagogical tradition has stressed that education instils both skills and moral comportment, mental habits and skills together with the dispositions to make them productive. Without the dispositional element, learning just does not 'take', a fact that every teacher comes to learn, usually the hard way. The dispositional element is conveyed tacitly, and acquired tacitly, through the routines and modelling of the everyday pedagogical context. The question that arises with technology is: Does the disposition as well as the skill survive the relay intact? Can the tacit disposition to learn be technologically relayed?

On this, as with much else to do with technology and learning, the jury is still out. For the sceptics, learning technologies, or borderless learning, can only work if paired with quality interaction between small groups of learners or teachers, that is, if linked to contexts where the tacit is traditionally conveyed and acquired. Here the debate centres on whether the distributed tutors have sufficient embodied expertise to do the job properly, and on whether this is not either a false economy, an exploitative labour practice, or whether it is even cost efficient at all (see the discussion in Hall, Section Four Chapter 2 of this volume). The sceptics can of course be dismissed as nostalgic for the high-cost liberal arts education which technology is precisely designed to replace. Nevertheless, the question as to whether especially technologically transmitted higher level skills can 'take' has yet to be answered. A second group, more pragmatic than sceptical, finds the answer to the question, 'Where is the disciplinary or dispositional agent then to be found?' in the habitus of the middle class. It is now well known that the cultural capital of the middle-class home predisposes the disposition to learn (not unfailingly, but regularly nevertheless), and the enthusiasm with which the middle class has taken to the new information and educational technologies might seem to confirm this supposition. But will this not simply harden the class divide? In other words, is educational technology not simply a structural agent that will attenuate social inequality? The public school at least attempted to provide dispositional access; technology will progressively restrict it to the middle class who have the dispositional habitus to access it productively. Technology may then become a new instrument of exclusion.

Interestingly enough, Castells concedes this possibility in his discussion of 'computer-mediated-communication':

> Increasingly computer-mediated-communication (CMC) will be critical in shaping future culture, and increasingly the elites who have shaped its format will be structurally advantaged in the emerging society. Thus, while CMC is truly revolutionising the process of communication, and through it culture at large, it is a revolution developing in concentric waves, starting from the higher levels of education and wealth, and probably unable to reach large segments of the uneducated masses and poor countries. (Castells 1996: 360)

Is this just tough luck? Partly. But we must remember that in Castellian sociology, the actional dimension is ever present, and Castells is confident that people are always going to react in unpredictable ways to the structures and strictures they are dealt. Here we reach the limits of analysis and reach the threshold of 'forecasting', a threshold Castells will not follow Touraine (1998) or Bell (1976) in crossing. There is, to be sure, a more optimistic response, which sees the ubiquity of technology in popular culture as a particularly effective means for disseminating cultural models and morals: if television, play stations and arcade games can disseminate a remarkably shared popular culture, why not a disposition to curiosity and learning? Why not indeed. The field is ripe for innovative research with all these questions begging:

there is just too much we currently only guess at. All we know for the moment is that the innovators have yet to find the right button to push to engage learners pedagogically in the public sphere. Public broadcasting, as Castells himself admits, is mainly boring. And if it can't capture an already attuned middle class, it stands no chance with the young of the generic underclass.

Some of these difficulties are visible in the two chapters in this volume dealing explicitly with education, by Hall (Section Four Chapter 2) and Moja and Cloete (Section Four Chapter 3). Both of them deal, in different ways, with educational knowledge as unproblematically productive. For Moja and Cloete, the politics of education lies with the politics of the institutions rather than with knowledge or technology. Hall, on the other hand, starts with a convincing account of some of the difficulties with technology in education, but goes on to vest his faith in it. In the end, both Hall and Moja and Cloete have an individualised notion of learning. It is plausible to suspect that this notion will have to be socialised along the lines indicated above in order to advance the discussion around technology and education. Besides, difficult times lie ahead for technological innovators. On-line trading ventures, or dotcoms, are failing at an unexpected rate, the reasons for which are, on reflection, obvious: the communicational infrastructure is simply not sufficiently developed. David Streitfeld explains with a neat analogy:

> It's like 1849: most of the dotcoms tried to get to California in a Conestoga, and most fell by the wayside ... Once we build the transcontinental railroad and make it routine to get there, entrepreneurs can be settlers instead of pioneers. (Streitfeld 2001)

Much the same could be said for the technological educators, who are currently more pioneers than settlers, setting in place untried and hugely expensive systems without either the relevant knowledge or communicational infrastructure. We can expect some expensive failures.

Finally, it may be useful to revisit Carnoy's suggestive account in Section One Chapter 2 of this volume. Recall that under industrialism the state, primarily through the school, had the job of individualising labour albeit in a selective and hierarchical way, and wrapping it up in a collective civic religion of citizenship (with America being by far the most successful case: see Appleby 2000). Under informationalism the workplace, says Carnoy, directly individualises the worker, and he goes on to speculate whether it doesn't now become the task of the school to collectivise the learners. Yes, but it surely now, more so perhaps than before, remains the task of the school to impart individualised learning skills, on the basis of which the individualising labour market will make its selection and allocation. At a point, as I said above, where the labour market will discriminate most specifically in terms of achieved individualised skills and dispositions, it surely behoves the education system as the principle cultural arm of the state to make sure that the state institutions provide these opportunities to the poor and disadvantaged, as a premier matter of social justice. (It does seem ironic that it is often just those countries that disclaim most publicly about social justice – Zimbabwe comes to mind, for example – that fail to grasp the centrality of this point).

Net and self

The theme of identity looms large in Castells' work, taking up the middle volume of his trilogy. This should not be surprising; culture, identity and meaning are the 'people' side of globalisation, and 'the dialectic between the net and the self [is] the central dialectic of our world' (Castells in Section Two Chapter 1 of this volume). What are the central formats of self in network society? His first distinction is between local identities and national identity, or between local cultural identity and national cultural identity. Local cultural identities usually precede or predate the state. State-sponsored identity – nationalism, or some or other identification with the nation-state – can either accommodate local identities, or seek to suppress them. A central theme in Castells is that suppression always incurs a terrible cost, even when it fails, as it all too often does. In the possibly single most successful case, that of revolutionary France, 'French identity' was created largely through a centralised school system, but only through destroying scores of local dialects, languages and local identities. In Castells' view, the price paid outweighs the gain. In revolutionary Russia, the state tried and failed to create the 'new man', and the partial accommodation of regional identities proved to be the undoing of the Soviet Union. Castells' message, perhaps deliberately crafted for the South African audience, is that socio-cultural engineering should not be pursued as an antidote to the depredations of globalisation. Indeed, these local identities, including ethnicity, are what cushion us from the abrasions of the network world.

Alexander (in Section Two Chapter 2 of this volume) agrees with Castells that local identities predate the state, and that we ignore them at our peril. But, like many South Africans, he has a far less benign view of these local identities which, in his view, should not be encouraged, much less institutionalised as Castells proposes. At stake here are two kinds of conceptual disagreement.

The first is that, although both Castells and Alexander agree on the 'constructedness' and 'constructability' of social identity, Alexander has a far stronger version of it than Castells has. For Castells, identity grows out of shared experience and over time; the French case notwithstanding, there are limits to the identity that can be created or 'imagined'. Alexander is far more persuaded by the French case. Because local identities precede the state, says he, does not give them any ontological or political priority. Because colonialism so frequently created identities in order to exploit differences, we should not, says Alexander, treat them with exaggerated respect.

Alexander agrees too with Castells that a superordinate national identity can and should be built, but he differs on the way it should relate to the local identities. Where Castells evinces and prescribes an additive 'live and let live' schema of national and local identities, the identity schema for Alexander is a zero sum one: the greater the plenum of ethnic or local identities, the weaker will be the national identity. The latter can only prosper if the former are held in check.

... we ignore at our peril Castells' message that we need national and local cultural concord in order to prosper in the global world.

With these two differences, we can see again that Castells has a pronounced culturalist bent to his analysis, Alexander a much more pronounced political bent. Alexander thus clearly inclines to the national reconstructors; Castells, as befits a member of the much-persecuted Catalans proud of his heritage, to the necessary vitality of local and national culture, even or perhaps especially ethnic culture. South African common-sense sides with Alexander, and it is noteworthy how the local experience with apartheid has shaped a preferred form of social analysis suspicious not only of knowledge but of the divisive and potentially exclusionary effects of local cultures too. This does not of course make it right, and the common-sense has been wrong before. Soudien (in Section Two Chapter 3) sympathetically brings out the confusions and equivocations that arise whenever South Africans talk about what it means to be South African. Castells' position however stands as a challenge to African scholarship, to seek examples of states in Africa where the relation of the superordinate identity to the local identities is not always and inevitably one of conflict and mutual antagonism. To paraphrase Alexander, we ignore at our peril Castells' message that we need national and local cultural concord in order to prosper in the global world. It would be a shame too if the apartheid experience closed us off to the healing *heimat* of local culture in network society, and left us with a politicised and unsociological appreciation of local life.

Having said that, there is an aspect of Castells' treatment of culture and identity that appears to me to be less than satisfactory. It has to do with his culturalist approach to social belonging. To summarise briefly, Castells believes that 'In this end of millennium, the king and the queen, the state and the civil society, are both naked, and their children-citizens are wandering around a variety of foster homes' (1997: 355). This leaves only the cultural havens of the local, the national and increasingly the global as sites of communal association – 'that is, for the time being, ecologists, feminists, religious fundamentalists, nationalists and localists – are the potential subjects of the Information Age' (Castelle 1997: 361). Two points arise here. The first is that this is not necessarily sociologically or socially wholesome. Castells is fond of reminding us that 'civil society is not necessarily nice people'. But neither are nationalists or localists: this above all is the warning sounded by Alexander. And if Alexander over-estimates the political and under-estimates the cultural, is it possible that Castells' culturalism leads him to the converse? What happens to national citizenship in network society? Calhoun (1999) reminds us that there are three crucial forms of association in any functioning society. The first is local community, based on interpersonal relationships and dense personal networks; the second is nationalism, based on cultural or jural equivalence; the third is citizenship, based on rights established in the public sphere. These are all distinct. Indeed, citizenship is not only different to the 'locally different' and 'nationally same', it is in fact a constitutively different form of association created precisely as protection against the potentially oppressive ambitions of both. Even though citizenship is thus a 'meaning-giving' belonging, it is juridical rather than cultural (or at least cultural as defined by the other two spheres). Culturalism is inclined to collapse this difference: collapsed upwards, we get citizenship as nationalism, and the sorry sagas of the Balkans and the Middle East are at least partly rooted here; collapsed downwards, we get citizenship as multiculturalism, and postmodern Babel. Both forms of collapse tend toward homogenisation of membership, and citizenship is there to remind us that collectives are the same in some respects (hence their belonging together) but heterogeneous in others, nevertheless having equal rights of participation and protection in the polity. An indubitably positive spin-off of the end of apartheid has been the entrenchment of an exemplary human rights ideal if not quite yet 'culture' in South Africa, the foundation for any contemporary idea of citizenship.[3] Perhaps it is just this very strong sense of citizenship, in a country after all, as Castells says, that is a state without a nation

there are three crucial forms of association in any functioning society. The first is local community, based on interpersonal relationships and dense personal networks; the second is nationalism, based on cultural or jural equivalence; the third is citizenship, based on rights established in the public sphere.

(1997: 51), that constitutes the essential part of our distinctiveness, and perhaps even the fecund source of our sometimes difference with Castells, who, we will all remember, defines himself pre-eminently as Catalan, a member of the community of Catalunya, that nation without a state. Feeling at home is therefore undoubtedly a deeply felt need, but being able to negotiate our differences rationally and accountably is a human right. As Calhoun's subtitle puts it, 'feeling at home is not a substitute for public space'. It will be a dark day if this most serviceable of commoners were to disappear along with the royalty of state and civil society in the wake of global network society.

Envoi

I have at home a bookmark commemorating 23 April, World Book Day, issued by the Generalitat de Catalunya, the government of Catalonia. On the front there is a red rose in a wine glass. On the back it reads, 'The people of Catalonia are proud that their tradition of giving roses and books to those they love should have extended throughout the world.' We must be grateful to Manuel Castells who, with great generosity of mind and spirit, provided this rare opportunity to appreciate book and rose together, sinuous intellectual argument about the global wrapped up in Catalan *joie de vivre*. Think local, act global, indeed.

Notes

[1] Bruno Latour puts this point with Gallic pungency: '... we have other resources with which to think, not just the idea ... that critical theory is the only repertoire of the intellectual – that denouncing and unveiling is the only work to do ... Denouncing and unveiling is not a very interesting practice, and it is not a good definition of the intellectual' (Latour 1993: 257).

[2] The distinction between knowledge and information in Castells is not always clear. He follows Bell (1976) in defining knowledge as a set of organised statements communicated systematically, and follows Porat (1977) in defining information as data that has been organised and communicated (Castells 1996: 17 fn 27). Castells clearly wishes to emphasise the secondary elaboration of data (information) rather than its genesis in scientific activity (knowledge), but he continues to use the terms almost interchangeably, or in conjunction, as in 'knowledge-based information'. The key point is less the distinction between information and knowledge as

it is between industrialism (which also used, or rather applied, knowledge and information) and informationalism, where information technology itself becomes a productive force and information itself a product:

> What characterises the current technological revolution is not the centrality of knowledge and information, but the application of such knowledge and information to knowledge generation and information processing/communication devices, in a cumulative feedback loop between innovation and the uses of innovation. (Castells 1996: 32)

[3] It does not always work as it should, of course. Columnist Max du Preez records the case of a friend, a 34 year old married man with two children, who was forced into a painful initiation and circumcision ritual against his will. When it was reported to the police, their response made it clear that in this liberated land culture can still trump rights: 'The Bill of Rights is for the cities. This man is a Mosotho. This is a tribal matter. The Bill of Rights does not apply here' (*Cape Argus*, 4 January 2001). Encouraging ethnic culture all too often empowers it at the expense of citizenship and rights.

References

Althusser, L (1971) *Lenin and Philosophy, and Other Essays.* London: New Left Books.

Appleby, J (2000) *Inheriting the Revolution: The First Generation of Americans.* Cambridge, Ma.: Harvard University Press.

Bell, D (1976) *The Coming of Post-Industrial Society: A Venture in Social Forecasting.* New York: Basic Books.

Bernstein, B (1971) *Class, Codes and Control.* Volume 1. London: Routledge & Kegan Paul.

Bourdieu, P (1986) 'The forms of capital', in JG Richardson (ed.) *Handbook of Theory and Research for the Sociology of Education.* New York: Greenwood Press.

Calhoun, C (1999) 'Nationalism, political community and the representation of society – or, why feeling at home is not a substitute for public space', *European Journal of Social Theory.* 2, 2: 217–232.

Castells, M (1996) *The Information Age: Economy, Society and Culture. Volume 1: The Rise of the Network Society.* Oxford: Blackwell.

Castells, M (1997) *The Information Age: Economy, Society and Culture. Volume 2: The Power of Identity.* Oxford: Blackwell.

Castells, M (1998) *The Information Age: Economy, Society and Culture. Volume 3: End of Millennium*. Oxford: Blackwell.

Collins, R (1979) *The Credential Society*. New York: Academic Press.

Du Preez, M (2001) 'Hard-won Bill of Rights should not be ignored', *Cape Argus*. 4 January.

Durkheim, E (1915) *The Elementary Forms of the Religious Life*. London: George Allen & Unwin.

Eder, K (1999) 'Societies learn and yet the world is hard to change', *European Journal of Social Theory*. 2, 2: 195–215.

Howie, S (2001) *Mathematics and Science Performance in Grade 8 in South Africa 1998/1999: TIMSS-R 1999 South Africa – Executive Summary*. Pretoria: Human Sciences Research Council.

Judt, T (2000) 'The story of everything', *The New York Review of Books*, XLVII, 14: 66–69.

Kuhn, TS (1970) *The Structure of Scientific Revolutions*. Chicago: Chicago University Press.

Latour, B (1993) 'An interview with Bruno Latour with T Hugh Crawford', *Configurations*. 1, 2: 247–268. Online: www:press.jhu.edu/demo/configurations/1.2crawford.html

Pels, D (1998) *Property and Power in Social Theory: A Study in Intellectual Rivalry*. London: Routledge.

Porat, M (1977) *The Information Economy: Definition and Measurement*. Washington DC: US Department of Commerce, Office of Telecommunications.

Poulantzas, N (1980) *State, Power, Socialism*. London: New Left Books.

'SA pupils come last again, survey shows' (2000) *Business Day*. 7 December.

Stehr, N (1994) *Knowledge Societies*. London: Sage.

Streitfeld, D (2001) 'Dotcoms buried as fast as they are born', *Cape Times* Business Report. 9 January.

Touraine, A (1998) *Return of the Actor: Social Theory in Post-Industrial Society*. University of Minnesota.

Johan Muller is a Professor of Education and Head of the School of Education at the University of Cape Town. He has taught at the Universities of the North and the Witwatersrand. He has been widely involved in the field of education policy development and has published extensively on the impact of globalisation on the production of knowledge and on the organisation of the higher education curriculum, higher education governance and conceptual and theoretical issues in the sociology of knowledge. His book, *Reclaiming Knowledge*, was published by Falmeroutledge at the end of 2000.

INDEX

D

E

O

P

Q

R

X Y Z

A John Hope [illegible]

Next Wave: New Directions in Women's Studies

A series edited by Inderpal Grewal, Caren Kaplan,

and Robyn Wiegman

A Joh[illegible]

LEEDS BECKETT UNIVERSITY
Leeds Metropolitan University
17 0546935 9

Next Wave: New Directions in Women's Studies

A series edited by Inderpal Grewal, Caren Kaplan,

and Robyn Wiegman